THE DISCOVERY OF
JEANNE BARET

ALSO BY GLYNIS RIDLEY

Clara's Grand Tour: Travels with a Rhinoceros in Eighteenth-Century Europe

A Story of Science,

the High Seas,

and the First Woman to

Circumnavigate the Globe

THE DISCOVERY OF

JEANNE

BARET

GLYNIS RIDLEY

BROADWAY PAPERBACKS   NEW YORK

Library of Congress Cataloging-in-Publication Data
Ridley, Glynis.
The discovery of Jeanne Baret : a story of science, the high seas, and
the first woman to circumnavigate the globe / Glynis Ridley.
Includes bibliographical references and index.
1. Baret, Jeanne, 1740–1807. 2. Explorers—France—Biography. 3.
Women explorers—France—Biography. 4. Botanists—France—
Biography. 5. Women botanists—France—Biography. 6. Commerson,
Philibert, 1727–1773. 7. Bougainville, Louis-Antoine de, comte,
1729–1811. 8. Bougainvillea. 9. Voyages around the world—Early
works to 1800. I. Title.

G440.B225R53 2010
910.4092—dc22
[B]
2010016778

ISBN 978-0-307-46353-1
eISBN 978-0-307-46354-8

PRINTED IN THE UNITED STATES OF AMERICA

Book design by Ellen Cipriano
Cover design by Mumtaz Mustafa
Cover illustration: (image of Jeanne Baret) The Mitchell Library,
State Library of NSW, ML 980/C01/22A2. Volume 2, A2327004

First Paperback Edition

J's book

CONTENTS

Baret, with her face bathed in tears, owned to me that she was a woman;
she said that she had deceived her master at Rochefort, by offering to
serve him in men's clothes at the very moment when he was embarking;
that she had already before served a Genevan gentleman at Paris, in
quality of a valet; that being born in Burgundy, and become an orphan,
the loss of a law-suit had brought her to a distressed situation, and in-
spired her with the resolution to disguise her sex; that she well knew
when she embarked that we were going round the world, and that such
a voyage had raised her curiosity. She will be the first woman that ever
made it, and I must do her the justice to affirm that she has always be-
haved on board with the most scrupulous modesty. She is neither ugly nor
pretty, and is no more than twenty-five.

—LOUIS-ANTOINE DE BOUGAINVILLE, JOURNAL, MAY 28–29, 1768

I swear that man
never knew animals. Words
he lined up according to size
. . . I strung words
by their stems and wore them
as garlands on my long walks.

The next day
I'd find them withered.

I liked change.

—SUSAN DONNELLY, "EVE NAMES THE ANIMALS"

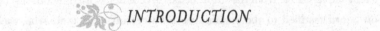 *INTRODUCTION*

In April 1768, two French ships, the *Boudeuse* and the *Étoile,* rode at anchor off the coast of Tahiti as 330 officers and men took their first shore leave in nearly a year. The ships constituted an expedition, under the command of Louis-Antoine de Bougainville, to circumnavigate the globe and claim lands for France.

On the beach a single woman stood surrounded by a group of men whose looks required no translation. Fearing herself in danger of an imminent gang rape, she screamed an appeal to a French officer to save her. But to the wonder of the French, the woman was not an islander but one of their own crew. As one of the French observers recorded the event, with a striking restraint given what was being described, "They have discovered that the servant of Mr. Commerson, the doctor, was a girl who until now has been taken for a boy."

For two years on board, Jeanne Baret had presented herself as a young man, using the name Jean Baret, and had worked as principal assistant to the expedition's naturalist, Philibert Commerson. When an old leg wound prevented Commerson from collecting specimens around Rio de Janeiro, it was Baret who had ventured inland and had brought back the showy tropical vine that would be named in honor of the expedition's commander: *Bougainvillea*. When the ships made slow passage through the Strait of Magellan, Baret and Commerson had been put ashore, their every move visible from the ships' decks. Accounts written by observers on board testified to the stamina of Commerson's assistant, who was always lagging behind him laden with boxes and papers—the cumbersome paraphernalia of eighteenth-century plant collecting. In an effort to avoid suspicion that she was anything other than a strong young man, Baret imagined the work that such a man might be capable of and then worked even harder. With her breasts flattened by strips of linen wound tightly round her upper body, she sweltered when others chose to strip, and checked every impulse that might expose her true identity.

But once ashore on Tahiti, Baret found herself surrounded by male islanders, whose gestures made plain the same offer of multiple sexual partners that Tahitian women were extending to the rest of the crew. Easily seeing through Baret's disguise where the Frenchmen did not, the Tahitians effectively forced the end of a nearly eighteen-month-long charade: Baret abandoned the fiction she had worked so hard to maintain to save herself from what seemed certain to be a sexual assault.

Or so official accounts of this extraordinary story would have us believe.

In addition to maintaining an expedition log in spare, navy board–mandated prose, Bougainville also kept a more expansive journal that he intended to publish upon his fêted return to an adoring France. But in neither document could Bougainville admit any knowledge of the rumors that had started circulating about Baret within a few days of the expedition's launch from Rochefort. For Baret's behavior was soon noted to be odd on several counts. Doubled up with retching from acute sea-sickness, the naturalist Commerson found his symptoms eased if he sat on deck, feeling the reassuring solidity of the main mast behind him. Baret was also sick, but kept to Commerson's cabin: an unprecedented privilege for the mere assistant of a gentleman scientist. Novice sailors quickly grew accustomed to relieving themselves at "the heads"—holes cut into an area of decking that jutted out over the open ocean—but Baret was never seen there. When the expedition sailed on to the equator and the crew stripped for the ritualized anarchy of "Crossing the Line," Baret was noticeable as the only clothed figure among the participants. Confronted by a handful of the crew determined to know the truth, Baret insisted that she was a man, though, as she expressed it, a man of the sort from which the Turkish sultan chose the guards of his harem. Baret's claim that she was a eunuch was well calculated; the traumatic past that it implied would, she hoped, prevent further inquiry, either verbal or physical.

But on all of these aspects of the voyage, Bougainville's official log and his private journal are silent. To acknowledge that there had been rumors of a woman on board ship, in contravention of French naval regulations, would be to acknowledge that the expedition commander had done nothing to investigate a possible breach. And from Bougainville's point of view, an investigation at sea would have been ugly. Had Baret refused to admit to her disguise, only a forcible stripping would have settled the question. Yet what commander in his right senses would want to reveal to his crew that there was a lone, physically vulnerable woman among 330 men? In saving herself from the Tahitians by admitting her lie, as Baret was supposed to have done, she also saved Bougainville from having to act upon an increasingly untenable situation.

Yet other members of the party—gentlemen travelers and scientists for whom the circumnavigation was not a stepping-stone in a naval career—recognized a good story when they saw it, and they were less concerned about official censure than Bougainville. In fact, eight accounts of Bougainville's expedition survive, all telling versions of the same story, each in a different voice. In addition to Bougainville's account, there are memoirs by Pierre Duclos-Guyot and Philibert Commerson (sharing a journal and both sailing on the *Étoile*); Charles-Nicolas Othon, Prince of Nassau-Siegen (paying gentleman passenger on the *Boudeuse*); François Vivès (surgeon of the *Étoile*); Jean-Louis Caro (first lieutenant of the *Étoile*); Charles-Pierre-Félix Fesche (volunteer, sailing on the *Boudeuse*); Joseph Hervel (pilot, joining the *Boudeuse* in Mauritius); and the chevalier Walsh. Baret features in the writings of four out of the eight: Bougainville, Nassau-Siegen, Vivès, and in the journal kept jointly by Commerson and Duclos-Guyot. Various details in these men's stories may be corroborated in accounts of the expedition kept by Caro, Fesche, d'Hervel, and Walsh.

Out of these eight narrators, only Bougainville revised his expedition journals for publication and saw them become a success. But the unpublished journals—especially those that feature Baret—are each written by such distinct characters that they do not merely duplicate Bougainville's account but instead present us with alternative views of the expedition that are at times more descriptive, more judgmental, and more unsettling than anything Bougainville writes. Among this group of journal keepers is the perennially well-groomed Prince of Nassau-Siegen, a gentleman who paid his way on the voyage for the experience of it, and whose velvet suits and full-length wigs maintained the illusion of style even as their wearer was reduced to eating his ship's rats on a deathly still sea. Mistaken for a woman himself on more than one occasion (generally because of his wig), the prince represents a glorious historical irony: a man whom many island peoples assumed to be the sole woman among 330 men, even as Baret worked in full view, collecting plant specimens under Nassau-Siegen's sympathetic and interested gaze.

Others were hostile to Baret: ship's surgeon François Vivès insinuates throughout his journal that Baret bought the silence of key crew members by prostituting herself. At one point his prose lingers on a description of Baret on New Ireland (to the northeast of Papua New Guinea), cornered by sailors who strip her and prove she is no eunuch. Vivès is careful to describe the incident as an examination rather than a gang rape but leaves his reader puzzling over a series of equally nauseating possibilities: that Baret was raped and Vivès thought it of no great importance; that Baret was not raped but was subjected to a humiliating examination, which Vivès found amusing; that the incident never happened but Vivès would like to imagine that it did. And if it did, what role did Vivès himself play? Either the episode was described to him, or Vivès recorded it from memory. In any case, Vivès is damned by his own prose as a sadistic voyeur of a woman's misery.

Baret's European crewmates were not the only ones to record their impressions of her. Unusually for an expedition of this nature, we can refer to the observations of those whom the French set out to observe. The Tahitians' version of events is available in the testimony of Aotourou, the brother of the Tahitian chief, Ereti, and the hightest-ranking islander to greet Bougainville on his first landing on Tahiti. In the course of the expedition's monthlong stay, Aotourou spent more and more of his time on one or the other of Bougainville's two ships. By the time the expedition sailed on, Aotourou was conversant enough in French to insist that he be taken back to France. Bougainville was only too willing to oblige, believing that Aotourou might be a useful pilot and translator in the short term and finally a lucrative figure of wonderment to the French king. While Aotourou has not left us his impressions of the expedition beyond Tahiti, his description of Baret as she appeared to the Tahitians offers rare insight into what the islanders were thinking.

Closest to Baret was the man she served, the internationally renowned botanist Philibert Commerson, who maintained after Baret's exposure on Tahiti that he was as surprised as anyone. That he was ignorant of Baret's real identity defies common sense and could be true only if Commerson failed to recognize in his assistant the young woman who, prior to the expedition, had lived with him in Paris for two years and had already borne him a son. Fortunately for Commerson, Bougainville had neither the means nor the desire to investigate the couple's history, and Commerson's integrity remained unquestioned in the official paperwork.

A brilliant scientist whose work had caught the attention of Louis XV, Commerson also tended in time to antagonize everyone around him. Even as a student, he had aroused hostility in his professors: He had no hesitation in interrupting a lecture to apprise the speaker that he was behind on the current scientific thinking. Commerson's precocity and far-ranging botanizing even brought the undergraduate to the attention of Carl Linnaeus, the greatest botanist of the age. And he could be charming when necessary: Commerson's royal appointment to Bougainville's expedition was thus facilitated by letters of recommendation from Voltaire, Queen Louisa Ulrika of Sweden, and the chief object of her royal patronage— Linnaeus himself.

Commerson's shipboard journal was a joint enterprise with an eager young sailor aboard the *Étoile,* Pierre Duclos-Guyot, one of three members of the same family to take part in the expedition. Pierre's father, Nicolas-Pierre Duclos-Guyot was the captain of the *Boudeuse,* and had used his influence to see that positions were found for his sons, Pierre and Alexandre, both of whom were interested in a naval career. Alexandre traveled on the *Boudeuse* with his father and was charged with preparing new charts of the South Atlantic. Out from under his father's gaze, Pierre displayed the same draftsman's skills as his brother and, while charts of the Strait of Magellan can be attributed to him, he clearly thought it much more exciting to contribute to a journal that might be published by a gentleman like Commerson. For his part, Commerson

was glad to be able to call on the technical knowledge of the young cartographer, who wanted desperately to be useful. When Duclos-Guyot
finally tired of Commerson's unsystematic approach to record keeping,
the journal fell silent. Today it is of interest mainly for the exquisite
watercolors contained within its pages, whereby Commerson faithfully recorded new species of flora and fauna from land and sea. But the
number of illustrations in the Duclos-Guyot journal is dwarfed by the
number of specimens that Baret and Commerson collected. More than
six thousand items would finally require cataloging and, until the collection could reach French shores, Baret and Commerson lived and worked
in its midst.

So the disparate narratives of all these men must be brought together
to finally allow Baret's story to be told, for Baret herself is silent. Sharing
a cabin with Commerson for the duration of the expedition, how could
she keep a journal without her relationship with Commerson forming one
of its central themes? Yet to write about him, and her relationship with
him, would have been to create a document with the power to destroy his
career. Commerson's appointment to the expedition came from the king
himself: To flout his royal ordinances prohibiting women on board ship
was dangerously tantamount to making light of his patronage. Whatever
the nature of the pact between Baret and Commerson, a running commentary implicating Commerson in the charade formed no part of it.

Baret may have allowed herself to be silenced by Commerson's need
for discretion during the voyage, but why did she not write her own
memoirs on her return to France? The reading public's appetite for trav-
elogues, factual and fictional, seemed inexhaustible. Seventeenth-and
eighteenth-century readers sailed the world's oceans vicariously from
the comfort of an armchair, mapping their own literary progress on the
quintessential accessory for any gentleman's library: a terrestrial globe.

Unfortunately for Baret, her timing was not propitious. Setting
out on the circumnavigation in 1766, she would not return to mainland
France until 1775—six years after the return of Bougainville's expedi-

tion. Only Baret, Commerson, and the astronomer, Véron, were absent from Bougainville's triumphant 1769 homecoming: They had remained with the French colonial settlement in Mauritius. Where she should have walked ashore and into the history books, she landed in a protracted legal case, caught between an impassive French government and Commerson's hostile relatives. Meanwhile, Bougainville's version of events was already entrenched in the public mind; his account of the circumnavigation had been published in Paris in 1771 and translated into English the following year. The philosopher Denis Diderot had even used Bougainville's descriptions of island peoples as a starting point for his own speculations on the nature of civilization; his *Supplément au voyage de Bougainville* presents a seamless continuation of the themes started in Bougainville's original. Underscoring the difficulty Baret faced in making herself heard, Diderot's book repeated Bougainville's story of Baret's exposure on Tahiti (not because Diderot was interested in what happened to Baret, but because he was curious about the Tahitians' apparently superior senses).

What hope could there be for a working-class woman to challenge a national hero? A woman who had hoped to deceive her shipmates for two or more years would readily invite the charge that she was a liar. Worse still for Baret, contemporary views about the proper sphere of female activity guaranteed that any display of her botanical knowledge in print would have branded her a whore.

Taxonomy—the classification of all living things, plant and animal, according to perceived "family" resemblances—may seem an improbable arena for a protracted historical battle of the sexes. But throughout the eighteenth century, women's attempts to engage in this male-dominated field generated a torrent of vitriol. The systematic exclusion of women from the field of taxonomy is so much a part of Baret's story that the historical silence surrounding her cannot fully be explained without understanding something of taxonomy's history. Anyone who has sought out the name of an unfamiliar but attractive plant in hopes of adding it to a garden will be familiar with the frustration of learning that the plant has no "common name," only a Latin one, or rather two. This binomial classification system, formulated by the Swedish botanist Carl Linnaeus in the first half of the eighteenth century, identifies all living things by genus (or family) and then species, using the Latin that was the universal language of scientific discourse in Linnaeus's time. No matter that DNA analysis has now redefined previous certainties about plant families, or that plant breeding has produced generations of hybrids that may boast three or four names, we still rely on the framework of Linnaean taxonomy to describe the natural world.

This would certainly be a revelation to contemporaries of Linnaeus, for it was by no means obvious to his fellow scientists that his proposed classification system would gain widespread acceptance. As the memorably named William Smellie explained in the first edition of the *Encyclopædia Britannica* in 1768, "Obscenity is the very basis of the Linnaean system." How can a taxonomic system be obscene? Linnaeus placed plants in family groups based on what could be observed of their reproductive strategies: the number and arrangement of male stamens and female pistils at the heart of each flower. Gardeners may effectively clone a plant by taking cuttings or splitting root-balls, but in the natural course of things, the vegetable world turns on the same principle of sexual reproduction as does the animal one. Trying to help his readers grasp the idea of vegetable sexual reproduction, Linnaeus explained the sexual reproduction of plants with analogies taken from human relations. Smellie warmed to his theme of the "obscenity" of the Linnaean system by asking readers to consider that "there is such a degree of indelicacy in the expression as cannot be exceeded by the most obscene romance-writer. For example, [Linnaeus says] 'the calyx is the bride-chamber in which the stamina and pistilla solemnize their nuptials.' "

For the aspiring female student of botany, Linnaean taxonomy invited a frank consideration of reproductive ability, both animal and vegetable. The protofeminist writer Mary Wollstonecraft even recommended in 1792 that women receive a botanical education to promote both cultivation of the mind and greater awareness of the body. Wollstonecraft contrasted the female botanist with Eve in the Garden of Eden, arguing that the educated woman could maintain "purity of mind" even when possessed of the "fruit of knowledge." Predictably, eighteenth-century male commentators, as typified by William Smellie, were less sanguine about the presence of Eve's daughters in the garden.

Baret lived then in a time of intense debate about women's exposure to scientific knowledge. A "proper" appreciation of nature was considered a mark of eighteenth-century female refinement, yet it was considered "unladylike" to go so far as to seek out the accurate Latin descriptor for a plant species. Even if she had returned to France with the rest of Bougainville's expedition in 1769, Baret could not have expected any public recognition of her work for the expedition: A female stowaway was a curiosity, but a female botanist was a breach in the natural order of things. As the book of Genesis reminded Baret's contemporaries, it was Adam who was granted the privilege of naming what was found in Eden. When Eve aimed for more knowledge, the world changed forever.

Part of the privilege of naming new discoveries in the natural world is the opportunity to commemorate individuals who assisted in the find. As Bougainville's expedition circled the globe, rivers, bays, and islands were named for members of the party. Most of these names survive only in the cartographic record: As colonies have achieved their hard-won independence, the names of history's colonizers have been erased from the landscape. In the field of natural history, however, the names of great botanists, zoologists, and explorers survive, built into the Linnaean taxonomy of genus and species. Commerson did not hesitate to celebrate himself in all branches of creation, and today over seventy species bear the name *commersonii* (though some were named in his honor after his death). He is commemorated in birds and mammals, ferns and flowers, mollusks and insects. He honored his commander with the *Bougainvillea* and his fellow officers with a handful of the more than six thousand specimens he collected with Baret.

Baret, on the other hand, received the acknowledgment of a single genus (comprising just three species): *Baretia*. It is not unknown for taxonomists to reclassify both genera and species and to rename them in the process, and while Commerson's commemoration of himself has remained largely untouched by taxonomic history, the plant genus *Baretia* no longer exists: Species named for Baret have been included in the genus *Turraea*. Nothing that Baret collected and preserved now bears her name.

To those of Baret's contemporaries who bothered to consider the wider implications of her story, it seemed unlikely that she would provide a model for other women. As Bougainville wrote, "She will be the only one of her sex [to circumnavigate the globe] and I admire her determination . . . Her example will hardly be contagious." Certainly, the stark details of Baret's day-to-day existence would be unlikely to inspire imitators. For over two years, Baret endured seasickness, loneliness, and starvation; the extremes of the world's weather on deck and onshore; endless work making every joint ache; and no possibility of relaxation, physical or mental, throughout the whole voyage. Bougainville was right: These things are no advertisement for emulating Baret.

But Baret's desire to experience more of the world does not seem so extraordinary for someone born into the lowest class of the French peasantry whose lives played out within twenty miles, at most, of their birthplace. Even as snow accumulated on the deck of the *Étoile* and Baret contemplated another cold, difficult trudge along the shores of the Strait of Magellan, the waters around the ship thronged with life-forms—penguins, sea lions, southern whales—of which a French rural laborer could never have conceived. When the ships finally broke into the Pacific and the sweat soaked through Baret's tightly bound disguise, was the physical discomfort lessened by the sight of pods of dolphins chasing flying fish? What did she make of the stately manta rays and lugubrious sea turtles recorded from this stage of the voyage? When Aotourou sat for her and asked her to dress his hair, did she pause to reflect on the fact that the physical distance traveled from home was far less than the imaginative one?

Bougainville thought Baret's example was not likely to be contagious because of the physical privations and brutality she experienced. But Bougainville overlooked the allure of the idea she embodied: that one human being, irrespective of the hand dealt by fortune, can have as much curiosity about the world as another. And that, like race and class, gender should pose no barrier to satisfying that curiosity and discovering how far it may take you.

ONE

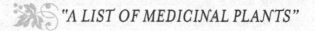 *"A LIST OF MEDICINAL PLANTS"*

The Botanist and the Herb Woman

THIS IS AN entry from local parish records kept in the town of Autun in France's Loire valley from the summer of 1740:

> On the twenty-seventh of July 1740 was born and on the twenty-eighth was baptized Jeanne, the legitimate issue of the marriage of Jean Baret, a day laborer from Lome and of Jeanne Pochard. Her godfather is Jean Coureau, a day laborer from Poil, and her godmother Lazare Tibaudin, who are not signing.

From the moment we are born we begin creating a paper trail. The only similarity between the infinite variety of those paper trails is their starting point in the same official document: a birth certificate that deals in simple facts. Jeanne Baret's life begins not with a standard factual record but with this story and, like all stories, it can tell us more than we might first imagine about its subject, the writer, and the circumstances in which they came together.

The unsteady handwriting and archaic spelling of the original suggest that the parish priest, Father Pierre, was old, and so his description of the child's godfather as being "à poil" (literally "nude") rather than "à Poil" (from the village of Poil) can be safely attributed to infirmity rather than mischievous creativity in the legal paperwork. Indeed, there was little for the priest to smile about as he contemplated the family's situation. Not only are there no signatures of any of the adults named in connection with Jeanne Baret's baptism, but the new father did not even place a cross against the record. What would be the point of such an action at a time when illiteracy rates were as high as 80 percent for men and 90 percent for women in this enclave of feudal culture, a place to which social commentators from across Enlightenment Europe flocked to gaze in horrified fascination at many of the last serfs in France?

Jeanne Baret's parents owned nothing, but they rose with the sun each morning to sell their labor for that day, their work changing with the seasonal cycle of sowing, tending, harvesting. Despite living in the middle of prime hunting and farming country, within walking distance of the vineyards for which the region is now famous, they starved through the winter when they could not work. As other regions of France traded local tyrannies for a more centralized exercise of the law, Burgundy continued under the immediate rule of local lords of the manor, or seigneurs, who were notorious for enforcing their property rights. The Barets' seigneur owned the collection of rotting wooden shacks where his workers slept, owned the land they worked, owned the produce they harvested.

If his agents chose not to use a laborer on any given day, the man had no paid work.

The modern reader might wonder why families such as the Barets did not simply move on, taking their most valuable commodity, their capacity for hard labor, to a place where conditions were better. But inertia is a powerful force and, prior to the Industrial Revolution in the nineteenth century, the average European country dweller never went more than twenty miles from home. Jeanne Baret's parents knew little of the wider world, even as its citizens periodically passed through the Loire valley, recording the wretched poverty of its laborers' lives.

One such observer, the great French military engineer Sébastien Le Prestre de Vauban, could hardly contain his incredulity at what the ordinary population endured, his description making it clear that the distance between farm laborer and farm horse was negligible: "They live on nothing but bread of mixed barley and oats, from which they do not even remove the bran, which means that the bread can sometimes be lifted by a straw sticking out of it. They . . . seldom drink wine, eat meat not three times a year . . . Add to this what they suffer from exposure: winter and summer, three-quarters of them are dressed in nothing but half-rotting tattered linen, and are shod throughout the year with clogs and no other covering for the feet. If one of them does have shoes he only wears them on saints' days and on Sundays." Against this background, it is sobering but unsurprising that those whom Vauban described, both men and women, would typically die in their mid to late twenties (twenty-six years was the average life expectancy of this class).

But when the baby girl born to Jean Baret and Jeanne Pochard was twenty-six, she would be living in a fashionable Paris apartment, organizing papers and preparing natural specimens for the eminent but often unsystematic botanist Philibert Commerson. When Jeanne Baret was twenty-six, she would see Rio de Janeiro, sail through the Strait of Magellan, and stare at the waters of the Pacific Ocean stretching to the farthest blue horizon. What combination of circumstances allowed Baret to go beyond the confines of her parents' lives?

Baret's association with the botanist Philibert Commerson—a relationship begun at some point in the early 1760s—undeniably helped to raise her out of poverty. Whether attempting to explain Baret's literacy or her facility with arranging and caring for Commerson's scientific collections, previous writers have always maintained that Baret was very much Commerson's creation. But their assumption that Commerson swept Baret up into his affluent world because he was captivated by some combination of beauty and good nature on her part is as flawed as it is romantic. Even if Baret had been an extraordinary beauty as a child, she was born into a world where nothing childish could last, and where the backbreaking routine of grubbing for subsistence wages would have afforded little opportunity to meet a man of Commerson's class. (After all, Cinderella had to be made to look like a princess before others could see her as one.) Even supposing that Commerson was seduced by his first sight of the downtrodden Baret, an illiterate, uneducated day laborer would have held little long-term appeal. Given that Commerson had no hesitation in publicly correcting his university professors' errors in the middle of their lectures, his tolerance for those he considered less capable than himself might reasonably be seen as limited.

So what is the intersection between the world of the mid- eighteenth-century Loire peasant and the gentleman scientist? Baret and Commerson came together at the meeting point between two views of the natural world: a folkloric, feminine tradition surrounding the medicinal properties of plants and the emerging field of taxonomy, which aimed to name and classify the natural world. Baret captured the attention of Commerson because she possessed botanic knowledge that lay well beyond the competence of his professors and mentors. She was an herb woman: one schooled in the largely oral tradition of the curative properties of plants. Herb women were for centuries the source of all raw materials to be prepared, mixed, and sold by male medical practitioners, and as botany crystallized as a science in the eighteenth century, a handful of male botanists did not think it beneath them to learn from these specialists. In this light, Baret was not Commerson's pupil, but his teacher.

The herb women of the eighteenth-century Loire valley were, unknown to them, part of one of the longest-running battles of the sexes in Western culture. From the beginnings of classical Greek medicine until the early nineteenth century, countrywomen supplied town-dwelling men—who were largely ignorant of how any given species might look in the wild and who considered plant collecting beneath them—with the dried and drying herbs that were a staple of the druggist's store.

Many male-operated businesses relied on the herb women's supply: apothecaries, who were general medical practitioners as well as pre-parers and sellers of drugs for medical purposes; druggists, who were in theory shopkeepers rather than medical men but still dispensed healthy doses of advice along with powdered compounds, dried leaves, seeds, and barks; physicians, who boasted university medical school training and kept quantities of the most useful herbs on hand; and surgeons, who alone were qualified to open the human body or remove its dis-eased parts, relying on narcotics and plant-based sedatives to render patients insensible. Dentists (then commonly known as tooth-drawers) also needed to supply their unfortunate clients with painkillers, and vet-erinarians liked to leave salves and potions with the owners of prize ani-mals. And last but not least among an eighteenth-century herb woman's clients was one of the most surprising innovations of the century: a male midwife (or obstetrician). Prior to the eighteenth century, midwifery had been the exclusive practice of women, and many herb women also served their local communities as midwives. But as the eighteenth century progressed, "man midwives" became the birthing accessory of choice for upper-class women and the aspirant middle classes, though they relied on herb women to supply them with drugs supposedly beneficial to both mother and child. Herb women thus possessed an unrivaled knowledge of the plant kingdom, while male medical practitioners enjoyed social status and power.

Professional in-jokes are rarely funny to outsiders, but an anecdote told by the Renaissance scholar Otto Brunfels provides such a perfect illustration of the centuries-old disconnect between the scholarly pursuit of botany and practical day-to-day engagement with plants that it is worth risking quoting an example of early-sixteenth-century humor. According to Brunfels, a contemporary physician named Guillelmus Copus of Basel gave a dinner party for his fellow physicians from the Paris Faculty of Medicine. Pulling a leaf from the salad, Copus asked his guests if any man could identify the herb. None could, and all agreed the tasty addition to the salad must be some newly introduced exotic. Calling in the kitchen maid to see what she might say on the matter, Copus watched the surprise on his guests' faces as the woman announced the "unidentifiable" herb to be parsley.

Even if the anecdote is the sixteenth-century botanist's equivalent of an urban myth, the gender and class dynamic that gives the story its punch line translates across centuries and cultures: the female servant displaying more commonsense knowledge than all the educated men in the room can muster. And more to our specific point: Ordinary women know what plants look like in the field and in the kitchen, while supposedly educated male scientists know only what they are told.

The establishment of the first university botanic garden in the Western world at Padua in 1533 was meant to remedy these gaps in male scholars' knowledge. Professors of botany and of physic (that is, medicine) were now able to observe the staples of the druggist's store within the safe environs of college walls, without experiencing the inconvenience and embarrassment of being seen to scour the countryside for herbs they knew only from imperfectly illustrated reference books. In an age of crude woodcut illustrations that only served to obscure identification, when the concept of the petal had not yet even been formulated, even the best herbaria (botanical reference books) were inadequate as field guides. Other respected universities followed suit, establishing their own botanic gardens at Pisa and Florence.

But for a handful of male botanists across the centuries, it remained obvious that the most expansive knowledge of the power of plants resided with herb women, who passed their accumulated wisdom through the female line of their families. Few educated men were willing to swallow their pride and learn from the herb women. In the 1530s, the stupidity of his fellow parsley-eating diners obviously made such an impression on Brunfels that he declared the value of learning from "highly expert old women." In 1534, the German physician Euricius Cordus also admitted to seeking knowledge from "the lowest women and husbandmen"; Anton Schneeberger, a Polish botanist, declared in 1557 that he "was not ashamed to be the pupil of an old peasant woman." When these rare declarations occur, they oscillate so wildly between the combative and the furtive that we have to remind ourselves the clandestine product being traded is the botanical knowledge of peasant women.

And this knowledge conferred an incalculable professional advantage. The greatest British botanist of the eighteenth century, Sir Joseph Banks, who christened Australia's Botany Bay in 1770 and whose collection ultimately contained over twenty thousand plant specimens, signaled his difference from his contemporaries at an early age: While still a schoolboy at Eton, he paid local herb women sixpence for every specimen they brought to his rooms and taught him about. Whatever smirks the visits produced among his classmates, Banks knew more about the plant kingdom than any of his contemporaries, and that knowledge brought him fame, influence, and wealth—not to mention its contribution to Britain's eighteenth-century imperial trade.

Philibert Commerson belonged to the self-selecting ranks of those well-to-do male botanists who sought out local herb women. But unlike those botanists previously named, all of whom seemed at pains to specify that their female instructors were old, Commerson's teacher was the youthful Jeanne Baret.

When Baret's birth and baptism were being recorded in the Autun parish register in 1740, Philibert Commerson was already twelve years old and living over one hundred miles farther south, in a manner far removed from the Baret family's daily hand-to-mouth existence. Commerson's birth on November 18, 1727, gave his father, Georges-Marie, his first son in a family that would eventually include seven children. Georges-Marie Commerson had benefited from his own father's conviction that the law offered a way up and out of the burgeoning ranks of provincial shop-keepers and traders, and he in turn harbored even greater ambitions for his eldest son.

The Commerson family lived in the town of Châtillon-sur-Chalaronne, a prosperous village of just under two thousand inhabitants, nearly thirty miles north of the city of Lyon. For modern visitors to France who are fearful that no place can possibly realize their ideal of French country living, Châtillon (though now over double its eighteenth-century population) is immensely reassuring: Its half-timbered houses trace a medieval street plan that, in combination with a ruined eleventh-century castle and seventeenth-century covered market, is richly suggestive of a long history of prosperity and domestic comfort. In such towns, the triumvirate of priest, doctor, and lawyer constituted the pinnacle of local power and influence: a position the lawyer Georges-Marie Commerson underscored by letting it be known that his clientele included the resident local aristocrat, the Prince de Dombes.

Across eighteenth-century Europe, ambitious members of a burgeoning middle class aspired to move within the ranks of the nobility, whether through professional preferment or judicious marriages. Within France, one of the most coveted signifiers of exalted status within the ranks of the middle class was the right to use what the French refer to as the *particulaire*: the word *de* before a surname, signifying the user's ownership of an estate. No matter that growing numbers of prosperous eighteenth-century businessmen were buying the tracts of land that entitled them to the *particulaire*: It was (before the Revolution of 1789) and *is* a form of French nomenclature omitted at the risk of causing great social offense. So it is perhaps unsurprising to find that, even as he stretched his lawyer's income to maintain a home for his growing family in Châtillon itself, Georges-Marie Commerson also invested in a property in the neighboring countryside: the gentleman's residence with accompanying vineyards, woods, and farmland entitling him—and his heirs—to that precious mark of social status, *de Commerson*.

To the father, it now seemed that nothing would hinder his eldest son's social and professional advancement. Philibert de Commerson had only to walk down the path envisaged for him, following his father into the law. Here it was assumed that ambition, application, and parental underwriting followed by a judicious marriage would undoubtedly lead to national prominence. Those great unknowns of inclination and aptitude played no part in the plan.

As a boy, Philibert de Commerson gave every indication of being likely to repay his father's financial and emotional investments. A quick study, taught on his own and therefore unused to accommodating his slower peers, he had exhausted the educational resources of the local clergy by the time he was thirteen. (Given that the staples of the eighteenth-century schoolboy's curriculum included arithmetic, geometry, grammar, Greek, history, Latin, logic, and rhetoric, the adolescent Commerson clearly possessed a good memory and reasoning capability.) Deciding the time had come (rather sooner than he expected) to send his son away for his education, Georges-Marie de Commerson unwittingly chose the institution that would facilitate the unraveling of all his carefully laid plans.

In 1740, the year of Jeanne Baret's birth, the twelve-year-old Commerson entered the Jesuit College of Bourg-en-Bresse. Today, a visitor to the region of Bresse, in eastern France, will find it promoted as the "land of one thousand lakes," the limestone geology of the region having caused the formation of hundreds of small bodies of water studded across the rolling pastureland. To the delight of amateur naturalists, both now and in the eighteenth century, the Bresse supports a unique ecosystem: Armfuls of wildflowers peculiar to the region grow at ground level, while overhead the changing seasons bring swirling flocks of migratory birds attracted to the waterways glinting in the sun. Both in terms of its overall appearance and localized detail, the landscape was alien to Commerson.

No one had ever suggested to Commerson that he could study the natural world around him by walking through it and experiencing it firsthand. Like the university professors whose ignorance of plants in the wild had led university botanic gardens to be built, schoolboys were supposed to gain their scientific knowledge from books and anything that could be demonstrated in the immediate environs of the college. But here at school, Father Garnier's favorite subject of instruction was what his contemporaries called natural philosophy (what would today be called natural history and the life sciences) and his preferred classroom was the wide expanse of the Bresse.

The unconventional teacher who transforms pupils' lives with nonstandard methods may be something of a cliché in literature and film but that does not make the influence of such individuals any less potent when they are encountered in real life. Father Garnier's habit of taking his classes into the countryside ignited Commerson's lifelong passion for botany. Where other masters' classes required the rote learning and recitation of lengthy passages in Latin and Greek, which pupils dutifully memorized if only to escape a flogging, Father Garnier invited students to observe the world around them firsthand, employing that hallmark of Enlightenment science: the empirical method of deducing basic natural principles from repeated observations. Father Garnier and his fellow teachers of natural philosophy saw no incompatibility between the Jesuit defense and promulgation of Catholic doctrine and the pursuit of scientific truth. On the contrary, close observation of the natural world revealed that it operated according to a system of laws, constituting infallible proof of the existence of a divine lawmaker: a rationale known as theophany. Under the principle that every observable species of plant and animal on the plains of the Bresse had been deliberately differentiated from all others by a wise and benevolent creator, Father Garnier encouraged his classes to identify as many examples of the divinely creating Word as possible.

For Commerson, the realization that he passed thousands of plant species every time he took a walk was a revelation: What purpose did such variety serve? Were all plants useful to man? Had all plants been identified by man? Commerson's questions, simultaneously impossible to answer and potentially valuable in their pursuit, led Garnier to take note of his pupil.

Commerson's passion for botany can be described in words, to be sure, and Commerson himself can tell us how rapidly his awareness of the natural world grew at this time, but it is often easiest to appreciate the depths of an individual's passion by looking at what he is prepared to do in pursuit of his interest. And Commerson's surviving notebooks from his school days with Father Garnier show a striking determination to arrange dried specimens in related groups, with additional commentary and verification of measurements. As a record of the flora of the Bresse in the mid-1700s, Commerson's notebooks are so accomplished that they should properly be termed herbaria, placing them in a long line of botanists' journals across the centuries that seek to freeze a plant at a specific point in time for future reference. Medical practitioners relied on these reference works, which showed useful plants at all stages of their life cycles, although all too often early herbaria only serve to highlight how little was understood of plants in the field. When Commerson was only fifteen, his multivolume herbarium was already one of the very best of its kind in terms of the variety of specimens preserved, though the adolescent could report only commonplace knowledge about individual species. He lacked the specialized knowledge that was the preserve of herb women alone.

With their pages of seemingly fragile yet perfect leaves and flowers preserved across two and a half centuries, the volumes represent hours of painstaking labor taken at the expense of Commerson's other studies. Georges-Marie de Commerson was furious at Philibert's newly declared intention to become a botanist and threatened to sever all financial support. As an uneasy compromise, both agreed that Commerson's interest in botany could be turned toward a medical career: Not only were many medicines derived from plants, but a dominant school of contemporary thought held the circulatory systems of plants and animals to be identical, and medical students found themselves sitting through many botany classes.

Commerson therefore enrolled at the University of Montpellier on France's southeast coast, near the salt flats and windswept plains of the Camargue. The medical school had a fine reputation, but it was hardly coincidental that Commerson's new institution also oversaw France's oldest botanical garden, founded in 1593. From Montpellier, Commerson kept up a vibrant correspondence with his closest friends from Bourg-en-Bresse, including a schoolmate named Jérôme Lalande. (Just as Commerson had been seduced by Father Garnier's botany classes, Lalande had succumbed to the appeal of astronomy, and his life's work would include a catalog of over fifty thousand stars. He is commemorated, most notably, in the name of a lunar crater.) In the public eulogy that Lalande gave years later upon learning of Commerson's death, he recounted how Commerson's obsessive plant gathering had resulted in his being banned from Montpellier's Jardin des Plantes. From Lalande's account, it is easy to see why Commerson provoked the faculty.

> Since he was compiling a herbarium intended to be the most complete of its kind in the world, he did not pause to observe any niceties when presented with the chance of adding to his collection: rare plants, even single specimens were not safe. The Professor [of botany, François Boissier de Sauvages] and the Gardener were always reprimanding him, until finally, Professor Sauvages gave orders banning him from the Gardens. This did not deter him, as he could climb over the walls at night, but it did cause him to resent this famous Professor, so that he looked for every opportunity to correct him or challenge him, particularly when errors were found in the Professor's class text on Botany.

The young naturalist clearly believed himself to be above the regulations and prohibitions within which others lived their lives. But Commerson's previous biographers have been mistaken in assuming that he despised all those who taught him and who tried to restrain his activities in the botanic garden. As a satirical pamphlet originating with the Montpellier medical school in the 1750s makes clear, the errors to which Lalande refers were in fact part of a rite of passage for Montpellier medical students, involving the deliberate sabotaging of the botany professor's lectures through a creative rearrangement of plant pots and name markers. The scene is easy to imagine: the hapless professor reading from notes and instructing his class to look at a given specimen, only to stand corrected when a member of the class points out that the plant in question is surely something quite different. (One favorite substitution was the broad, nodding fronds of the banana swapped for the shrubby, ovoid-leaved coffee bush.) Feeling himself superior to his slower peers, Commerson was no doubt a smirking orchestrator of this recurring practical joke.

But even if Commerson did not admit it to Lalande, Sauvages was more than a match for his undergraduate tormentors; indeed, watching Sauvages pivot effortlessly to consider the plants substituted by his students for those he was expecting to discuss might have been part of the pleasure of this little Montpellier ritual. Sauvages knew that the Montpellier garden accounted for, quantitatively speaking, the merest fraction of botanical knowledge, and for the second time in his brief experience as a student, Commerson was exhorted to leave herbaria behind and to get out into the field (where, presumably, he could also do less damage to the University's own living collections). The language Sauvages used may strike us as hyperbolic, but it is easy to imagine its inspirational effect on a lecture theater full of young men living in an age of exploration: "Botany is a science you cannot master just by sitting at your desk or from books. After reading and study it will demand a healthy constitution to survive all sorts of weather conditions; strength to climb the most inaccessible and exposed rock faces; courage to descend into deep crevasses. You see, Nature routinely hides her best treasures in such wild places, keeping them only for those explorers who are willing to seek them out." For contemporaries, such sentiments would instantly identify Sauvages (and Commerson's earlier tutor, Father Garnier) as a disciple of the Swedish botanist Linnaeus, and in fact Sauvages and Linnaeus were good friends.

If Commerson's father had believed that medicine would replace botany as his eldest son's first love, then he was disabused of such a notion when, in 1754, shortly before his twenty-seventh birthday, Dr. Commerson announced his intention of leaving Montpellier for an undetermined period of botanizing in the Pyrenees. Whatever he lacked in terms of ambition for a medical career, Commerson's personal drive was more than apparent as he set out on his first botanizing expedition. From the Pyrenees in southwestern France, Commerson headed northeast for a comparative study of the flora of the Jura Mountains that straddled the Franco-Swiss border.

Next, Commerson invited himself to the Geneva home of France's

most famous thinker: Voltaire. At once a dramatist, poet, writer of satirical fiction, and general thorn-in-the-side of the French body politic,
Voltaire maintained a town house in the independent city of Geneva,
finding the residence an especial comfort whenever he heard rumors that
he had upset the French royal censor (again). In Geneva, Voltaire was
beyond the reach of French royal *lettres de cachet:* the warrants by which
writers found themselves woken in the night, removed from home, and
imprisoned at the king's pleasure, indefinitely and without trial. For
those who self-consciously saw theirs as the Age of Enlightenment, Voltaire was one of its brightest stars; the pull he exerted was so powerful
that he began to style himself "the innkeeper of Europe" (*l'aubergiste de
l'Europe*) as a stream of visitors made their way to his door.

For Voltaire, Commerson's formal scholarly achievements would
hardly have distinguished him from his similarly educated peers, but the
writer found his young visitor interesting for several other reasons. Voltaire, like Commerson, had despised his own father's best efforts to force
him into the legal profession. And his interest in gardening had recently
expanded as he considered the purchase of a country estate (at Ferney,
just across the border, in France).

Voltaire's conversations with Commerson were evidently so agreeable that, in February 1755, he offered Commerson the post of his secretary and estate manager. Since Voltaire could have secured the services
of almost anyone he chose, it is reasonable to conclude that Commerson
could be extraordinarily good company—witty, informed, obliging—
when he respected others or wished to please them as much as he generally pleased himself. Had he accepted, the position would have placed
Commerson in the middle of Voltaire's correspondence that would grow
to include heads of state (such as Catherine the Great) and some of the
most original minds of the Enlightenment. But in a display of both his
single-minded pursuit of botany and his unwillingness to trade a father's
direction for that of an employer, he declined the post. At the age of
twenty-seven, with no income and no obvious prospects, Commerson

appeared to all the world to be a wandering dilettante with a high opinion of himself and little regard for others' approval.

Commerson's confidence that he could make a career—and a name—out of his love for botany risks rendering him a somewhat detached figure. But as Commerson and Voltaire well knew from their animated discussions of botany, the science was believed to hold the key to revitalizing the French national economy and making France the premier imperial power of the day.

Across the Enlightenment world, thousands of men (and considerably fewer women) enjoyed the feeling that they were contributing to humankind's intellectual and material progress as they tirelessly observed, measured, and recorded the natural phenomena around them. The French laborer's dependence on wheat for bread encouraged a range of entomological, geological, and meteorological inquiries: Bugs, soil, and weather were recurring elements of the equation by which an empire determined how much of what food it could grow. The addictive luxuries of tea, sugar, chocolate, and coffee, as well as silks, muslins, damasks, and cotton, were produced for the masters of the sprawling French and British empires through the unremitting physical labor of slaves and native peoples. At the outposts of empire where all these goods originated in their raw, growing state, it was feared that demand might outstrip supply, for the millions of slaves and workers on whose backs empire was built also had to be fed and clothed.

French and British statesmen, considering their long and often tenuous supply lines, started to wonder if exotic plants could be grown more intensively and closer to home. Spinning their terrestrial globes, they dreamed of Pacific discoveries that might change the imperial status quo by providing new sources of hardwood for their navies, or cheap, reliable sources of carbohydrates for their slave drivers. As both Voltaire and Commerson would have known, to be Voltaire's secretary was perhaps not the most useful thing that Commerson could do.

By 1755, Commerson's wanderings around France and Switzerland had finally exhausted the limits of his father's patience. Georges-Marie wanted Commerson to settle down and take seriously the establishment of a career. So when Commerson was offered employment, albeit a temporary position, he was relieved that it was something he wanted to accept. Queen Louisa Ulrika of Sweden had learned that her most eminent scientist—Linnaeus—needed researchers to help him complete his monumental *Systema naturae*, the tenth edition of which would be published in 1758. (From an eleven-page first edition in 1735, the book had grown as knowledge of the natural world had expanded, and the tenth edition cataloged over 4,000 species of animals and twice as many plants.) As the queen promised to underwrite some of his research expenses, Linnaeus was able to ask his friends to recommend their best students to undertake fieldwork. Despite his undergraduate antics, Commerson found his name put forward by his Montpellier botany professor, François Sauvages. His work for Linnaeus gave him his first real exposure to the sea, as he reported on the fish of the Mediterranean. More important, the triumvirate of Linnaeus, Queen Louisa Ulrika, and Voltaire provided Commerson with the letters of recommendation that secured his place on Bougainville's circumnavigation and so sealed his fate.

With a testament from Linnaeus to his knowledge and application, and with a demonstrable contribution to the Linnaean system, Commerson was finally approaching the position of esteem that he believed he deserved. France's community of natural philosophers took notice. The director of the Jardin du Roi in Paris (renamed the Jardin des Plantes after the Revolution), Bernard de Jussieu, invited Commerson to work for him. Agonizingly for Commerson, his father was unmoved by the Jussieu family's prominence in French botany and threatened to sever all financial support unless Commerson returned home and started practicing medicine. As with every previous occasion on which Georges-Marie de Commerson had tried to bend his son to his own ideas of the best path to take, he again enabled the very outcome he wished to avoid. For in demanding that Commerson give up botany and settle down to a profession—and preferably a wife, too—Georges-Marie laid the foundations for his son's meeting with Baret.

Commerson continued to botanize, even as he gave the appearance of being serious about a respectable professional career. Lalande's eulogy describes the lengths to which Commerson regularly went to prove himself worthy of Sauvages's adventurous ideal: "He would frequently come back from his collecting expeditions in a shocking state, injured by falls from the rocks he had climbed, exhausted by all the effort. Once, he snagged his hair by a waterfall and had to tear it out, piece by piece, teetering on the point of drowning or falling." (Lalande obviously seasons his story with generous helpings of poetic license. But the climax of the passage was far from a laughing matter.) The qualified doctor became a patient when a plant-collecting interlude in the French Alps nearly proved fatal: "—Collecting plants in the Dauphiné [in southeast France], he was bitten by a dog thought to have rabies; the bite was on top of an existing leg wound and so excruciatingly painful, and the cause of so much anxiety, that despite the remedies he obtained from the monks of the Grande Chartreuse, he couldn't stand. He had to stay in bed for three months." Close to the Dauphiné, the nearby monastery of the Grande Chartreuse was home to some of the most skilled plantsmen in Europe.

Over four thousand feet up in the French Alps, this ancient home of the Carthusian order is best known today for the production of its eponymous green liqueur, first recorded in 1764. According to the monastery, the recipe for Chartreuse is known to only three monks at a time and is blended from 130 different plants. Like herb women before them, today's monks also guard their botanical knowledge and with it their livelihood. But the worldwide sale of Chartreuse does more than testify to the appeal of this eighteenth-century herbalists' invention, it demonstrates the monastic knowledge that Commerson saw as a patient. Although it is highly unlikely that the monks who treated Commerson's leg had a herbal cure for rabies, the botanist seems to have feared that his suppurating wound was a prelude to full-blown symptoms of the disease. Genuinely believing himself to be infected, he regarded it as little short of miraculous that the monks' plant-based salves and herbal teas apparently warded off his decline into hydrophobia, madness, and death.

As a medical student, Commerson had learned about plants' circulatory systems, which were believed to possess the same mechanisms as those of animals. He had also learned about common plant-based remedies for the most frequently encountered ailments, but as a practicing doctor, he would have expected to buy those remedies or their raw ingredients from local herb women. Commerson could identify most species that he found in the field and all those he preserved in his ever-expanding herbarium, yet he was ignorant of all but their most mundane medicinal uses. Now that Commerson believed he owed his life to the monks' closely guarded herbal knowledge, he wished to acquire more of that knowledge himself. Commerson needed a teacher with knowledge of a kind not to be found in the books of Father Garnier or Professor Sauvages.

As he was recuperating and looking for someone who could teach him folkloric beliefs about the curative properties of a wide range of plants, Commerson found himself teaching the rudiments of botany to a very special pupil. As he wrote to his friend Gérard in 1758:

I have found a delicate flower that I am going to press, not in my herbarium, but in the marriage bed . . . By a happy combination of circumstances she has agreeable looks, a good mind and reading knowledge and, last but not least among these minor attractions, she commands a fortune of 40,000 francs, most of which is already hers to dispose of. In marrying her, I don't believe that any compromise will be necessary because I'm sure that I can make her share my interests. I've already introduced her to natural history and our walks are now little botanizing expeditions.

The object of the thirty-one-year-old Commerson's attentions (and predictable gardening metaphors) was thirty-eight-year-old Marie-Antoinette-Vivante Beau (known simply as "Antoinette"), the daughter of a lawyer from the rich dairy lands of the Charollais.

Tempting as it is to see Commerson as a fortune hunter, it is worth bearing in mind that he may just as easily have been the hunted. An eighteenth-century unmarried woman in her late thirties had long ago been mentally consigned by family and friends to a life of dependence, first on her parents and then on her married siblings. That Antoinette remained unmarried even with a sizable fortune suggests both that previous fortune hunters may have been summarily dismissed and that the "good mind" Commerson praises was far from attractive to all prospective suitors. As their daughter's single life wore on, Antoinette's parents perhaps looked more favorably upon any respectable bachelor who came into their circle, and it is entirely possible that the Beau family courted Commerson with the sort of urgency typically associated with Jane Austen's fictional matriarchs.

The wedding took place on October 17, 1760—after protracted discussion among the parties of Antoinette's money—and the newlyweds settled in the small Loire town of Toulon-sur-Arroux, where Commerson practiced medicine and where Antoinette's beloved brother, François, was the parish priest. Within a year of the marriage Antoinette was pregnant, and Commerson was becoming well known locally for his "Swiss Tea," a remarkable concoction of twenty-two herbs and spices that would today be marketed as a detoxicant.

In searching for the means by which Commerson arrived at his

Swiss Tea we find evidence of Jeanne Baret's skill as an herb woman, evidence of how and where Baret and Commerson first met, and—most remarkably of all—a manuscript by Baret herself, when none has been thought to exist. As if encapsulating the process by which Baret has escaped the history books, her manuscript notebook from this period is currently cataloged as Commerson's; it is entitled simply "A list of medicinal plants." In finding this text, a unique survivor from the world of the herb women and their predominantly oral culture, we discover both Baret and an eighteenth-century ethnobotanical tradition.

Commerson's surviving notebooks and papers are held at the Muséum national d'histoire naturelle in Paris. Working through them, it is apparent that material before 1766—that is, before the Bougainville expedition set sail—can be divided into three distinct categories: Most visually striking are the herbaria (including his earliest known journals begun when he was just fifteen), full of carefully pressed specimens that form solid masses of green among an inky sea of written observations. The languages of the herbaria are, as would be expected, Latin for all the descriptors and French for the field observations. These field guides (in which category we may include all the observations of fish made for Linnaeus) can be contrasted with a second group of manuscripts, in which Commerson may be found copying out the work of natural philosophers whom he admires (including Linnaeus and Sauvages), interspersing their accounts of their travels and working hypotheses with his own thoughts on what they report. In this group of manuscripts, Latin is not simply the language of genus and species but is used as the preferred medium for scientific reflection. The third category of pre-1766 manuscripts comprises notebooks on human anatomy and plant biology, and these are self-evidently Commerson's undergraduate class notes from Montpellier.

Today, a reader seeking access to this pre-1766 material will find it cataloged as part of an extensive sequence with Commerson's later papers, representing all of his materials from the Bougainville expedition. One of the higher cataloging numbers, representing the later material, refers to a thirty-two-page notebook in which a spidery handwriting lists a range of French native plants and the ailments that each was thought to cure. Though attributed to Commerson, one does not need any graphological expertise to see that the handwriting is plainly not his. Moreover, it makes no sense for this anonymous, dateless notebook to come from the years of the expedition—that is, after 1766—since the notebook refers exclusively to native French plants, not the exotics that Commerson encountered in South America, the Pacific, Mauritius, and Madagascar. In an effort to keep the unbound leaves of the notebook together and perhaps to distinguish this document from surrounding papers, the written pages have been placed within a plain green folder that bears the date 1840 on the inside cover, in a hand that is different from both the writing of the notebook and Commerson's own.

Because of this date, the notebook appears at first glance to be a nineteenth-century interloper that has inexplicably come to reside with Commerson's life's work. But an entry for the notebook in a nineteenth-century library catalog from the Bibliothèque de Jussieu provides compelling evidence that the notebook predates 1766 (and that the green cover dated 1840 is not part of its original makeup). The natural history collections of the Bibliothèque de Jussieu, which were incorporated wholesale into the stacks of the Muséum national d'histoire naturelle in the nineteenth century, originally included only those materials of Commerson's that predate 1766. In other words, the notebook's provenance from the Bibliothèque de Jussieu suggests that it belongs with Commerson's earlier papers, and has little relevance to the later materials among which it is now sequenced.

To the separate facts of the notebook's composition before 1766 and in a hand other than Commerson's must be added its representation of a highly specialized body of knowledge. True to its titular promise of *Tables des plantes medicamenteuses*, the notebook offers a series of tables, or lists, of herbal remedies for common ailments. The twenty-two different species from which Commerson's popular Swiss Tea was blended are undoubtedly here, but the ingredients of the Swiss Tea are the least that the volume has to offer. For the notebook is that rarest of survivors: a herb woman's list of folkloric plant remedies from early modern Europe. The notebook holds the once-secret knowledge that, when it was divulged to outsiders at all, was only given piecemeal for payment (as Joseph Banks paid the herb women who taught him, one specimen at a time).

That Commerson's marital home of Toulon-sur-Arroux was just over twelve miles from the village of Baret's birth, La Comelle-sous-Beuvray, indicates that in all the years Commerson had botanized across France and her borders, Baret (typical of her class) had traveled no farther than her own legs could carry her in a single day.

La Comelle-sous-Beuvray (or La Comelle, as it is more conveniently called) takes its name from its abundance of surviving Roman architecture. (*Comelle* is thought to be a corruption of *columella*—Latin for a small column.) Architecturally, the Loire is best known today for its moated châteaus, though the region's extensive Roman remains amply repay the decision to visit even a fraction of them. The natural beauty that attracted Romans and modern tourists alike to the Loire is complemented by an extensive navigable inland waterway: a rich prize indeed in the province of Roman Gaul.

For a village with a modern population of 199 citizens, La Comelle has a disproportionately large share of architectural treasures evoking the area's centuries-old settlement. Baret's girlhood home existed alongside what must have seemed inexplicably fantastic structures to the subsistence laborers of the area: a Roman Temple of Janus (the two-faced god looking backward and forward) in a field next to the river Arroux;

the soaring Romanesque twelfth-century cathedral of Saints-Lazare in Autun; and even an Autun museum (the Musée Rolin) justifiably proud of its display of the twelfth-century sculpture Gislebertus's *The Temptation of Eve*. For those who believe in fate, it seems prophetic that Baret's childhood home was situated between the dual faces of Janus and an iconic representation of Eve in the Garden of Eden.

La Comelle's tourist board rightly celebrates all of these man-made wonders alongside the area's unspoiled natural beauty, and the town's promotional literature also notes that "La Comelle has a person of renown, who was born 'Jeanne Baret', who between 1766 and 1773 was the first women to make a tour of the world." Like Baret's notebook, which was absorbed into Commerson's papers, her circumnavigation is here made coterminous with Commerson's journey: He died in Mauritius in 1773, though she did not return to France until 1775. Even this short history from the village of her birth finds her elusive. Yet we can sketch her early years with some confidence.

Returning to the story of Baret's birth, scratched out by Father Pierre in the Autun register, her mother is named as Jeanne Pochard. Pochard was the daughter of Nicolas Esaic Pochard and Elizabeth Grandjean. The surnames Pochard and Grandjean are significant for they are among those accepted by the International Huguenot Society as being indicative of Huguenot (that is, French Protestant) ancestry. To bear a surname accepted by the society as being a Huguenot surname is not, of course, an infallible guide to the religious beliefs of one's ancestors, but to find a Pochard in combination with a Grandjean strongly suggests that Jeanne Baret's maternal grandparents were part of the French Protestant community. This aspect of Baret's family history is important to her story: Early modern Protestant communities generally had higher levels of literacy than their Catholic counterparts, since they placed great emphasis on an individual's ability to read the Bible in the vernacular (as opposed to listening to Mass celebrated in Latin).

Under King Henry IV of France, the Huguenots had been granted religious toleration, enshrined in the Edict of Nantes (1598). Henry IV's religious pluralism was, however, not to everyone's liking, least of all that of his formidable mother-in-law, Catherine de Medici. When Henry IV was assassinated in 1610, the Huguenots lost the best-placed advocate they had ever had. Their freedoms were progressively eroded until the Edict of Nantes was finally revoked by Louis XIV in 1685. Thereafter, they became a persecuted minority within France. Many emigrated, resulting in the moving of entire literate communities of skilled workers from France to Protestant northern Europe and North America. For Huguenots who could not or would not emigrate, life in eighteenth-century France was both harsh and heavily scrutinized. Children of self-confessed Huguenot parents had to be baptized according to Catholic rites within two days of birth, and both parents and children had to be seen worshipping at their local Catholic church. Whatever beliefs were promulgated behind closed doors, the French state would enforce the appearance of religious conformity within the community. Jeanne Baret's baptismal record indicates that she was baptized the day after her birth, which may indicate Huguenot conformity with French law, rather than family fears over the child's immediate prospects for survival.

If Jeanne Pochard was indeed of Huguenot parentage, then she was likely literate. But even though she was capable of signing the register of Jeanne Baret's birth, she did not since only the father's signature had any legal value or meaning. Unlike Pochard, the surname Baret is not a recognized marker of Huguenot ancestry, suggesting that the Huguenot-born Jeanne Pochard, weary of living a restricted life in an ostracized community, and forced from an early age to make a public observance of Catholicism, ended up marrying the Catholic Jean Baret. He may have been beneath her in terms of educational achievement, since he was illiterate, but he was a hard worker. By law, their daughter, Jeanne Baret, had to be baptized a Catholic, and the family conformed with the injunction placed on Huguenots to arrange such baptisms speedily: Life was difficult enough without inviting any further scrutiny. As a woman and a member of a religious minority in a rigidly hierarchical society, Jeanne Pochard could hardly use her literacy to help raise her family out of poverty, but she could at least teach her daughter to read. Commerson, then, did not teach Baret to read as many have claimed; she understood the rudiments of reading and writing as a child.

Baret must have first met Commerson at some point between 1760 and 1764 while she was collecting plants a few miles from La Comelle and he was botanizing a few miles from his home in Toulon-sur-Arroux. Unlike Antoinette, who had to be instructed in the rudiments of botany, Baret could easily answer Commerson's many questions about the likely herbal composition of the remedies he had received at the Grande Chartreuse. Undoubtedly Commerson initially paid Baret for sharing her expertise, as Joseph Banks paid the herb women who instructed him, but at some point in the four years after they met, she and Commerson became lovers. And what really stoked the gossipmongers of Toulon-sur-Arroux was that the doctor started living with his lover so soon after the death of his wife.

Antoinette's pregnancy within a year of her marriage in October 1760 had led to the birth of a son, François Archambaud, on April 16, 1762. Three days after the birth, Antoinette died. Given Baret's knowledge of plant remedies, and certainly of plant poisons, it should be stressed that Antoinette's death resulted from complications arising from her son's birth, and not from any nefarious activities on Baret's part. Indeed, it is not certain that Commerson and Baret had become lovers before the death of his wife. That death left Commerson, aged thirty-four, a widower with a new baby son, whose existence also happened to secure Commerson's command of Antoinette's dowry.

In the years since he turned down Jussieu's offer of a position in the Jardin du Roi, Commerson had surely speculated at length about what he might have achieved there had he not been in danger of losing the financial lifeline provided by his parents. Now he was free to plan his future, so long as it would accommodate the demands of a growing child. Beyond whatever grief he felt, there were practical matters to be considered. Like any well-to-do wife, Antoinette had overseen the management of the household servants, who continued to cook and clean for Commerson as before. But Commerson had no interest in providing the kind of direction that such household staff expected—reviewing weekly menus, paying tradesmen's bills. And so by spring 1764, Commerson had installed a housekeeper to take care of all such details that might distract a gentleman from his studies. The housekeeper was Jeanne Baret.

From their first chance meeting in the countryside between La Comelle and Toulon-sur-Arroux, Baret and Commerson had grown close. It is easy to imagine Baret's initial delight that an educated gentleman asked her to share her expertise with him, and we know that Commerson could be engaging company when he chose. Many professional men no doubt lodged their orders with Baret but, as the previous history of herb women has shown, such men presented a largely united front in their condescension toward the women who underpinned their businesses. In contrast, Commerson, who had charmed a well-to-do heiress where others must have failed, and who liked a woman with a "fine mind and good reading knowledge," was entirely easy discussing botany with Baret as with an equal. In Baret, Commerson had the perfect complement to his own fund of classical botanical education and the void in his domestic arrangements: a woman capable of being at once his teacher, assistant, and all-around aide.

It was an unequal partnership, to be sure, in that Commerson had wealth and social status, while as an herb woman from a community of day laborers, Baret was used to a precarious existence on the margins of financial stability and social respectability. In Commerson's household, she had a solid roof over her head and a ready supply of food on the table. One imagines her herb woman's notebook as a lover's gift to Commerson: the ethnobotanical wisdom of centuries being something tangible she could offer in return for her newfound domestic comforts. And whatever the history of their relationship in the early 1760s, they were certainly lovers by spring 1764, for in late summer of that year, Baret was visibly pregnant and Commerson was widely assumed by his neighbors to be the father.

Baret's presence in Commerson's house had been, almost from the first, a source of endless interest and, increasingly, publicly voiced outrage among the townspeople. A housekeeper who was free to come and go in her master's study and who stood side by side with him in consideration of papers and plants was clearly something more than a mere servant. Even worse, the doctor's brother-in-law was the parish priest, yet the doctor seemed careless of any offense he gave, either as a family member or as a congregant. Eighteenth-century etiquette required that a respectable family who found an unmarried servant to be pregnant should turn her out immediately, to avoid the moral contagion and impropriety associated with her sin. It was untenable that the pregnant Baret should continue living with and working for Commerson, and right under the nose of the priest. But Antoinette's death—and her dowry—had freed Commerson from the need to stay in a village in which his lifestyle was not accepted. Why should he now be dictated to? In August 1764, Commerson made arrangements for Baret to see an attorney in the town of Digoin, some eighteen miles south of Toulon-sur-Arroux.

Royal law required any woman who was unmarried and with child to obtain a certificate of pregnancy. The concept of the certificate may seem like a bureaucratic folly, but it stemmed from the Enlightenment state's desire to measure and account for the body politic as effectively as Enlightenment experimentation was inquiring into the human frame. Certificates of pregnancy of the region and period repeatedly offer a window into the desperate lives of poverty-stricken, typically illiterate young women, naming their child's father before witnesses of their own class, or of the presiding attorney's choosing. Just as Baret's baptismal record is a short narrative, rather than a series of answers to standard questions, so Baret's certificate of pregnancy also deviates from its expected form.

Dated August 22, 1764, it states that "the woman concerned (who is five months pregnant) declined to name the father" and is signed by Baret herself and witnessed by two men of consequence: "Hughes Maynard de Bisefranc, esquire. Lord of Lavaux and Cypierre of St Louis" and "Henri Alexandre Laligant, doctor." A local major landowner, Bisefranc, and the Autun doctor, Laligant, had somehow been co-opted into riding over twenty miles to sign Baret's legal declaration that her unborn child's father would remain anonymous.

As Baret traveled to Digoin, Commerson said his good-byes to his two-year-old son, Archambaud, and delivered the boy to Antoinette's brother, Father François Beau, presumably in an atmosphere of strained politeness and lengthy silences. Commerson would never see Archambaud again, though the priest would always be a zealous advocate for his godson's best interests. Together, Baret and Commerson now took a coach for Paris. Baret was twenty-four and Commerson thirty-six. Though they did not know it, they had begun a journey that would help to redraw the known world.

Two

 "TO JEANNE BARET, ALSO KNOWN AS JEANNE DE BONNEFOY"

A Changed Identity in Paris

THE MODERN TRAVELER can complete the 212-mile drive from Digoin to Paris in approximately four hours, most of which will be spent on the well-maintained, northward-heading A77. In late 1764, as Baret sat in a horse-drawn coach for only the second time in her life (the first being for the twenty-mile journey from Toulon-sur-Arroux to Digoin), she faced at least a four-day journey to Paris at Commerson's side. Throughout this time, a pregnant Baret was jolted against Commerson as they occupied two of the four inside seats in a post chaise typical of the period:

a coach lacking in suspension and pulled by a team of four horses that was changed at wayside inns. Such coaches often permitted four or more poorer travelers to sit outside, muffled up against all kinds of weather alongside luggage, the postillion [driver], and bags of letters—the transportation of the mail being the raison d'être for most coaching routes. Neither comfortable nor relaxing, eighteenth-century coach travel was a necessity that one endured if the occasion demanded it and if funds allowed.

Given Baret's provincial background, it is easy to imagine the physical rigors of the journey being somewhat mitigated by the ever-changing scenery. En route from Digoin to Paris, Baret encountered landscapes and cityscapes that were wholly new. The Loire, bigger than any river Baret had ever seen, accompanied them for two days. As the post chaise made its bone-jarring way along the river's side, the city of Orléans came into view; with its midcentury population of approximately sixty thousand, it was easily the largest city that Baret had yet experienced. Despite the cramped, sweltering confines of the coach and her aching joints that had registered every rut of the road, Baret saw more in four days than anyone of her class would typically expect to see in a lifetime. The real astonishment of the journey, however, lay at its end: Paris.

The population of mid-eighteenth-century Paris was easily ten times larger than that of Orléans and vaster than anything known to the few residents of La Comelle. What many regard as the quintessential landmarks of the city—the Arc de Triomphe and the Eiffel Tower—are nineteenth-century innovations, as are the city's most famous wide boulevards. The Paris that Baret approached on the Orléans mail coach was a city dominated by churches and royal palaces: the dense medieval street plan of districts such as the Marais yielding to the honey-colored sandstone facades of neoclassical mansions on the Île de la Cité. Gliding between the buildings of five centuries, the river Seine was freighted with wooden barges bearing cargoes representative of the extent of France's imperial reach. The city absorbed both luxury goods and raw materials, its legions of workers fed the great markets of Les Halles, into which livestock, fish, and produce poured from the surrounding countryside.

In addition to its rapacious physical appetites (for clothes, food, goods, and services), Enlightenment Paris was also consumed by a collective hunger for knowledge. Baret's Paris was the center of a publishing phenomenon that had far-reaching implications for the city's population and economy, and that would shape Baret's own life. Between 1751 and 1772, the writer Denis Diderot and the mathematician Jean Le Rond d'Alembert designed and edited one of the greatest publishing projects in history: the twenty-eight volumes of the *Encyclopédie*, a work so vast in scope and unprecedented in its success that at least one out of every one hundred Parisians are thought to have been employed on the project across its complex twenty-one-year printing history. It was not simply the obvious trades of papermaker, printer, bookbinder, and bookseller who were affected by the *Encyclopédie*'s gravitational pull: Ink (made from cuttlefish) became in short supply; the linen trade found it impossible to meet the papermakers' demand (linen rags formed the basis of good-quality handmade paper). Eleven of the *Encyclopédie*'s huge volumes are occupied by engraved plates, and most of these plates fall into two distinct groups: representations of contemporary technology, including industrial processes, and newly commissioned images of the natural world. From fleas to elephants and from bats to sea lions, the totality of known species was there.

But even as it aspired to be comprehensive, the *Encyclopédie*'s images and entries acknowledged the limits of Enlightenment knowledge. In the process, it questioned the claims of church and state to absolute authority. When Baret arrived in Paris, the success of the early volumes of the *Encyclopédie* had demonstrated the reading public's desire to know what lay beyond their immediate horizons. A French circumnavigation of the world not only offered government ministers the prospect of new lands to colonize but also promised scientists rich additions to zoological and botanical knowledge. Paris was a knowledge economy and it was booming.

Among the considerable amount of building work taking place in mid-eighteenth-century Paris, some of the most desirable developments were rising around the city's botanical garden, where Commerson had once been offered a position. Created in 1626 and first opened to the public in 1640, the Jardin du Roi was constantly evolving. As Baret and Commerson arrived in Paris in 1764, work had already begun on extending its walkways and increasing the size of its hothouses to accommodate an increasingly diverse collection. Commerson, wishing to live as near to the Jardin du Roi as possible, engaged an apartment for Baret and himself a few minutes' walk away in the rue des Boulangers.

Walking down the street today, it is possible to see some eighteenth-century exteriors, their smooth, unadorned, stone facades punctuated by green window shutters and tiny wrought-iron balconies sprouting pots of carmine-colored pelargoniums. Once inside, it is evident that the allure of rent by the square meter has been too tempting for generations of landlords, and once-spacious sets of eighteenth-century rooms have been divided and subdivided into efficient rental apartments making maximum use of every centimeter of space. Even so, it is still possible to look out at the city skyline beyond, knowing that what we see is much the same as the view Baret took in. For Paris, unlike its rival London, prohibited the kind of skyrise developments that have obliterated most pre-twentieth-century cityscapes. We can imagine green fields and woods still visible beyond the eighteenth-century city limits (which would easily sit within the modern Paris ring road, or boulevard Périphérique), and wonder at the impact of all this upon a twenty-four-year-old woman who had previously never traveled farther than twenty miles from her birthplace.

Baret and Commerson took possession of a fashionable second-floor suite of rooms with access to a communal courtyard. When Baret took the housekeeping money and headed for city's markets, she occupied an unusual position. Many of the female servants bargaining for produce at the vegetable stalls undoubtedly knew what it was to share the bed of the master of the house, willingly or not, but surely very few knew what it was to share his lifestyle as well. The laboring class into which Baret was born had neither money nor use for luxuries such as candles, but Baret now lived in a world in which daylight activities could be extended into the evening—not to mention the special entertainments of the Paris night: theater, music, opera. Living in La Comelle, Baret had no notion of a playhouse or a pleasure garden, but in Paris she was able to observe the rich cultural life of the city as she went about her errands.

To her relief, the provincial morality of Toulon-sur-Arroux did not extend to the capital: The neighbors who shared use of the block's communal areas speculated on her pregnancy, to be sure, but Baret was not ostracized because of it. Nor was there any need to explain anything to Commerson's growing circle of Paris acquaintances, for one of the most feted of contemporary thinkers, Jean-Jacques Rousseau, lived openly in Paris with his working-class mistress, Thérèse Levasseur, who would eventually bear him five children. In the last months of her pregnancy, Baret became accustomed to a spacious, solidly built home with good-quality food on the table, a warm hearth, and everything that could make life agreeable. Her only duty, in addition to ensuring the smooth running of their rue des Boulangers apartment, was to observe and care for the collection that Commerson was already amassing, rapidly turning its elegant rooms into one large hothouse.

Though Commerson had no paid work at the Jardin du Roi, the apartment's proximity to the gardens meant he could conveniently effect introductions to leading Enlightenment scientists. Commerson had only to leave his calling card in order to secure a meeting with a particular individual, since his work for Linnaeus was well known and still admired. In 1764, the director of the Jardin du Roi was Georges-Louis Leclerc, comte de Buffon. Just as Diderot and d'Alembert had angered both church and state with the ongoing publication of their egalitarian *Encyclopédie,* so

Buffon was laboring over his own equally controversial, equally monumental multivolume reference work, the *Histoire naturelle*. Where Diderot infuriated his critics and delighted his supporters by insinuating criticisms of the established order in what should have been the most innocuous entries (for example, descriptions of foreign cities often discussed alternative forms of government), so Buffon drew anger from the doctors of the Sorbonne with his speculations arising from the infant sciences of geology and paleontology. As Commerson introduced himself at the Jardin du Roi in 1764, fifteen volumes of the *Histoire naturelle* had already appeared and had proved to be a resounding commercial success, the engraved plates bringing a world of exotic fauna and avifauna to armchair travelers across Enlightenment Europe. At the Jardin du Roi, Commerson and Buffon became good friends, and Commerson finally met Jussieu.

The minutiae of Baret's Paris home life at this time are unknown, but Buffon's domestic arrangements are worth mentioning as an example of the *philosophe*'s life unconstrained by social niceties or regular family responsibilities. When not in Paris, Buffon could be found rambling about his Burgundian château in the village of Montbard: A perplexing master for the château's servants, he found it easiest to study the habits of native French mammals, birds, and reptiles by giving them the run of the house. To Buffon's scientific contemporaries, this was regarded less as a chaotic eccentricity and more as the most practical means of collecting empirical data. Visitors' reports therefore conjure up scenes of badgers luxuriating in front of the fire, hedgehogs defecating in the kitchen pots, and wolf pups chasing frantic farmyard birds, all playing out as Buffon's pet capuchin monkey, Jocko, scampered around doing exactly as he pleased. (Madame Buffon, we are told, could often be found in the relative tranquillity of the château's purpose-built aviary.)

Baret and Commerson's shared interest being flora rather than fauna, the apartment in the rue des Boulangers was certainly less animated than Buffon's Montbard home, but it was presumably no less dedicated to the study and preservation of specimens, be they dried, drying, or very much alive. The nature of Baret's contribution to Commerson's work at this time is best understood if we examine mid-eighteenth-century interest in a plant with which we are all familiar: coffee.

The first coffee of the morning is today considered a necessity for many, but in 1760s Paris it was a luxury, albeit an addictive one. Visitors to Paris today can still enjoy an excellent cup of coffee at the city's oldest coffee-house and restaurant, Le Procope, which first opened its stylish paneled rooms in 1686, and established its civilized custom of allowing the coffee drinker to linger over a single cup while reading or writing. Pictures of philosophes such as Voltaire that now adorn its walls are no mere decoration, but rather a who's who of Procope's satisfied customers. The early success of Procope naturally encouraged imitators across Paris, all of which found the combination of a relaxed ambience and good coffee to be a recipe for commercial success. Soon, as individual coffeehouses became associated with particular political factions or social movements, Le Procope was—and, to a certain extent, still is—the writers' coffee-house of choice.

But the availability and price of coffee in Paris in the 1760s depended on fragile ocean supply lines, which could be interrupted by the outbreak of hostilities between the European powers, or the revolt of colonized peoples. The Dutch had succeeded in transplanting coffee trees from Asia to their Indonesian island stronghold of Batavia (Java) in the early seventeenth century, and as a result coffee was much cheaper in the Netherlands than in France. Seeing the burgeoning domestic market for coffee, French merchants dearly wished that their own country's botanists could find a means of guaranteeing a regular supply of good-quality coffee beans from an unproblematic French colony. The Dutch were certainly not about to share their expertise. And coffee is a plant with a very particular set of needs.

The many species of coffee all share the basic likes and dislikes of *Coffea arabica*, a ten- to twelve-foot subtropical tree that sickens if not grown in a properly alkaline soil and dies if exposed to freezing temperatures. Today it is an easy and inexpensive matter for gardeners to test the acidity of their soil. But in the mid-eighteenth century, botanists stared at precious specimens of *Coffea arabica* in Europe's hothouses and tirelessly recorded every measurable variable of water, soil, and light, tracking a plant's development through the growing year and desperately hoping for a harvest of beans. Even when the plant fruited and beans were harvested, eighteenth-century botanists had no way of knowing if a particular combination of conditions was optimal until growers at a variety of sites could replicate the cultivation. The French eventually established lucrative coffee plantations on their Caribbean colony of Saint-Domingue (now Haiti) and by the 1780s were able to export French-Caribbean coffee across the world. But a slave revolt in Saint-Domingue in 1791 demonstrated—among other things—an inability to rely on a supply of exotic plants from colonial outposts.

Commerson's obsessive determination to understand as much about the plant kingdom as he could guaranteed engagement with the sorts of botanical puzzles that were thought to hold the key to economic development. And whether the plant being studied was coffee or cinchona (the source of the antimalarial drug quinine), a network of reliable, competent growers was needed beyond the nation's botanical gardens. The correspondence of André Thouin, director of the Jardin du Roi in 1786, shows that 403 amateur growers across France and its empire were regularly sent specimens of exotic seeds to experiment with in their own homes. The amateur growers included leading thinkers such as Jean-Jacques Rousseau, who visited the Jardin du Roi in November 1770 and wrote delightedly that its botanists "have gladly given me samples of plants."

As they indulged their own passion for gardening, such amateur growers could be counted on to record faithfully a plant's apparent likes and dislikes, providing data that could be used in the commercial development of a species. For example, if gardeners across France reported that coffee plants died when planted in soil that was also used for potatoes, it would be easy to deduce that coffee hates the acidic soil in which potato plants thrive.

From thousands of such observations, undertaken across an equally broad range of species, the botanists of the Jardin du Roi oversaw a vast virtual garden and learned how best to feed France. (If the process sounds haphazard, it may be a surprise to discover that amateur gardeners engage in similar work today. In *The Botany of Desire*, Michael Pollan describes how the diversity of the world's apple crop lies in the hands of enthusiasts prepared to grow and report on previously unrecorded varieties of apple gathered from ancient orchards in Kazakhstan. Not all crop research and development takes place in research facility greenhouses.)

Commerson was precisely the sort of individual who could be trusted to care for and keep accurate records on a precious specimen, whether a seed, a rhizome (a tuber), or a living plant. And whatever he brought back to the rue des Boulangers to study, Baret could help him. Baret did not need formal instruction or a working knowledge of the Linnaean taxonomy that Commerson, Buffon, and Jussieu used with ease. Equipped with her herb woman's knowledge of native French species, she could immediately see resemblances between the familiar and the unfamiliar: If X looks like Y, perhaps it has the same properties as Y; perhaps it likes the same conditions; perhaps its leaves, its flowers, its roots have the same medicinal benefits.

As Baret had been Commerson's teacher back in Toulon-sur-Arroux, she now became his coresearcher, living with him amid the subjects of their investigations newly arrived from the Jardin du Roi. Everywhere Baret looked, there were stalks, leaves, and flowers hanging upside down to dry, awaiting immortality between the sheets of Commerson's herbaria: fronds in water waiting to be sketched; brittle seed pods getting ready to burst and shower their ripe contents across the room; bulbs and fleshy roots to be dissected; and living potted plants of all shapes and sizes filtering the Paris light through leafy window shades of green. And with her country upbringing, Baret was unlikely to become hysterical if an iridescent tropical beetle should emerge from an outsized seed pod and fly about their rooms, mesmerized by the candlelight. It was the perfect environment for a plant lover but a highly impractical home in which to raise a child—and in December 1764, the tranquillity of this apartment herbarium disappeared. Baret gave birth to a son.

The few modern histories of Baret typically ignore this period in her life or pass over it as quickly as possible. The events of the months from December 1764, when Jean-Pierre Baret was born, to December 1766, when Baret presented herself as a man in order to join Bougainville's circumnavigation, are, however, key to understanding her relationship with Commerson, as well as her way of thinking. Just as she had refused to name her child's father on the certificate of pregnancy, she gave the boy her own surname. But the father who was so glaringly absent on paper was all too present in the rue des Boulangers apartment, and was temperamentally unsuited to the demands made by an infant who cried at all hours of the day and night. Whether we see men like Commerson and Buffon as driven by uncontrollable obsessions or simply as selfish, we can be certain that the intellectual passions that made them potentially interesting companions also made them frustrating ones. Commerson clearly reacted badly to Jean-Pierre's birth and wanted nothing to do with the child, for in January 1765, the boy was placed in the care of the Paris foundling hospital, whose staff entrusted him to a foster mother.

Nearly two hundred and fifty years later, this simple statement of the facts still has the power to shock. Throughout history, few charges are guaranteed to arouse more hostility across the world than the accusation that a mother is devoid of any maternal feeling, and Baret risks becoming an unsympathetic figure for evidently preferring her lover over her child. Because this part of Baret's history has the potentially corrosive power to undermine every other aspect of her life, we need to consider how she saw things in December 1764.

With the exception of the classical Roman world, at no point in Western history has the abandonment of one's own children been seen as anything other than a taboo subject. Parisians in 1764 were perhaps even more acutely sensitive to this than any community before or since, due to two scandalous publications that appeared in the month of Jean-Pierre Baret's birth. The book that started the controversy was a weighty 550-page work of political theory by Jean-Jacques Rousseau, alternately the darling and the punching bag of intellectual circles, depending on how combative his paranoia was making him at any given time.

To be sure, Rousseau's *Letters Written from the Mountain* has nothing to say about the reprehensible action of abandoning one's child, but its lofty sociopolitical pronouncements so angered Rousseau's nemesis Voltaire that he responded with an eight-page anonymous pamphlet. In *The Sentiment of the Citizens,* Voltaire revealed the dirtiest secret he knew about Rousseau's history: From 1746 to 1752, Rousseau had caused his working-class mistress, Thérèse Levasseur, to entrust the five children born to them to the Paris foundling hospital. Voltaire had skewered Rousseau, not only for disposing of five infants in succession as though they were some sort of recurring annual pest but also because Rousseau was celebrated across Europe as the author of *Émile, or on Education,* a 1762 novel detailing what Rousseau believed to be the ideal upbringing of a male and female child. And parental abandonment formed no part of *Émile*'s paternal vision. Rousseau stood revealed as a hypocrite and a monster—and easily the best subject of city gossip since April of that year, when the king's former mistress, Madame de Pompadour, had died.

Baret did not move in the world of the literary salon, where educated, aristocratic women discussed art, politics, and social scandal, but Rousseau was such a force in contemporary European culture that no one with access to newspapers or public forums of any kind could have re-mained unaware of the revelation regarding his private life. Going about her business in Paris in December 1764, Baret could not have avoided hearing virulent condemnation of mothers and fathers who resorted to abandoning their children.

But the statistics relating to child abandonment in France in the 1760s suggest that many of those professing to be scandalized by Rous-seau's actions must have been hypocrites: Approximately sixty thousand babies were left in French doorways every year of the decade, and over one-quarter of live births in the capital were thought to result in aban-donment. The most celebrated Parisian to acknowledge that he was a foundling—left in a box on the steps of the church of Saint-Jean-le-Rond—was the coeditor of Diderot's *Encyclopédie*, Jean Le Rond d'Alembert. Against this background of helpless infants being consigned to city doorways, to live or die as fate would have it, the Paris found-ling hospital where Baret sent her son was intended to provide a humane answer to a desperate mother's prayer.

The Paris Hôpital des enfants-trouvés was founded in 1670 as a con-tinuation of work begun by Saint Vincent de Paul to stem the tide of tiny corpses—frozen in winter and the prey of rats in any season—that greeted the early-morning pedestrian. Neither an orphanage nor a hos-pital as we understand these terms, the institution took its name from another meaning of hôpital—hospice (a word that used to denote an in-stitution offering temporary care of any sort, not necessarily to the ter-minally ill). An estimated six thousand babies passed through its doors every year. The nuns in charge of the foundling hospital directed teams of wet nurses to provide immediate sustenance for any admitted child, until such time as he or she could be moved to a foster home outside Paris, where the child would live with other foundlings, his or her care sub-sidized by an allowance paid from the hospital to the caregiver. Finally, between the ages of six and eight, the children would return to the city as apprentices, to learn some useful trade.

This was the grand vision of Saint Vincent de Paul, but at his death in 1660, the forerunner of the Paris foundling hospital was still a small-scale operation. In 1670, a dedicated building allowed a huge increase in the number of infants that could be cared for, but no one stopped to consider the rapid spread of disease among a tightly packed population of newborns: Mortality rates were typically 70 percent in the first twelve months of a child's entry into the system.

Critics were, however, less concerned by these unnecessary deaths than by a lack of transparency in the hospital's admissions process: With an intake of approximately six thousand children per year, against an annual total of at least five times that number of abandoned children in Paris alone, the hospital clearly could not help all who might benefit from its services. Some charged that the foundling hospital primarily helped wealthy Parisiennes who paid to rid themselves of the products of extramarital affairs, both within their own class and across the class divide. Others believed that it was necessary to know an administrator of the hospital to secure a place for a child. For mothers lacking money or friends in the right places, a lottery determined their baby's admission. The trinkets that many of these desperately poor women chose to leave with their children, in hopes of future recognition and reunion, may help to illuminate Baret's thinking.

In the London Foundling Hospital, endowed in 1739 by a benevolent merchant named Thomas Coram, a museum has grown in the anteroom where ordinary women once drew lots to determine their child's admittance or rejection. Most poignant among its exhibits are the keepsakes that the poorest women left with their children, such as walnut shells or thread bracelets. These fragile identifiers allowed mothers a tiny glimpse of hope, imagining a prosperous future in which they might return to the hospital and trace their child, the precious, pitiful object finally confirming its bearer's true identity. Rousseau insisted that he had written a cipher on a piece of paper sewn into the cloths of his first relinquished child (the implication being that he wished to leave open the possibility of tracing it).

D'Alembert was in fact eventually reclaimed by his father, suggesting that the hopes of relinquishing mothers were not wholly futile. (These were the improbable family reunions on which swaths of sentimental fictions were based, causing satirists to mock plot devices involving identifying jewelry and birthmarks.)

Perhaps Baret gave up Jean-Pierre fully persuaded that some of the most influential women in Paris saw merit in the Hôpital des enfants-trouvés, and firmly believing that the separation would be temporary. Thinking that Commerson could be persuaded to own the boy, or that she might save enough out of the housekeeping to somehow make a life for them both, Baret may have clung to the hope embodied in the pathetic tokens at the London Foundling Hospital Museum: the hope that one day, in the not-too-distant future, she could reclaim her son and see him made his father's heir.

Certainly some communication between Paris and Toulon-sur-Arroux must have hinted at the possibility of a wedding, since Commerson's brother-in-law, Father François Beau, appears to have written to Commerson seeking clarification. The likely contents (and probable destruction) of Father Beau's letter can be deduced from Commerson's surviving rant of a response, alternately combative and sarcastic: "Your assumption of a second marriage is as stupid as it is untrue and I take offense at your prying into my business. No one has any right to interrogate me on this subject but, since you have been so kind as to make inquiries, let me assure you that I'm doing very nicely." Comfortable in his new life in Paris, Commerson saw no need to contract a marriage to a woman who was already living in his apartment, assisting him with his work, taking care of the housekeeping, and sharing his bed. Even if he had felt a moral obligation to marry the mother of his child, Baret's humble origins made this socially unthinkable.

Lacking journal reflections from Baret or Commerson on the possibility of their marriage, we can turn to the well-documented, almost parallel relationship between Thérèse Levasseur and Rousseau to see how Rousseau's friends ridiculed the background of his working-class mistress and her unfamiliarity with their carefully choreographed social rituals. Levasseur's presence at the table was enough to visibly disconcert Rousseau's middle- and upper-class friends, who preferred that she not be invited to join their gatherings. Rousseau did eventually marry Levasseur, but he had by then hemorrhaged so many friends through his obvious emotional instability that this apparently romantic defiance of social convention was not likely to be imitated. And Commerson, though a great admirer of Rousseau's written work, was clearly too desirous of acceptance in French intellectual circles to countenance a marriage with Baret.

And so, while it is easy to rush to judge Baret, to think her foolish for believing that Commerson might finally legitimize their relationship and their child in the eyes of the church and state, Baret would be neither the first nor the last woman to persist in a relationship in hopes of her lover's change of heart.

Any hope of an eventual reunion with Jean-Pierre would be shattered when he was reported dead in the summer of 1765—a trauma whose statistical likelihood did not make it any easier to bear. Agonizingly for Baret, she could not turn to Commerson to share her grief because Commerson himself was seriously ill.

Commerson's eighteenth- and nineteenth-century biographers identify a "pleurisy" at this time, but the modern understanding of this painful lung inflammation holds that it can arise from a wide range of underlying causes, including a cracked rib or a pulmonary embolism. We have already heard his friend Lalande's dramatic rendition of the rigors to which Commerson subjected his body, and Commerson may well have sustained a rib fracture when scrambling about in search of specimens. As he lay in bed, sweating and contorted with chest pains, his every breath resulting in agony, Baret must have considered the ever-present menace of tuberculosis: a death sentence in 1765.

Baret knew that, in the event of Commerson's death, she would be destitute. The apartment was rented in Commerson's name—indeed, prior to the French Revolution of 1789, women in France could not enter into a legal contract in their own right. Since Baret was not Commerson's wife, his death would have led to her expulsion from their home, with only the clothes on her back and any ready cash to which she had access. In the eyes of the law, and Commerson's in-laws, she was technically a housekeeper, and therefore liable to the suspicion regularly attached to domestic staff, on whom the wealthy depended even as they fundamentally mistrusted servants as a class. If life with Commerson was emotionally wearing, with its tantalizing though remote possibility of marriage, life without him would be physically hard: Baret would need to make her way back to the area she knew and return to the life of an herb woman, always reliant on the vagaries of weather, clients, and the land itself. She had left all that behind in the few square miles between La Comelle and Toulon-sur-Arroux. Irrespective of any genuine feelings Baret had for Commerson, life in Paris was good and Baret surely wanted it to stay that way.

Baret took care of Commerson, letting him rest in bed as she continued to run their home, tending to all of the specimens surrounding them. Most time-consuming and tiring were the larger potted plants that had to be watered with ice-cold water pumped in the communal courtyard and carried up two flights of stairs. Day in and day out, Baret ran up and down, caring for Commerson and their collection. During his illness, Commerson was offered an appointment to the royal menagerie housed at Versailles, but he was not in a position to visit the menagerie or to imagine starting work there. To be a naturalist of the royal menagerie, by appointment to Louis XV himself, would have silenced the criticisms of Commerson's father and in-laws forever, and he would surely have taken the post if he could have comfortably raised himself out of bed. That he did not is indicative of the severity of his illness, and how much Baret must have feared losing him.

With Baret's nursing, Commerson slowly resumed his correspondence and returned to a long-standing though intermittent project, a book he was writing called *Martyrologe de la botanique*. In translating the title as *Martyrs of Botany* and speculating on whether Commerson saw himself among their number, we risk overlooking the controversial nature of his choice of words. In 1760s France, "martyrs" were those who had given their life for the Catholic faith and were good candidates for canonization. In associating martyrdom with botany, Commerson was elevating science as a credo in its own right, with a wink to his readers to acknowledge that he was being provocative. Like Diderot and d'Alembert in their *Encyclopédie* or Buffon in his *Histoire naturelle*, Commerson was ready to declare his membership in the congregation of the philosophes in print. Now, he just had to find the project that would make him known outside intellectual circles.

In the latter half of 1765, his friends at the Jardin du Roi seemed to have just the project; government ministers were earnestly discussing the need for a French circumnavigation of the globe. Vessels from Britain, the Netherlands, and Spain had already made the journey, claiming far-flung territories for strategic or commercial use. From 1756 to 1763, France and Britain had fought to determine the imperial fate of North America and India. This conflict, variously known as the French and Indian War or Seven Years' War, is often held by historians to be the first truly global conflict, with rival European powers exporting their antagonisms around the known world. The Treaty of Paris that concluded the war in 1763 effectively made Canada British by bringing seventy thousand disgruntled French residents of Quebec under British rule. In 1765, a proposed French circumnavigation was not simply a vanity project, but an economic imperative. If France were to stand any chance of retaining or improving its standing in the race for empire, a Frenchman had to discover the last great prize that was believed to lie in the Southern Hemisphere: the Great Southern Continent, or *terra australis incognita.*

Reasoning that the landmasses of the Northern Hemisphere had to be balanced by an undiscovered Great Southern Continent, imperial rivals Britain and France made repeated attempts to find a land already thought of as *terra australis incognita;* that is, British and French explorers had continued to try to find the land they *hoped* Australia would be. As early as 1606, the Spanish explorer Pedro Fernandes de Queirós recorded landing on the coast of present-day Darwin. But as his cursory inspection failed to find any evidence of a gold-working culture to rival that of the Incas, he and his successors across nearly two hundred years convinced themselves that riches to rival those of South America were still to be found in the hinterland of some other coast.

Any expedition would need a naturalist to collect exotic flora and fauna, describe previously unknown species, and assess the commercial usefulness of a range of tropical and subtropical greenery. Commerson had only to express an interest in the post for his name to be put forward.

Baret must have thought 1765 the most tumultuous year of her life to date. She relinquished her son; heard Commerson dismiss the idea of marriage; learned of her son's death; then feared losing Commerson himself. Stability of any sort—emotional, physical, financial—must have seemed elusive. And now a seemingly recovered Commerson announced his enthusiasm for a venture that would take three years, assuming all went well. Commerson's plan had no part for Baret, for how could she accompany him? French royal ordinances expressly prohibited women from being on board ship, in contrast to the British Royal Navy, which allowed the wives of officers and key personnel (such as the ship's carpenter) to accompany their husbands. (Though arguably good for the morale of individuals, the British policy risked stoking discontent among the majority of the crew.) Having served Commerson indispensably in the establishment of his herbal tea business in Toulon-sur-Arroux and during their time in Paris, having abandoned her child for him and nursed him through months of illness, Baret now found that Commerson was making plans that could not possibly include her.

Commerson was virtually assured of the post from the start. His nominator, Pierre Poissonnier, was a doctor with direct connections to the Minister of Marine (that is, the minister in charge of naval matters) Étienne de Choiseul. (And Étienne was one of two Choiseuls in government—his cousin César Gabriel de Choiseul, duc de Praslin, swapped ministerial appointments with him throughout the 1760s so that, by the decade's close, both had held the portfolios of foreign affairs, war, and the navy.) The botanist Jussieu and Commerson's astronomer friend Lalande seconded the nomination. Letters of reference came from Voltaire, Queen Louisa Ulrika of Sweden, and the chief jewel in her scientific crown, Linnaeus himself. The post paid an annual salary of two thousand livres and allowed Commerson six times that amount in expenses. In addition, Commerson was to find himself a servant equally capable of pressing specimens and dressing his master. Baret would have been the obvious choice, had she not been a woman.

At some point in the latter half of 1765, the plan to dress Baret as a man and have her act as Commerson's valet must have begun to germinate. As Commerson made a point of writing to his father, father-in-law, and brother-in-law with news of his appointment and its generous terms, the need to engage an assistant for the voyage was inevitably very much on his mind. Family and friends, eager to promote the interests of Commerson's nephews and more distant relatives, suggested a host of young candidates. For the socially aspirant bourgeoisie, the chance to place an adolescent on this most prestigious naval venture held out greater long-term social advantage (and less expense) than three years at boarding school. "I'm assured that when I get back I'll have honors, job offers and an annuity. There will be nothing I can't do," Commerson greedily wrote to a friend.

While Commerson's assistant could not hope for as much, he might still expect participation in the circumnavigation to translate into social and professional advancement, with an annual stipend for particularly meritorious service. That Commerson is not recorded as having pursued any of the candidates (even though he actively tried to secure for his younger brother Georges-Marie the post of expedition chaplain against the wishes of their father) suggests that Baret and he began discussing the audacious idea of her disguise at an early stage. What might have begun as an improbable joke between them clearly acquired momentum, as "How could I?" was succeeded by "What do I have to lose?"

It is tempting to imagine certain influences behind Baret's decision to attempt to pass herself off as a man. We could rehearse the history of women's exclusion from the stage until well into the seventeenth century, with female parts being taken by specialist boy actors. Many of these roles involved a female character disguising herself as a young boy, resulting in a spectacle familiar to early modern theatergoers of young men playing young women playing young men. We could speculate on whether Baret had seen any such production (most Shakespearean comedies feature such a role) and whether it inspired her. Or we could consider what impact the so-called breeches parts in eighteenth-century opera might have had on Baret's thinking (that is, youthful male characters who were scored as sopranos, clearly requiring a female opera singer to play a male part). But these sorts of speculations are culturally and chronologically inappropriate for Paris in 1765.

In that year, in both France and England, women had been playing women's parts on stage for just over a century, while the role of the page Cherubino in Mozart's *Marriage of Figaro*—probably the most famous breeches role in the opera world—would not be written until 1786. In 1765, as Baret considered whether she might make a convincing male adolescent, no young French actress generated a frisson on the Paris stage by her shapely appearance in knee breeches and a tight-fitting waistcoat. The dramatic hit of the year was Pierre-Laurent Buirette de Belloy's newly premiered tragedy, *The Siege of Calais*, which fooled no one with its fourteenth-century setting. The play's depiction of medieval Anglo-French hostilities allowed frank discussion of French losses in the 1756–63 war—losses that Bougainville's expedition was meant to remedy.

Could Baret's cross-dressing have been informed by a handful of eighteenth-century books detailing the exploits of women who had disguised themselves as men to make their living? Anne Bonny and Mary Read were mentioned in popular accounts of pirates and had apparently dressed as men while living with pirate crews; Hannah Snell's purported memoir, *The Female Soldier* (1750), described its author's career disguised as a man, serving in the Royal Marines from 1747 to 1750. But *The Female Soldier* was not translated into French in Baret's lifetime, probably because the author, Hannah Snell, claimed to have been present when the British defeated the French at the siege of Pondicherry in 1748. As for the exploits of Bonny and Read—assuming that Baret had heard of them—the pirate histories in which they appeared were long on swashbuckling and short on the practical details of how a woman might conceal her sex from a crew of men in the middle of the ocean. (Both Bonny and Read also had an influential lover among their respective pirate crews, and were never seen by their crewmates as anything but women spoken for and out of bounds.)

Might Jeanne Baret have been influenced by an earlier female cross-dresser, French national saint Jeanne d'Arc, the Maid of Orléans, who dressed as a man and led French resistance to the English during the Hundred Years' War? This is unlikely. Joan of Arc was canonized in 1920 and her iconic status is largely a twentieth-century phenomenon. (She is not invoked by Belloy's tragedians in *The Siege of Calais*.) So Baret could never have gazed wonderingly at a statue of this other Jeanne, dressed as a man, for the first French statues to her were erected in the nineteenth century. Tempting though it may be for some historians to place Baret in a tradition of female cross-dressers on land and sea, gaining inspiration from what other women had done, it is exceedingly unlikely that Baret knew of any of them.

Two descriptions of Baret have survived, and while neither yields specifics, we can deduce that the charade would have been unthinkable had Baret been conventionally pretty. In his journal, Bougainville makes her an Everywoman in terms of her appearance, if not her actions, saying simply that she "is neither ugly nor pretty." The only other eyewitness account comes from the expedition surgeon, François Vivès, and it, too, is highly generalized. A single image is known that claims to be Baret, though its first appearance in an Italian book of voyages published in 1816 suggests that the artist read Bougainville's account of his expedition rather than meeting Baret and drawing her from life. But even if this nineteenth-century watercolor is a generic "woman in a sailor suit" concocted by an artist who never saw Baret, it accurately depicts the outfit worn by ordinary eighteenth-century seamen: loose-fitting drawers closed with drawstrings and a roomy square-cut tunic. Baret would not have been expected to wear this regulation outfit since she was serving as Commerson's valet and general factotum rather than as a crew member, but the painting nevertheless shows a style of clothing she could have adopted—loose and as shapeless as possible, trying her best to disguise her curves.

After Baret was stripped of her disguise, it became evident that she had spent nearly two years of the voyage with linen bandages wound tightly around her upper body to flatten her chest. The bandages impaired Baret's ability to take deep breaths when she exerted herself, as she did regularly, carrying all the equipment needed by a botanist in the field. Modern confirmation of the restricting nature of chest binding comes from New York journalist Norah Vincent, who spent eighteen months presenting herself as "Ned" in a selection of male-only or male-dominated environments, and whose *Self-Made Man* brings us as close to Baret's experience of physical transformation as anyone is likely to get:

First I had to find a way to bind my breasts. This is trickier than it sounds, even when you're small breasted, especially when you're de-

termined to have the flattest possible front. First I tried the obvious . . .
bandages. I bought two of the four-inch-wide variety and strapped
them tightly around me, fixing them in place with surgical tape to
make sure that they wouldn't unwind midday. This made my chest
very flat, but it also made breathing painful and labored.

Vincent finally abandoned the bandages in favor of a sports bra. Baret
did not have that option and so the bandages that Vincent found unreliable by midday must have been a constant source of anxiety and chest
pains. Vincent confirms that baggy and layered clothing helped safeguard her disguise; that a voice coach trained her to use fewer words
in conversation and to concentrate on accessing the deeper tones in her
natural register; and that she felt more confident after building muscle
bulk in her shoulders and arms through weight training. Since Baret was
called a "beast of burden" by Commerson himself and by officers and
men who marveled at her strength on the ice-sculpted banks of the Strait
of Magellan, we can deduce that Baret—through some combination of
genetics and habituation to a working life outdoors as an herb woman—
had already developed this kind of physical strength.

Slowly, Baret begins to take physical shape for us: an ordinary
woman, neither remarkably attractive nor unpleasant to look at; strong
enough to do physical work expected of the opposite sex; slender enough
to be able to disappear in oversize men's clothes; and with facial features
that were presumably gamine enough, combined with a rough haircut, to
let her pass as a clean-shaven, gentle-looking young man.

Undoubtedly, the new identity would have been tried out on the
streets of Paris, perhaps initially at night, with Baret gradually gaining
enough confidence to eventually attempt running errands during the
day. And so what might have started as teasing pillow talk about how
different things would be if Baret were not a woman had acquired a momentum, until it seemed possible that Baret would be able to sustain her
presentation as a young man and deceive her shipmates. From Commer-

son's point of view, Baret's disguise offered the perfect solution to the tedious problem of finding a botanizing servant with whom he could bear to be cooped up at sea for the best part of three years. The man who had not hesitated to dig up specimens from the Montpellier botanic garden because he placed his wants above mere regulations was not about to be constrained by a royal prohibition forbidding woman on French naval expeditions.

But for Baret, the voyage was a high-stakes gamble. It must have occurred to Baret that she would be one woman among over three hundred men, isolated at sea for long stretches of time, and if anything should happen to upset the expedition hierarchy—a shipwreck, a mutiny, a pirate attack—she would become a property claimed by whichever faction survived and triumphed.

Perhaps Baret was genuinely, passionately in love with Commerson and thought it better to see and understand what he experienced on the voyage rather than trust he would return an unchanged man after three years at sea. Perhaps Baret hoped that her devotion on the expedition would convince Commerson to disregard social conventions and legalize their relationship, giving her the status and respectability of being Madame Commerson.

But while Baret might well have loved Commerson and loved being with him, if we see this as the sole factor motivating her to join the expedition then we continue to make Baret an unthinking drone, moving only at Commerson's will. To construct and sustain the fiction of Jean Baret required keen powers of observation, a quick wit, a good sense of humor, an abundance of drive, and endless reserves of stamina: These qualities were not in Commerson's power to bestow, but were Baret's alone. And though her resolve to join the expedition pleased Commerson and accommodated his needs, we should not lose sight of the fact that Baret was surely also pleasing herself.

Her work as an herb woman was informed by an extensive knowledge of plants and their properties—the chance to botanize with

Commerson everywhere that the ship made landfall must have been a tantalizing prospect. Baret could see the charts that Commerson spread around their apartment and could wonder at their representation of the earth's lands and seas. Spinning a globe, Commerson could show her that their journey to Paris, marvelous though it had seemed, could not even be distinguished on a model of the known world: If France seemed vast to her after their coach journey of four days, she could barely comprehend the distance that would be traveled in a voyage of three years. Remembering that when she chose to attempt to join the expedition, she had never even seen the ocean, we can see Baret as a woman ready to surrender to the power of wonder.

Baret had no financial or legal affairs to put in order before the couple left Paris to join their ship, but Commerson had a web of obligations to attend to, including making provision for his money and effects should he not survive the voyage. The will that he drew up is an elaborate document that gave directions for the disposal of his body before making bequests to family and friends. Commerson's preference was that his corpse be used by a medical school for a public dissection; were this not possible, he asked to be buried at sea, or on land with no formal ceremony. This surprising beginning to the will is matched by an equally strange conclusion, in which Commerson makes a provision for Baret as though there were no plans for her to accompany him:

> To Jeanne Baret, also known as Jeanne de Bonnefoy, my housekeeper, I leave monies to the total of six hundred livres to be paid in a single lump sum. Wages are owed since September 6th, 1764, at a salary of one hundred livres per annum. In addition, I declare that all the linen, all the women's dresses and clothes in my apartment are

her own property, as well as all the furniture, including chairs, tables, armoires, beds, excluding only my herbaria, books and my own personal effects bequeathed to my brother as previously detailed. I desire that all the furniture be handed over to Jeanne Baret and that there not be any difficulties made, even if she chooses to stay in the apartment for one year after news of my death, which residence may provide time to organize the natural history specimens that are to be sent to the Royal Collection [Cabinet des estampes] as is detailed above.

For some modern commentators, the passage is an elaborate ruse designed to deflect suspicions of premeditated disguise and deceit. The problem with this explanation is that if Baret was revealed to be a woman while at sea and Commerson was to declare himself as shocked as the next man (which is exactly the reaction he feigned when the moment came), then the will would prove that Baret and Commerson were already known to each other. A man nearsighted enough not to realize that his constant companion is a woman dressed as a man strains belief: A man unaware that his constant companion is the woman with whom he has been living for the past two years is either a character straight out of a farce or a consummate fraudster.

The reference to Baret was more likely intended to address the possibility of Commerson's death during the expedition, upon which Baret would return to Paris, claim the goods in the apartment, and organize Commerson's specimens. And considering all that has been said about Baret's experiments with cross-dressing, it also seems highly likely that the will sought to provide for Baret if her disguise was detected as she tried to board the ship. Commerson could then claim he had not had any suspicions of the "young man" who offered to work as his assistant, and could go on with the voyage; Baret could return to Paris knowing that, should any legal dispute arise—with the Beau family, for example—she could point to Commerson's wish that she be allowed to reside in the apartment for up to one year after confirmation of his death.

The will also offers some intriguing insights into the couple's life-style. Before she became one of the boldest cross-dressers in history, Baret was clearly far from indifferent to clothes, Commerson's will taking pains to confirm what was apparently an abundance of women's apparel in their rooms. The separate reference to "linen," meaning both bedding and table linen, together with an itemization of furniture, is richly suggestive that the rue des Boulangers apartment exuded comfort and some style in the middle of tropical greenery. For all the obsession with botany, Baret and Commerson were clearly not indifferent to their surroundings. Notably, this is the first mention of Baret's use of a pseudonym: de Bonnefoy. People who hide their identity under an alias usually do not choose one at random. Rather, most people show a strong preference for retaining their own initials and appear to derive comfort from a name with personal meaning. If Baret's mother's family were Huguenots, Bonnefoy—literally, "good faith"—may attest to the role religion played in Baret's life. But why did Baret feel the need to use a pseudonym for at least part of her time in Paris? Remembering that Father Beau had written to Commerson concerning rumors of a marriage, it is clear that Commerson's family were interested in receiving intelligence of what went on in the rue des Boulangers. In becoming "de Bonnefoy," Baret ensured that verbal inquiries about Commerson no longer linked him to the scandal to Toulon-sur-Arroux—that affair had involved the housekeeper Jeanne Baret, who was gone, supplanted by Jeanne de Bonnefoy.

The most striking of all the information given in the will is Commerson's desire that Baret be allowed the space and time necessary to organize his natural history specimens, that is, assorted shells, dried fishes, and plant specimens intended for the royal collection. This clause of Commerson's will provides the clearest proof of the reciprocity of their relationship. Just as Baret had shared her herb woman's lore with Commerson, he had obviously taught her enough about Linnaean taxonomy for Baret to be capable of arranging the jumble of his collection into tidy classificatory groups. From the time of the couple's decision that Baret should try to join the expedition to the day when they finally left Paris to go to their ship, Commerson could teach Baret anything he thought she still needed to know.

Commerson and Baret (traveling as Jean) left Paris by coach on December 15, 1766, heading for the port of Rochefort in the middle of France's western coast. There they were to have their first sight of the ship that would take them around the globe. At first the coach retraced the path of their original entry into Paris, heading from Paris to Orléans, then keeping company with the river Loire to Tours. From Tours they headed south, via Poitiers, then turned west to the coast.

The first great port that Baret saw was La Rochelle, but she had little time to marvel as the coachman lashed the horses on to Rochefort. Inside the coach, the mood was subdued. Baret was out in the world as a man and could not escape to the apartment if she suddenly felt her disguise on the point of betraying her. Aware that the close confines of the post chaise and length of the journey afforded four to six inside passengers a chance to scrutinize one another closely, she doubtless shrank as far into her greatcoat as possible and resisted any temptation to discuss the scenery with Commerson. Besides, conversation between the strangers jolting through the freezing winter weather was informed by a somber mood in the country at large: the death of the Dauphin, heir to the throne, in December 1765, seemed to be a depressingly apt symbol for the stagnation of political and social institutions, not to mention imperial ambitions. France needed a boost to the national psyche, and it was hoped that the circumnavigation would, in time, provide that.

The two vessels undertaking this journey would first rendezvous in Rio de Janeiro. The larger and faster of the two, the frigate *La Bou-deuse*, carried expedition commander Louis-Antoine de Bougainville. In December 1766, he was already heading south to one of the most contentious groups of islands in the world. Known to the French as the Îles Malouines, to the Spanish as the Malvinas, and to the British as the

Falkland Islands, these granite outcrops in the South Atlantic had originally been claimed by France. Indeed, Bougainville had been the one to propose to the French government that the islands would provide a fine strategic base from which to monitor maritime traffic heading for the Strait of Magellan or Cape Horn.

But in the aftermath of the Seven Years' War in 1763, France was perceived by her European rivals as weakened on the international stage, and Spain successfully lobbied for control of the Îles Malouines. As Baret and Commerson arrived in Rochefort, Bougainville was already en route to ferry French colonists from the Îles Malouines to Rio de Janeiro, from where they would have to find their own passage back to France. Bougainville would then wait on the *Boudeuse* for the arrival of the flute, or storeship, that was to accompany him on his circumnavigation: *L'Étoile*. Smaller, slower, and heavier than the *Boudeuse*, the *Étoile* was docked in the harbor as Baret drank in her first view of the sea and of the vessel that was about to become her oceangoing home.

As pallets stacked with dried goods swung through the air, straining the hoists from which they dangled, barrels of freshwater and beer were rolled across the gangplank connecting the *Étoile* to the quayside. Some provisions disappeared down into the hold while personnel busied themselves above and below deck. Officers who were new to one another moved rapidly from the rituals of gentlemanly introductions to choreographing the movements of the crew. In the following days, the *Étoile* would have to be stored with everything that might conceivably be needed on a voyage of three years, including trinkets for bartering. In fact, a tiny group of senior officers had quietly decided to forgo a quota of provisions to make way for more cheap consumer goods, in expectation of an abundance of trading opportunities. They would come to regret their greed only when it was too late to do anything about it, and the prospect of starvation hung over both ships.

Amid all this maneuvering of goods, individuals, and influence, Baret and Commerson played their own carefully rehearsed parts.

Standing on the dockside disguised as a man, Baret offered her services
to Commerson as principal assistant to the naturalist. Commerson, who
would later claim that he had been unable to find an assistant who pleased
him in all the months of preparation for the voyage, acted as though
he had seized upon the last candidate who presented himself on the
day before leaving port. Baret must have felt that the chances of detection were strong as she boarded the *Étoile* with Commerson. She stood
behind him, laden with his bags and a portion of his field equipment,
finding herself motioned to as Commerson made his introductions to
the *Étoile*'s captain. For the captain, François Chenard de La Giraudais,
the naturalist's assistant clearly invited less scrutiny than the naturalist
himself, who seemed to have brought along far too much field equipment to fit in the tiny berth he had been assigned. Before Commerson got
comfortable—or rather, uncomfortable—La Giraudais offered his own
captain's cabin to the naturalist.

Without diminishing the generosity of the offer, La Giraudais may
have felt he gained rather than lost by the exchange. La Giraudais had
sailed with Bougainville before, but together on the same ship. As captain of the *Étoile*, La Giraudais was subject to Bougainville's overarching
command of the two-ship expedition, but was directly responsible for
the day-to-day running of his own vessel. By yielding his cabin to Commerson, La Giraudais astutely moved himself closer to the crew of the
Étoile, both literally and figuratively. No longer isolated by his privilege
in the great captain's cabin at the stern, La Giraudais slept closer to his
men and heard more of the discontents, petty rivalries, and gossip that a
captain needed to consider before they threatened to get out of hand.

The relative seclusion of the captain's cabin must have seemed like
a godsend to Baret, who was already registering the unexpectedly small
appearance of the ship as she and Commerson descended belowdecks.
By allowing Baret to isolate herself in the cabin, La Giraudais's offer
reduced the likelihood of detection before the ship set out for Rio, and so
sealed Baret's fate.

THREE

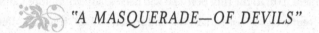 *"A MASQUERADE—OF DEVILS"*

Crossing the Line

"VOYAGE" MIGHT BE too grand a word for Baret's first taste of life afloat. Without even needing to make full sail, the *Étoile* was eased out of Rochefort harbor by a pilot's boat and towed down the river Charente to an anchorage by the offshore crescent of sand known as the Île d'Aix. At an early stage in Rochefort's naval history, it had become apparent that all but the lightest vessels had too much draft to sail down the Charente without running aground on the river's bottom. The fitting and loading of vessels begun in Rochefort was therefore routinely completed on Aix. Approximately two miles long and two thousand feet wide, Aix had looked like a sandy boomerang in the Atlantic until Louis XIV's great military engineer Vauban oversaw the construction of a fort there at the end of the seventeenth century. Housing cannon able to defend the docks of Aix and the mouth of the Charente, the fort transformed Aix and the surrounding waters into a vast naval stronghold.

In Rochefort, the *Étoile* had loaded men and some provisions, a task that would be completed at greater length in Aix. A system of ropes and pulleys known as block and tackle was used to fill the depths of the hold first with barrels of freshwater and beer. Serving double duty as provisions and ballast, the iron-ringed barrels sank into a securing layer of shingle that prevented the entire contents of the hold from rolling and pitching the ship with its movement. Beside the water and beer (the latter a necessity in an age when freshwater was often less than fresh) were barrels packed with dried salted meats, cheeses sealed in their own rinds, oatmeal, dried peas, and that favorite of weevils the world over, the tooth-jarringly hard confection of flour, water, and salt known as hardtack, or ship's biscuit.

As the *Étoile*'s hold filled with food and spare materials—timbers, anchors, iron for the blacksmith, sailcloth, rope—Baret could only watch and reflect on the enormity of what she was embarking upon. During the six weeks that the *Étoile* spent in harbor at Aix, Baret must have considered abandoning her plan. The more she learned of the ship, the less feasible her deception must have appeared.

The *Étoile* was technically a flute, or storeship, in contrast to the *Boudeuse*, Bougainville's faster, lighter frigate. The popular mental picture of a sailing ship is a ship of the line; that is, a three-masted vessel that takes its name from the linear battle-fleet formations typically employed in naval conflicts from the seventeenth to the nineteenth centuries. Such ships had multiple gun decks and might carry anywhere from 60 to 110 cannon. At 120 feet, the *Boudeuse* was as long as a ship of the line and had three masts, but it was lighter, narrower, and therefore faster than any military vessel. Because the *Boudeuse* was designed for reconnaissance work rather than military engagements, it had only a single gun deck. As a flute, the *Étoile* was lighter and smaller still: 102 feet long and 33 feet wide, drawing 480 tons. Whereas the *Boudeuse* carried a complement of 11 officers and 203 men, the *Étoile* accommodated only 8 officers and 108 men. But measure out a space approximately 100 feet by 30 feet—smaller than the average U.S. home lot—and imagine it peopled with 116 others split among four decks, and the reality of Baret's situation begins to take shape.

Baret's home and only refuge now was the captain's cabin she shared with Commerson. The captain's cabin was always located at the stern (or utmost rear) of the ship, placing the captain close to the wheel should he ever need to take personal control at short notice. Behind a screen at the side of the captain's day cabin, a hanging cot swung with the motion of the ship, in theory rocking its occupant to sleep. And like his most senior officers, a captain was spared the indignity of relieving himself at the "heads" (holes cut into a projecting area of decking to the fore, or front, of the ship). While all senior officers and gentlemen shared use of a single commode in the tiny enclosed space of the quarter galley leading off the officers' wardroom (or common room), the captain enjoyed exclusive use of the quarter galley leading off his cabin.

Baret could not go to the heads with the ordinary seamen, where she would be visible not only to the other crew members but also to any officer or marine who cared to go to the front of the forecastle deck that towered above. (The apparent perversity of the arrangement is mitigated by its practicality, since it gave potential mutineers one less place to begin fomenting revolution and men could not escape from their work.) But if she were known to be using the captain's cabin quarter galley, Baret would arouse hostility and suspicion among every callow junior officer and officer's servant forced to go to the heads—and the feeling of injustice would only grow as temperatures fell and aging rations made for queasy stomachs. It is a measure of Baret's complete ignorance of life aboard ship and of Commerson's inattention to anything that did not concern him directly that neither had foreseen this problem. But clearly Baret had no choice but to use the cabin's facilities and think of some justification for doing so if anyone should notice.

Baret must also have felt oppressed by the size of her shared cabin—no more than fifteen feet long and thirty feet wide at its widest point; its ceiling did not allow any man over five foot six to stand upright. Though not a woman used to a palatial home, she was an herb woman very much used to being able to walk outdoors. On the *Étoile*, as on all ships of the period, a strict social and naval etiquette dictated who was allowed to walk on which deck, in the company of whom. Ordinary sailors scrubbed the deck planks underfoot or climbed in the rigging overhead, but only officers were visibly engaged in taking leisure between their watches. On the foremost deck, the forecastle, Baret could stand and be refreshed by the sea air, but as a gentleman's assistant with the unheard-of privilege of sharing her master's cabin, she was sure to be scrutinized closely.

For his part, Commerson spent his days getting to know the officers and those on board who were nonnaval personnel like him. Between introductory conversations and the enforced conviviality of evening dinners in the officers' mess, Commerson wrote letters to friends. These are characterized by an almost childish delight in newly acquired vocabulary—Commerson insisting that he is no longer a "landlubber" and has found his "sea legs." With breathtaking insouciance, he routinely dismissed the possibility that seasickness might yet manifest itself.

Given that the *Étoile* was bobbing at anchor in the leeward environs of an offshore island, his confidence was spectacularly misplaced. But the letters help us imagine the whispered conversations between Baret and Commerson. Commerson was presumably all confident bluster: Here they were on board, the disguise had worked, and life at sea was not so bad, without even a trace of the nausea so often reported. And Baret's life would improve once the expedition really got under way. Then they would be able to go off botanizing—away from the enforced separation on deck. Baret would feel much more herself when they were once more in the field. And he *needed* her. From Commerson's point of view, the latter was undoubtedly true: Had Baret scrambled round the squat barrels rolling across the gangplank and jumped ship at Aix, Commerson would have faced the prospect of a circumnavigation without any competent botanical aid. To be told she was needed and to be begged to stay must have been intoxicating. At last on February 1, 1767, all conversation on the subject became moot. The *Étoile* made sail, leaving Aix a receding sandy speck on the immensity of the Atlantic. The next port of call would be Rio de Janeiro.

Both Baret and Commerson were soon gripped by a gut-wrenching seasickness. Commerson found his symptoms greatly eased if he sat on the poop deck (reserved for officers and therefore relatively calm), feeling the reassuring solidity of the mizzenmast behind him. Since seasickness results from the body's confusion at trying to process a world of constantly shifting reference points, one of the best remedies is to give the visual and tactile senses something stable on which to focus. With the mizzen rising at his back and the still horizon to lose himself in, Commerson was able to experience some relief. Baret, however, was terrified that if she were to go to the forecastle (the only deck permitted to her), her sickness would distract her from maintaining her male disguise. For a woman to pass as a man in front of over one hundred pairs of male eyes is hard enough: It is nearly impossible when her whole body is racked with a nausea beginning in her legs and rising in wave after unrelenting wave through the whole length of her torso. Nor could Baret have kept her breast-flattening linen bandages in place at this point; without that virtual straitjacket, she could at least curl up in her quarters and wish herself anywhere but *here*. Even in the cabin, the hanging cot only exacerbated the swaying motion that was the cause of her illness, and lying in a blanket on the floor was hardly better—what the brain knew to be a density of straight, massive oak planking defied the eyes' and guts' ability to account for its incessant rocking.

For days, Commerson surrendered to the air on deck and to more experienced colleagues who persuaded him to eat a little something "because with something for the stomach to work on, the nausea is not as bad." But Baret rolled around the cabin floor, trying to get comfortable and becoming progressively more dehydrated.

Commerson's journal entry for February 10, 1767 (a full ten days after leaving Aix), shows that a solid meal was still an impossibility for him, though one day later, Baret was improved enough to try feeding him some broth and he was finally in a position to keep it down. On top of the six weeks' anchorage at Aix, the couple had now been closely quartered for the best part of two weeks at sea. No other ship's servant slept, or convalesced, in the same cabin as his master. If anyone on the *Étoile* voiced a suspicion at this point that Baret was a woman, we might expect to find some hints of this in at least one journal from the expedition. In fact, repeated references of this nature do exist in the writings of one expedition member. His name was François Vivès and he was to prove Baret's and Commerson's implacable enemy.

As ship's surgeon on the *Étoile*, it might therefore be assumed that Vivès would have much in common with Commerson, given the latter's medical training. But when the *Étoile*'s officers and gentlemen had made their first hesitant introductions to one another at Aix, it quickly became apparent that Vivès and Commerson were awkward together. It is easy to understand what about Commerson so rankled this career surgeon. On board ship, Vivès was typically employed in dealing with the suppurating and the stinking, tending to seamen showing the ravages of venereal disease (rampant in European navies) and a lifetime of punishments meted out by man and the elements. Should the *Étoile* ever experience an accident, such as a falling spar or an explosion of gunpowder,

Vivès would become a butcher, sawing at limbs as he tried to maintain his own balance on a sand-sprinkled floor, his patients plied with alcohol yet shrieking in agony.

Men like Vivès were a necessity on board and, if they stayed in the service, they might hope for advancement to an admiral's ship and eventually a comfortable practice on land. Vivès did not have to learn much about Commerson's history to intuit that Commerson had despised the life of a country doctor to follow his botanical passion. Condemned to a voyage largely stuck belowdecks, contemplating the physical complaints of seamen, Vivès surely saw in Commerson what his own life might have been, had he been blessed with Commerson's money and prominent supporters. As far as Vivès was concerned, Commerson was a preening dilettante, hopping off ship at every opportunity to go wandering about onshore.

Alone among all the chroniclers of the expedition, Vivès has attracted the charge that he is unreliable because he writes from a position of hindsight and wants to appear wise after the event. Of course, this would not necessarily make his story untrustworthy, even if it were true—which it is not. Everyone who wrote their own account of the voyage can be shown to have described some events shortly after they occurred, and other episodes some time after they occurred. Where Vivès is thought to be suspect, Bougainville is always assumed to be credible, even when he has clearly written journal entries at some distance from the events described.

But given all the time Baret spent in Commerson's cabin, and her ongoing avoidance of the heads, what Vivès tells us is entirely credible: "After a few weeks, the calm that had descended was troubled by a rumor circulating among the men, concerning a girl in disguise on the ship. Everyone knew where to look—it was undoubtedly our little man." It was not that Baret's disguise was poor, but 116 men living in a self-contained world measuring 102 feet by 33 feet were quick to register oddities of behavior. Considering Baret's near-continuous presence in Commerson's cabin, either Commerson was guilty of the punishable crime of sodomy, or he was guilty of a blatant disregard for the royal ordinance that forbade women on board naval ships. Either way, La Giraudais had to be seen to act.

The captain's log that La Giraudais was required by law to keep on the *Étoile* has never been found. Perhaps it is just coincidence that the document that would have detailed how La Giraudais dealt with these rumors does not appear to have survived. Yet what we lack from La Giraudais is more than made up for by Vivès, who writes that La Giraudais sought to put an end to rumors of a relationship, heterosexual or otherwise, between Commerson and Baret by insisting that Baret sleep with the other servants.

No ship of the period had a dedicated sleeping area for men below the officers. Just as officers and gentlemen scientists enjoyed the use of private lavatory facilities in the quarter galley off the officers' wardroom, so they benefited from cozy berths in a variety of places off-limits to men outside the officer class. Commanders and captains had their own cabins, of course, but others enjoyed this privilege, albeit on a smaller scale. For example, a first lieutenant, such as Jean-Louis Caro on the *Étoile,* typically enjoyed his own tiny cabin complete with hanging cot. A ship's master, such as François Blanchard on the *Étoile,* also had an enclosed area for his cot. Surgeons, chief engineers, and captains of artillery would have private sleeping quarters—or areas reserved for their exclusive use—allocated according to their age and social class. Junior officers (ensigns) might have to bunk on the lower decks, among the ordinary men, or "ratings," if a captain thought them of inferior families.

Separate from all of these carefully defined groups, the officers' servants liked to stay together and to find sleeping space within earshot of their masters, though they still had to hang their hammocks among the ratings. Finally, a corps of marines kept to themselves, ever ready to quell mutiny and safeguard arms and ammunition. They placed their hammocks where they chose, the lower gun deck being a favored location when there was no prospect of battle. Banned from sleeping in Commerson's cabin, Baret was confronted by the bewildering naval hierarchy determining the placement of hammocks.

Hammocks of a regulation fourteen inches wide were slung anywhere on the lower decks that seemed to promise a quick descent into sleep, for sleep was a rationed commodity: A three-masted sailing ship does not sail itself just because it is night, and the *Étoile* required half her complement of hands to be on watch at any one time. Men slung their hammocks where they could for four hours' rest, then rolled and stowed them away when they were summoned on deck. Baret was not sailing as a deckhand (or naval rating) and was not subject to this shift system, but anyone caught enjoying extra sleep as men moved between watches risked a rude awakening as their hammock was cut down.

For Baret, the need for an undisturbed night's sleep was coupled with her fear of assault by suspicious sailors and the fact that Commerson had to accede to his captain's command, making him seem suddenly a less powerful and protective figure. Still weakened by nearly two weeks of seasickness, Baret surely felt nausea of a different sort as she prepared to sleep among a rotating cast of 108 sailors among whom the rumor was that she was a woman. Prudently, Commerson had thought to take a pair of pistols on the voyage (a gentleman needing to be able to defend himself in case of mutiny on board or altercations onshore), and Baret now prepared to go to her hammock cradling a fully loaded pistol. It was a desperate measure, but Baret knew she would have no time to load the weapon if a group of the men decided to settle the rumors—which is what inevitably happened.

Vivès makes light of the terrifying situation, mockingly employing the language of chivalric romance to suggest an attempted gang rape: "As soon as she came among them, her gentlemanly neighbors, having their interest piqued, desired to pay their respects; she cruelly rejected them and made complaint." Baret appears to have waited for the first approach from the men and then pulled a pistol, threatening to blow the head off anyone who took a step closer. Though eighteenth-century pistols were clumsy and as likely to backfire on the shooter as hit the target, none of the men who circled Baret wanted to risk a better acquaintance with the surgeon's clamps and saws. Like a cornered animal, she watched through the night, as others seized their only opportunity to sleep. In the morning, she retreated to Commerson's cabin, ostensibly to carry out her assistant's duties, but in reality to collapse on the floor in a state of nervous exhaustion, throwing up in the privacy of the adjoining quarter galley when she reflected on what might have happened.

Meanwhile, the dog bite that had once led Commerson to the master herbalists of the Grande Chartreuse had turned into ulcerated skin now oozing pus and beginning to stink in the close confines of the *Étoile*. An infection that Baret would have treated on land with her remedies was more problematic at sea, where familiar fresh herbs were not available. Yet the leg could also be used as an excuse for Commerson to have his assistant return to the cabin, ready to provide whatever the naturalist might need at all hours of the day and night. Vivès writes of La Giraudais's obvious exasperation that Baret and Commerson seemed intent on prolonging their charade.

The command that La Giraudais had so coveted was becoming more of a disaster as the *Étoile* sailed on. Livestock on board were dying because their keepers could not access hay bales in the hold, for the same reason that the ship's cook could not get to the store barrels: The cabal of officers who had ordered the hold packed with trade goods had seen it done clumsily. Vital day-to-day supplies were obscured by huge bolts of cheap cloth, chests of ornamental metalwork, sacks of glass beads, and boxes full of hand mirrors. Much of the cargo was poorly secured, and choppy waters would send huge packets skidding across the hold and areas of the lower decks, knocking over men and destabilizing the daily routine.

On top of this, La Giraudais now contemplated the equally destabilizing effect of the rumors surrounding Baret. Not wishing to have to explain any of this to Bougainville when the *Étoile* rendezvoused with the *Boudeuse* in Rio de Janeiro, La Giraudais demanded an interview with Baret, determined to ask her directly about the building discontent among the crew.

Once again, Vivès sneeringly describes something that should have been in the missing captain's log from the *Étoile*. Since Vivès confidently reports what was said at the interview between Baret and La Giraudais, one infers that the captain quickly reported the outcome of his investigations in order to quiet the crew. Standing in front of La Giraudais in an otherwise empty officers' wardroom, Baret met his eyes as she gave the only answer that could simultaneously deny a deception and account for her behavior: "Trying to show all our suspicions to be groundless, the false servant insisted that he was not a woman but was rather one of those individuals from among whose ranks the Ottoman emperor chooses the keepers of his harem."

In claiming to be a eunuch, Baret cleverly played to one of the great fears of European seamen of the period: being attacked at sea and captured by pirates who would sell their European captives into slavery in the Ottoman Empire. Here, in the European popular imagination, Christian men would be forcibly circumcised (to render them ritually clean) or even castrated (to make them impotent in their dealings with the women of the sultan's harem). Whatever national animosities they harbored, the peoples of Europe were united in their fear and antagonism toward the Muslim ruler in Constantinople, whose aim was popularly represented to be the destruction of the Christian West.

While European sailors in the Mediterranean and around Africa feared enslavement in the East, eighteenth-century novelists titillated their readers with stories of Christian women on captured vessels. Employing a trope at least as old as the Crusades, Western writers promised female readers that should they find themselves in enemy hands they would be auctioned off to satisfy the most lascivious and depraved imaginings of their Ottoman captors. (As the historian Linda Colley convincingly shows in *Captives*, the reality of Christian European enslavement in the Ottoman Empire was altogether more complex and infinitely less lurid than the eighteenth-century European imagination had been led to believe.)

Baret's insistence that she was a eunuch surely caused every man on the *Étoile* to shudder as they recollected all that they had heard about the fate of fellow sailors unlucky enough to be at the mercy of their collective enemy. Without actually claiming to have been a sometime prisoner in the Ottoman Empire, Baret nevertheless hinted at a traumatic past that had left "him" lacking in adult male features.

As crewmen wondered whether Baret might indeed be a eunuch, they knew that a man did not have to become a slave in the Ottoman Empire to suffer this fate. The castrated guards of the sultan's harem had an eighteenth-century European counterpart. Coming from Catholic France, Baret's fellow sailors would have been well aware of the church's practice of rendering chosen boys castrati in order to preserve a soprano, mezzo-soprano, or contralto range in an adult male. Since its regulations prohibited women from singing in church choirs, the Catholic Church sanctioned the castration of a select group of prepubescent boys, usually plucked from the local orphanage, intending that their lives should be lived in the musical service of God. In the eighteenth century, some of those unwillingly consecrated to divine service as boys had rejected God in favor of mammon, and celebrity castrati were the international opera stars of the age. (And though it is commonplace in histories of opera to note a decline in roles written for a castrato throughout the nineteenth century, an 1898 photograph of the Sistine Chapel choir identifies one-quarter of those pictured—seven out of twenty-eight men—as being castrati.)

By identifying herself as a eunuch, Baret brought an immediate end to her questioning. Everyone on board had heard the stories about castration at the hands of the Turks, and everyone knew about the church's policy at home. Whether it had come from Constantinople or from Rome,

Baret's story was the stuff of male nightmares. Baret was dismissed from the summary interview and given permission to resume sleeping in Commerson's cabin. Given that Vivès calls Baret a "false servant" as he sets the scene, he may have wished to imply that he would not have been fooled by Baret's lies, as his captain appeared to have been. But it is not simply a descriptive phrase: *La Fausse suivante* (*The False Servant*) was the title of a popular 1724 play by the celebrated French writer Marivaux. It is a play whose heroine disguises herself as a man, the better to observe her scheming lover. To Vivès, it seemed obvious that he was observing a cross-dressing performance, whatever the expedition command might say. Yet even if La Giraudais saw through Baret's story, there was precious little he could do about a woman who persisted in maintaining that she was a man. To expose Baret as a liar, she would have to be exposed physically—an action that could not be ordered without inviting chaos.

La Giraudais may also have hoped that the situation would resolve itself as the ship drew closer to the equator. In time-honored naval tradition, the transition of a ship from the Northern to the Southern Hemisphere would be marked by a day of carefully choreographed anarchy known as the ceremony of Crossing the Line. Anyone on board who had not previously crossed the equator would be expected to take part, naked and uncomplaining. If La Giraudais privately questioned Baret's story, he must have believed she would confess her charade rather than attempt to maintain it through this day.

At a time when no agreed method existed for gauging longitude at sea, the determination of latitude by observation of the sun overhead was as foolproof as it had been since the days of classical Greece. The *Étoile* slipped from the North to the South Atlantic on March 22, 1767, on calm waters—seemingly the only moving thing on an unending expanse of ink blue ocean, under an equally immeasurable canopy of cloudless sky. In contrast to the measured rhythms of wind and water that enveloped it, the *Étoile* was the scene of a grotesque frenzy of activity dedicated to the degradation of all novice members of the crew. Commerson's journal expresses his surprise at how elaborately and ritualistically the preparations for such anarchy had evolved: "The day before [we crossed the Line] we got the most ridiculous letter from 'Father Tropic' that warned La Giraudais not to forgo naval custom by allowing the uninitiated to cross the Line without the sacrament of baptism, and since several of the officers were not yet initiates, they should expect all that followed. It was signed 'Father Tropic,' son-in-law of Father Equator."

In practice, the "baptism" of the officers was a relatively tame affair compared to what ordinary seamen endured. Officers and gentlemen who had never crossed the Line stood together, tied by a thread that wound its way around each man's thumbs. Divested of their naval uniform jackets (since no one wanted to show disrespect to the physical appendages of office—epaulettes, shiny buttons, dress coats), officers did their best to maintain the appearance of good humor as a bucket of water was thrown in their direction. For a bribe of rum, an officer could ensure that the water was nothing more than seawater and that the bucket would be launched from a distance. Well-liked officers breathed easier than those who had already managed to throw their weight about, though sailors were not foolish enough to attempt anything that might return to haunt them should a junior officer one day become their commander. To show that they had embraced the spirit of the proceedings, the dripping officers then picked up bowls and buckets and threw water over each other as the men looked on. Everyone had to appear to be having a good time and to be participating fully.

When the officers were finally permitted to towel themselves dry, the orchestrators of the mayhem turned their attention to the officers' servants and sailors of no rank. Baret was in this group and Commerson describes the appearance of her tormentors, beginning with a sailor painted green to represent the god of the seas.

> A roll call guarantees that no one can escape Father Neptune, who descends from the rigging with all his followers. Think of a masquerade—of devils. The young men are all completely naked, their skin greased over with oil rubbed with soot or tarred and stuck with poultry feathers. The key players wear sheepskins adorned with horns, or sprout tails and talons. Some move about on all fours, others copy dancing bears—boys hang like monkeys from the rigging and everyone joins in a cacophony of barking, growling, meowing and neighing, accompanied by the blowing of goat horns and the bashing of all the pots and pans emptied from the kitchen.

At this point, anyone who had been unlucky enough to have crossed one of these actors would bitterly regret having done so. And any of the initiates who, like Baret, had drawn the crew's attention for any reason must have contemplated what lay in store for them with horror.

The spirit of carnival may be a joyous one when everyone is genuinely intent on making a good time for all, but it is terrifying when it gives license to a group to move in on its prey under the guise of communal celebration. Mob rule was allowed to mark the crossing of the equator (when even a hint of unruliness would on any other day have caused a ship's company of marines to shoulder their rifles) only because officers did not believe themselves or their command to be in serious danger, yet thought it important to allow the men a release of any tensions building among them. Under the guise of Father Neptune's rites of passage, hierarchies were established and reinforced among the mass of ordinary seamen; obligations were contracted; factions learned the limits of their power. The seaman who played Father Neptune signaled that belowdecks he and his friends were masters of their own oak-bound realm. Having watched Commerson be sluiced down by Father Neptune's protégés, Baret waited with approximately thirty others for what she was about to endure.

Commerson's journal describes the scene in vivid detail, though he is careful never to pay undue attention to Baret, or to confess his knowledge of her true identity. But as Father Neptune took his place "on a throne that had been knocked together for him," adjusted his elaborate "crown," and commanded the initiates to swear that they would "never be guilty of adultery with an absent shipmate's wife," Commerson confesses that he laughed out loud. Baret was not in a mood to find the private joke funny, since it was followed by an immediate and total immersion in "the pool." Surprisingly few sailors of the period were able to swim and generations of bitter experience had taught European sailors that swimming over the side of a ship was likely to attract sharks. The pool was a practical solution that ensured the safety and relative cleanliness of men in open water. It consisted of spare sailcloth, the edges of which had been fitted with eyes and attached to pulleys hanging from the catheads (beams projecting from the side of the ship, sometimes carved as domestic felines, sometimes as lions); like a giant sea-filled hammock, it trailed in the water, secured to the ship. Seawater ebbed and flowed through the canvas, but men inside were usually safe from shark attack, drowning, or getting lost at sea.

According to Commerson, "Men were made to sit over the pool, with an oar under them, that was let go as soon as they had taken the oath. The initiate was then submerged and often held under by strong men until, pretending to help him up, he was blanketed with soot. This was all happening under the longboat, which was brimming with seawater, and fifteen to twenty men were tipping buckets of it on all those below." Either because he did not experience the immersion, or because he hoped to publish his journal and did not wish to risk giving offense to his readers, Commerson refers to the sloshing contents of the pool as simply "water." But scores of maritime memoirs describe their authors' nausea at finding themselves in a mixture of water and excrement from the crew and the livestock pens.

Struggling to climb over each other, the men—six to eight of them in the pool at once—were pushed sharply back by the jeering hordes on deck, who thrust out oars to batter their victims under the viscous surface. From Commerson's description, it is evident that experienced deckhands on the *Étoile* had made unusually elaborate preparations for the day, since the longboat (secured to the deck) had been filled with seawater to pour down on the cesspit of the pool, floating in the sea below. Not surprisingly, those undergoing the ceremony generally opted for various stages of undress as a matter of practicality; Baret must have stood out as one of the few clothed individuals on deck. Since she could not reveal the linen bandages binding her breasts, she declined to remove even her shirt. Her insistence that she was a man, but a eunuch, had undoubtedly given many members of the crew pause for reflection and sympathy. But standing fully clothed, surrounded by naked and seminaked crewmen, when the only other shirts on deck covered officers and gentlemen, Baret must have appeared proud and stubborn. And in the slopping morass of the pool, the burly men who held new recruits under could easily grope her to satisfy their curiosity. While others concentrated on trying not to swallow a mouthful of the vile brew in which they found themselves, Baret also had to thrash against the probing hands of her tormentors, who pressed hard against her body as they pressed her down.

Depressingly, Commerson writes that immersion and a blanketing in soot were not the end of the barbarism: "After baptism, they were whipped round the forecastle where all those actors with buckets ran about, bashing into people, until everyone was exhausted." The painted, feather-adorned young men who had scooped buckets of water out of the longboat onto those in the pool below concluded the proceedings by running about the main gun deck and driving their buckets into all of the initiates, who were simultaneously trying their best to escape the flailing cat-o'-nine-tails (typically used to enforce naval discipline). Commerson himself calls the chief players in this bizarre spectacle "devils," and it seems appropriate to characterize the whole spectacle as a literal and figurative Pandemonium, as though the Renaissance visions of hell conjured by the painter Hieronymus Bosch had been realized in the middle of the Atlantic.

All Western ships marked Crossing the Line in some way, and the "baptism" of equatorial virgins appears to have been a constant. But few captains gave as much free rein to rabble-rousing crew members as La Giraudais did on the *Étoile*. That so many of the crew—approximately one-quarter—had never before crossed the equator seems an unusually high percentage, suggesting that Bougainville's ship, the *Boudeuse,* had already enjoyed the pick of experienced sailors willing to sign on for a projected three-year circumnavigation. For the duration of the voyage, the *Étoile* and the *Boudeuse* would be separate, self-contained floating worlds, the character of each largely determined by the men in command.

Baret is unlikely to have been consoled by anything that Commerson could say that evening. Battered emotionally and physically, retching as her stomach rid itself of everything she had been immersed in, she stripped off her soiled bandages and spoiled clothes. Whereas Commerson only had to hang his dripping shirt and breeches out to dry, Baret set to work scrubbing at the filth that caked her. The memories of the day were harder to eradicate. After the incident with the pistol below decks, Commerson had for the second time in two months proved unable to protect her, and there was nowhere she could go: The first opportunity to escape the confines of the *Étoile* would be the port of Montevideo, still over two months' sailing away. Not only did Baret have nowhere to go, she had nothing to do, other than tend to Commerson as a servant and an assistant. At this stage in the voyage, there was not even anything to see from the decks of the *Étoile* other than the unbroken surface of the South Atlantic, stretching to a steely blue infinity in every direction.

The world's oceans do not teem uniformly with life across their breadth and depth. Thousands of square miles of both the Atlantic and the Pacific may be considered marine deserts. Life is found in the nutrient-rich waters where ocean currents meet, or where thermal vents rise from the depths; it concentrates in waters above the troughs where the plates of the earth's crust buckle miles below; it throngs on coastal shelves and around reefs and islands. Because the *Étoile* was a French ship, its course south and west was designed to avoid the shipping routes preferred by British and Dutch vessels. Assuming it charted a course similar to that taken earlier by the *Boudeuse* (and for which a detailed log survives), the *Étoile* crossed the equator at approximately longitude 28° west— roughly halfway between the bulges of the west African coast at Conakry in Guinea and the South American coast at Natal in Brazil. A better illustration of the middle of nowhere would be hard to find, 540 miles from the South American coast. Commerson's journal from late March 1767 reveals his disappointment at hauling in nothing more than a single bonito (a relative of the tuna), and seeing a small pod of porpoises and a handful of presumably hungry sharks. A page from his notebook dated March 17–18, 1767 (just before the horror of Crossing the Line), shows a fish drawn to scale, in the middle of otherwise sparse entries. For Baret, this was far from the bounty of exotica she had been promised.

The tropical sun beat down on the *Étoile*, which now reeked of vinegar, above and below decks, in an attempt to thwart the spread of any disease that might affect men, timber, or stores. With temperatures rising into the eighties on a daily basis, Baret's torso erupted in the scaly, weeping patches of red skin indicative of atopic dermatitis, or eczema: her autoimmune system's verdict on the stresses of her life and the chafing of tight linen bandages soaked with fresh sweat on top of stale.

She watched as the skin of her upper body transformed into a crusted and flaking mass of raised welts, continually itchy and sore. The crew may have imagined various crudities taking place in the privacy of Commerson's cabin, but it seems more likely that relations between Baret and Commerson had never been worse. Baret was physically and emotionally drained and permanently uncomfortable; Commerson was moody and withdrawn without anything to see or do. Both longed for their first sight of the South American coast and its unfamiliar plant life—a reminder as to why they had come aboard.

On April 8, 1767, the lookout on the *Étoile* identified Cape Frio, a promontory on the coast just north of Rio de Janeiro. La Giraudais had orders to stand off from Rio and track a southwest course, roughly parallel to the coastline, to the Portuguese port of Montevideo in present-day Uruguay. In Montevideo, the question of whether the Portuguese authorities would be friendly to a French vessel rested upon the handover of the Îles Malouines then under way. (Though Spain and Portugal were once imperial rivals and were not always in accord, even in the eighteenth century, Portuguese authorities made a show of their support for Spain in this cause.) Bougainville and the *Boudeuse* were still anchored off the Îles Malouines, which were about to become the Spanish Malvinas, and Bougainville was making room on the *Boudeuse* for all those French residents who balked at the thought of either Spanish or British rule.

A few weeks after the *Étoile* made landfall at Montevideo, two Spanish frigates that had overseen the handover arrived in Montevideo, acting as couriers of orders from Bougainville. La Giraudais was now to take the *Étoile* back to Rio, retracing the earlier three weeks' voyage, and to wait for his commander there. Realizing that Bougainville would likely take a dim view of the excessive amount of *pacotillage*, or trinkets, in the hold, La Giraudais had used the preceding weeks in Montevideo to allow his officers to liquidate as much of the offending material as possible. The markets of Montevideo were therefore suddenly and unexpectedly glutted with beads, mirrors, and cheap cottons.

Baret and Commerson had also managed to get ashore themselves and, to Baret's surprise, Commerson had revealed a secret. Though he had previously expressed disapproval in his journal about the greed of the *Étoile*'s officers, he was acting as the agent of M. Dulaurent, a surgeon in Rochefort, who had entrusted Commerson with a quantity of items for sale. Ridding himself of Dulaurent's entire consignment in Montevideo, Commerson netted 628 livres. Yet Commerson had never haggled with merchants or shopkeepers in his life: Baret had run his household in Toulon-sur-Arroux and had shopped for the couple at the Parisian market stalls of Les Halles. With nothing else assigned to her to do in Montevideo, Baret undoubtedly helped Commerson dispose of his share of the *Étoile*'s clandestine cargo, learning two things in the process: that Commerson was a hypocrite and that botanical treasures were not his only source of profit on the voyage.

All over the port city, the *Étoile*'s officers were making money as the men spent what little they had in the brothels and taverns situated within stumbling distance of the docks. Baret's pleasures were of a different sort: solid ground under her feet, breathing air that was not rank with vinegar, moving about relatively freely without feeling herself the object of scrutiny or suspicion. Among the human flotsam of a major seaport, one more odd-looking individual was unlikely to attract anyone's notice. La Giraudais lingered ten days after receiving Bougainville's new orders on May 18 to cast off for Rio: a measure of how much needed to be done to ready the *Étoile* for Bougainville's inspection. This time La Giraudais had both wind and current with him and the journey that had taken three weeks from Rio to Montevideo now took just over two. The *Étoile* anchored in the roadway off Rio (that is, in an area of sheltered anchorage out to sea from the harbor) on June 13, 1767, and waited for Bougainville's imminent arrival. There was to be no carousing onshore; everything was to be orderly for the expedition commander's arrival. One week later, the *Boudeuse* hove into view.

FOUR

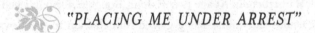 *"PLACING ME UNDER ARREST"*

*The Bougainvillea and
the South Atlantic*

THE *BOUDEUSE* WAS a new ship, only recently completed in the dockyards of Nantes in November 1766. At 120 feet long and 36 feet wide, she was only 18 feet longer and 3 feet wider than the *Étoile*, but at 550 tons she weighed 70 tons more than the *Étoile* and carried nearly double the number of men: 214 compared to the *Étoile*'s 116. Bougainville wanted his flagship to be fast and responsive, and he had a mathematician's attention to detail. Fearing that she was top-heavy when he first inspected her, Bougainville had ordered all twenty-six of the twelve-pound cannon on her gun decks to be replaced with eight-pounders. (The cannon capable of firing twelve-pound shots weighed eighteen hundred pounds apiece, so the substitution resulted in an estimated diminution of near twenty tons.)

Born in 1729 and therefore two years younger than Commerson, Louis-Antoine de Bougainville had, like the botanist, been regarded as something of a prodigy. His wealthy parents, who had moved to Paris from the northern region of Picardy early in his childhood, did not hesitate to find the best tutors for young Bougainville when he showed an interest in mathematics. An eminent astronomer, Alexis-Claude de Clairault, was recruited to teach Bougainville about the heavens (and their contemporary role in navigation at sea), while Jean Le Rond d'Alembert (Diderot's coeditor on the *Encyclopédie*) provided advanced mathematical instruction. At age twenty-four, Bougainville published a treatise on calculus that immediately gained him election to the Royal Society of London (then, as now, a mark of great scientific honor).

And his interest in theoretical conundrums was balanced by a passionate desire to help solve real-world problems. In 1756, at the outbreak of the Seven Years' War, Bougainville signed on to serve as aide-de-camp to the celebrated French General Montcalm. His commander died in Quebec City in 1759 when the British stormed the natural rock defenses of the French garrison stationed there, ushering in the end of a French dream of empire in North America. But Bougainville acquitted himself well and returned to France with a growing reputation as a soldier as well as a scholar. Out of all the books that he read during this period of his life, one stands out for its influence on his future career: Charles de Brosses's *Histoire des navigations aux terres australes* (1756), a compendium of all the disparate information known about the South Pacific. In its pages, Bougainville found a convergence of exploration and natural history— two subjects in which all Enlightenment gentlemen were expected to take an interest. Moreover, the book assured its readers that a Great Southern Continent existed and would surely be found in a systematic exploration of the region.

Ever since the conclusion of the 1756–63 war—a conclusion that left any self-respecting Frenchman dispirited—Bougainville had dreamed of a French expedition to the South Seas, where new imperial ventures might yet find success. That France had ceded the Îles Malouines to Spain was galling to him—doubly so, since his specific presence had been requested at the island's handover, but as the *Boudeuse* drew within sight of Rio and the *Étoile*, Bougainville could finally look forward to an expedition that no foreign emissary could spoil.

Trusting in the competence of La Giraudais, with whom he had previously sailed to the South Atlantic, Bougainville was therefore disconcerted to see the *Étoile*'s now half-empty hold, which La Giraudais blamed on the fault of port bureaucrats in Rochefort. (The frantic unloading of much of the *Étoile*'s cargo in Montevideo had not left any time to restock with food there.) But La Giraudais assured Bougainville that there was enough for the voyage, just so long as they could take on some fresh food when they stopped for freshwater on as-yet unknown islands in the Pacific. Bougainville had no wish to lose time with the sort of weeks-long process of stocking the hold that should have been accomplished at Aix, nor had he any desire to enrich the merchants of Rio. Bougainville therefore ordered that they would pause in Rio only for as long as it took to reprovision with "victuals for ten months"—a quantity of provisions thought sufficient to make it to the Pacific. Beyond this time, they would surely make landfall in the Pacific and find food.

As there was nothing to do but wait for these stopgap provisions to be loaded, the *Étoile*'s personnel came into sharper focus for Bougainville. The commander had already had six months in which to get used to those on the *Boudeuse*. The officers and gentlemen of the *Étoile*, being mostly unknown to him, now received the full force of his scrutiny.

To begin with, they were missing one of their number. Bougainville learned to his horror that the storeship's priest, Father Buet, had been murdered in port on June 17, three days before the commander's first inspection of the *Étoile*. Commerson's journal characterizes Buet as a drunkard who had spent the hours before his death visiting dockside taverns in the company of a young man referred to only as "Constantin." (This is presumably the same "Constantin" known to have been second pilot on the *Étoile,* though in the absence of a log listing all personnel on that ship, nothing is known about him beyond his last name.) Without specifying the nature of the relationship between the two, Commerson says that Buet's behavior would have made him the target of an attack in France as easily as in Rio, and it is hard to escape the implication that an inebriated Buet became the target of a homophobic assault by Rio dockhands.

Portuguese officials showed little inclination to investigate the attack. Indeed, the imperial masters of Rio were in general proving antagonistic to their French visitors: The Portuguese governor was never at home when Bougainville called, and contracts made between expedition members and Rio businessmen—for the purchase of an additional vessel and the short-term lease of a house near the port—were canceled without explanation.

Against this background of rising tensions and bureaucratic intransigence, Baret and Commerson began the work that had brought them on the expedition: striking out into the countryside around Rio in search of previously unrecorded species of plants that might be promising candidates for agricultural or other commercial development. Though Bougainville had ordered that no member of the expedition should go beyond the city's limits, the directive was no more of an impediment to Commerson than the walls of the Montpellier botanic garden had been in his school days. The best-known botanical discovery of the expedition dates from one of these field trips, and the truth behind its collection shows how unjustly Baret's name has been written out of history.

The showy subtropical vine that Commerson would name *Bougainvillea brasiliensis* is native to South America, growing in a continent-wide swath that runs from Brazil west to Peru and south to Argentina. Since Bougainville's expedition introduced the bougainvillea to Europe, it has gone on to literally blossom across the world, its cultivars clambering over gardens from California to Florida; draping themselves over balconies around the Mediterranean; splurging color across Australian gardens, Indian cities, and Vietnamese tourist resorts. To the uninformed eye, a typical bougainvillea vine appears to be a thirty-foot-long garland of densely packed, brilliantly colored flowers, most often in eye-popping shades of pink and mauve. But the gardener's eye quickly perceives that the plant's vibrant hues come from specially modified leaves, or bracts, that surround its tiny, unremarkable white flowers.

Any reference source for bougainvillea will attribute its discovery and collection either directly to Bougainville himself or, less often, to Commerson. Of course, the notion that Bougainville discovered the plant is absurd on two counts. First, as commander of a circumnavigation he traveled with a specialist whose sole purpose was to go into the field to collect specimens. And second, even had he wished to indulge his interest in natural history by taking a walk in the countryside around Rio, Bougainville had no time to do so, stuck as he was in diplomatic gridlock while investigating a murder and reprovisioning his storeship.

The idea that Commerson was physically fit to collect specimens of bougainvillea in the field is belied by Vivès's journal entries. Given the animosity that existed between the surgeon and the naturalist, Commerson must have been extremely worried by the condition of his leg to seek advice from Vivès (who in turn must have been delighted that Commerson had to seek his professional opinion). From the writings of both Commerson and Vivès, we can see that Vivès never passed up an opportunity to indulge in crude innuendo about the relationship between Commerson and Baret, while Commerson had a recurring delusion that Vivès was trying to kill him. Commerson's periodic paranoia with respect to the surgeon's intentions may have begun at this time.

With relish, Vivès recorded that the botanist's leg ulcers were verging on the gangrenous and that amputation of the limb would likely be required. Commerson, who had his own medical training to draw on, surely despised the alacrity with which Vivès offered his bone saw. Commerson was able to make the journey from ship to shore on a daily basis and hobbled as far as he could, but he was not in a fit state to wander any distance, to scramble down gullies, or to climb outcrops to get the lay of the land. Rather, Commerson sat in the best vantage point he could find, enjoying fresh air around him and solid ground under him. Having confirmed that he was comfortable, Baret would begin the day's work of scouring a new area for interesting specimens.

Over sixty years after Baret's forays around Rio, a young Charles Darwin visited exactly the same area and recorded the following impression:

> Following a pathway, I entered a noble forest, and from a height of five or six hundred feet, one of those splendid views was presented, which are so common on every side of Rio. At this elevation the landscape attains its most brilliant tint; and every form, every shade, so completely surpasses in magnificence all that the European has ever beheld in his own country, that he knows not how to express his feelings . . . I never returned from these excursions empty-handed.

Baret's main difficulty on these botanizing expeditions must have been choosing which plants among the tropical green multitude had the most potential for commercial development. This, of course, raises the question of what might have interested Baret about the showy vine that would be named bougainvillea. As an herb woman, she was not likely to be seduced by colored bracts simply for their beauty, no matter how spectacular. Though bougainvilleas are successfully marketed for their ornamental value today, Baret's brief was to find scientifically useful plants, not eye-catching ones, and we do her a huge disservice by making the stereotypical assumption that a woman would automatically seek out the prettiest flowers. The colored bracts may have been the first thing that caught Baret's attention, but her interest was likely sustained by a less obvious characteristic of the plant.

Across the world today, many of those who enjoy the plant's charms know it as a deciduous plant that sheds its leaves during dry seasons, but where the bougainvillea enjoys year-round precipitation and warmth, it is evergreen. In its native habitat, after the flowers have been fertilized by hummingbirds and insects, they go on to fruit. The trio of waving flowers in the center of the bracts then swell at their bases, resembling nothing so much as a humble bean plant. The effect is captured in a delicate watercolor by Sydney Parkinson, the principal artist on James Cook's first Pacific expedition (1768–71). Gardeners familiar with the scarlet flowers of bean plants nodding from the climber's supporting canes will agree that it would have been entirely reasonable for Baret, on her first encounter with a fruiting bougainvillea in 1767, to draw parallels between this new plant and the more familiar French species. Indeed, English herbalist Nicholas Culpeper's seventeenth-century description of "French beans" could easily be about bougainvillea:

> There is also another sort of French Bean commonly growing with us in this land, which is called the Scarlet-flowered Bean. This arises up with sundry branches . . . to the length of hop-poles, about which they grow twining, but turning contrary to the sun, having foot-stalks with three leaves on each as on the other. The flowers also are in fashion like the other, but many more set together, and of a most orient scarlet colour.

As we can see from Culpeper's description, any early modern European plantsman—or plantswoman—faced with a bougainvillea for the first time might take in its flowers and scarlet bracts and categorize it as a bean plant. An herb woman such as Baret would have been particularly attuned to the similarity since, according to Culpeper, bean flowers were commonly used in poultices "to assuage inflammations rising upon wounds" like the infection that was plaguing Commerson's leg. Baret's knowledge of folk remedies used in the treatment of gangrene is evident from the herb woman's notebook discovered among Commerson's papers in the Muséum national d'histoire naturelle. At the foot of the last page of the notebook, we find the promise of a plant-based remedy to *arêter et empêcher la gangrene* (to stop and prevent gangrene). (In addition to the notebook's titular use of the archaic word *medicamenteuses*, rather than *herbes/plantes médicinales,* it displays spellings such as *arêter* rather than the standard *arrêter* and *gangrene* rather than *gangrène*. These are not spelling variations typical of Commerson's vast archive of papers and may be further evidence of Baret's authorship.) Unfortunately, the notebook then ends abruptly, without the remedy known to Baret being given. The likely reason for the notebook's sudden end is that pages were deliberately removed in the nineteenth century for reasons that continue to reverberate today.

Immediately before the promised remedy—and preventative—for gangrene, the last page of Baret's notebook lists two plants that have a notorious history: *la Sabine* (savin, or *Juniperus sabina*) and *l'Aristoloche* (birthwort, or *Aristolochia*). Both plants were used by Europe's midwives (as the colloquial "birthwort" suggests) to start labor or cause expulsion of a retained placenta—and hence both also have a history as abortifacients, or plants that may induce abortions.

Modern research into the properties of these plants shows that they can be deadly: Many of the five hundred species of *Aristolochia* are acutely toxic; some are carcinogenic, and herb women such as Baret would walk a fine line between saving life and taking life with their use. The historian Londa Schiebinger coined the term "agnotology," or the deliberate act of forgetting, to describe the way in which such controversial folk medicines were written out of popular medical books in the nineteenth century, when "criminally induced abortion" began to be outlawed, starting in France in 1810. When Baret's notebook was given the green cover dated 1840, the censorship that Schiebinger describes was at its height in France. Seeing *la Sabine* and *l'Ariostoloche* on a page might have caused the remainder of the notebook to be destroyed in the belief that it contained forbidden knowledge.

So while Baret's remedy for gangrene can be guessed at but not recovered from her notebook, it is possible to reconstruct the European discovery of the bougainvillea with some certainty. As the *Boudeuse* and the *Étoile* lay at anchor in the Rio roadway, Baret and Commerson made daily journeys to the dock. The crew members rowing them ashore in the longboat most likely helped lift Commerson to a hired mule, then left the couple to their own devices until sunset, when everyone gathered back at the dock. Vivès describes Baret as always walking, visibly armed with at least one of Commerson's pistols in addition to the day's provisions, sheets of paper, and a cumbersome collection of eighteenth-century field equipment.

Sweat must have soaked the linen strips binding her chest as she struggled with the heavy leather satchel containing food, knives, a spade, some small glass vials for seeds and soil specimens, and matchbox-sized carrying cases for insect life. She also toted a precious box of portable optical instruments, including magnifying glasses and a small pocket perspective, or telescope. And then there was a compass, lest Baret lose herself in unfamiliar terrain. A fine mesh net tied to the satchel helped in the capture of bugs, birds, and butterflies. The sheets of paper Vivès mentions were not artist's paper for drawing specimens, for this would have been too time-consuming in the field. Besides, in a discipline where accuracy is crucial to the correct identification of species, neither Baret nor Commerson was an expert illustrator. Rather, this highly absorbent paper could be interleaved with freshly picked botanical specimens, which were then pressed flat with a portable field press that Baret also carried. Today field presses can be made of lightweight materials such as aluminium or fiberboard, but in 1767, they were made of wood.

With the cumbersome field bag over one shoulder and a wooden press hanging from leather straps over the other, Baret is often recorded as walking a few steps behind Commerson—a habit interpreted at the time as a servant's deference, but which we may read as sheer exhaustion from the burden that caused every muscle in Baret's body to ache. Walking apart from Commerson, Baret was also freed from having to listen to his exultations about unfamiliar plant life while she was physically enslaved to it.

When Commerson found a place where he was able to sit for the day, Baret could at least unload the food and strike off to explore on her own. Catching sight of the shrubby evergreen vine that would become known as bougainvillea, she must have thought it important to collect the plant to see if a bean poultice could be made from it for Commerson's leg. For if Commerson were well, she would not have to do everything in the field, and relations between them might return to a more even footing.

Even though Baret could see, close up, that what had looked like the scarlet flowers of a bean were actually leaves, she believed its vibrant color meant it would still be potent in treating gangrene. For one of the most basic tenets of Baret's kind of folk medicine was the "doctrine of signatures"—the belief that a plant's appearance was a clue to its medicinal use. Though the doctrine predates the fall of the Roman Empire and the spread of Christianity across Europe, the early church embraced the concept that a divinely creating force had intended the great book of nature to be read.

According to the doctrine, plants would reveal their godly purpose if inspected closely. So, for example, the doctrine held that a distillation of a barbed species like hawthorne would draw splinters; that decoctions of yellow flowers or roots would cure jaundice; and that red-hued flora would remedy blood disorders. Generations of European herbalists had therefore thought the scarlet flowers of the bean plant to be efficacious in drawing out infection from the body, precisely because a site of skin infection was typically an eruption of vibrant red. As the herbalist John

Gerard wrote, a decoction of red leaves or flowers was the best cure for blood poisoning, for "oile of the colour of blood . . . is a most precious remedy for deep wounds." So the colored bracts of the bougainvillea signaled to Baret their ability to calm and restore angry skin, while the green and black fruiting seed pods at the center of each cluster of bracts seemed a tangible representation of the necrosis attendant on gangrene. With Commerson one stage away from amputation on Vivès's operating table, Baret would do all that she could to save him.

If the doctrine of signatures were an infallible guide to plant-based remedies, bougainvillea—and bean flowers—would be widely used today in the treatment of gangrene. They are not. And yet Baret believed in the efficacy of her herb woman's cures, at least insofar as her long-term treatment of Commerson was concerned. We can reconcile the contradiction by understanding a little more about the nature of Commerson's condition. After the dog bite that sent him to the monks of the Grande Chartreuse, Commerson experienced a lifelong pattern: His leg wound appeared healed but would then reopen for no apparent reason; each reopening was worse than the last.

Because these symptoms are precisely those that plagued the English king Henry VIII (following a jousting accident), and because Henry's health has been extensively researched, we can feel confident in making a medical diagnosis. Commerson, like Henry VIII, suffered from varicose ulcers; that is ulcers caused by underlying problems with the varicose veins. Blood pools in the veins and leaks into the surrounding tissue. Before a modern understanding of this condition, sufferers and those treating them believed remedies from bloodletting to poultices had cured them. In reality, the appearance of a cure was only an abeyance of the problem. Bed rest and bathing of the leg undoubtedly helped ease symptoms but, like Henry VIII, Commerson would never be free of this debilitating disease. Intriguingly, a manuscript in the British Library shows that Henry VIII concocted a paste made of twenty-five different ingredients to apply to his ulcers. Modern re-creations of "The King's Majesty's Own Plaster" unfailingly produce a vibrant red mixture—just the color of bougainvillea.

Baret must have collected as many boughs of bougainvillea as she could possibly carry, since Commerson's suppurating leg was going to require daily dressing with a fresh poultice (made from both bracts and seeds) to draw the infection. A handful of the leguminous seeds in her field bag would be reserved to take back to France, for cultivation in the hothouses of the Jardin du Roi, and in the homes of men like Buffon and Rousseau. In addition to gathering seed pods that she hoped could be cultivated back in France, Baret placed a selection of pliable stems between sheets of paper, turning the screws of the field press to preserve them flat for eventual mounting in an herbarium. Other bracts were deftly stripped from their stems and bundled in a square of linen, to accompany Baret back to the *Étoile* in her field bag.

Excitedly, Baret showed Commerson what she had found and promised him that a plaster made of the bougainvillea's bracts would draw the infection from his leg. In the journal he kept intermittently, Commerson referred to the discovery in passing as "novissima planta"—a phrase often carelessly and simply translated as "the new plant." While "novissima" may be used to signify "the most recent" or "the latest," it also has a specific theological meaning. In Catholic doctrine, the Novissima are the four last things—death, judgment, heaven, hell. The term may therefore reflect Commerson's own grim prognosis for his health, should Baret's preparations fail to work, underscoring the extreme unlikelihood that the ailing Commerson had been capable of collecting the specimens of bougainvillea in the field. Continuing in the Latin preferred by European scientists, Commerson also recorded the date and location of specimen collection:"E. Brasilia. Rio de Janeiro et locii vicini, Julio 1767" (East Brazil. Rio de Janeiro and surrounding area, July 1767).

Whatever hopes he had for the promised remedy, Commerson must have quickly realized that the plant was showy enough to make an impact with the expedition command, and told Baret to set aside a couple of the most striking boughs for presentation to Bougainville himself. With Bougainville only just starting to acquaint himself with the personnel of the *Étoile*, Commerson likely thought to distinguish himself by offering Bougainville a fresh bough of the supposedly medicinal vine and declaring that it was to be named bougainvillea.

As an ingratiating maneuver, this was impossible for the other gentlemen and officers of the *Étoile* to surpass, but Commerson failed to see that the ostentatious nature of the gesture would invite more scrutiny than perhaps he and Baret could withstand. Having survived the brutal Crossing the Line ceremonies, and through her insistence that she was a eunuch, Baret appears to have won a grudging acceptance among the personnel of the *Étoile;* at any rate, they are not recorded as making any attempts to assault her as the ship sailed the South Atlantic. But Bougainville brought a fresh pair of eyes to bear on her and saw right through Baret's disguise. While the commander's papers give no indication that he saw anything odd about the naturalist and his assistant at this time, Bougainville's actions in Rio speak volumes about his attitude toward Commerson. For shortly after the triumphant presentation of the bougainvillea, Bougainville placed Commerson under house arrest, confining Commerson to his cabin for the best part of a month. As we will see, the evidence that Bougainville saw through Baret's disguise and sought to punish the lead botanist for his deception is overwhelming.

In a rare letter to his estranged brother-in-law, Father Beau of Toulon-sur-Arroux, dated September 7, 1767, Commerson wrote, "M. de Bougainville, always watching over me—and learning from M. Vivès, who was changing my dressings, that I was in danger of losing my leg—at the very least—to gangrene, chose to help matters by thoughtfully placing me under arrest until I was completely better, which only happened when we got to Buenos Ayres." The poultices prepared by Baret needed changing and renewing daily, and Vivès, not wishing that a royal appointee should die on his watch—and perhaps also fascinated by the efficacy of Baret's herbal remedies—had obviously undertaken a regular inspection of the patient in order to report back to Bougainville. But Commerson's distinct phraseology, "placing me under arrest," implies that medical exigency was but an excuse for the enforced confinement Commerson endured in his cabin between July and September 1767.

A royal ordinance dating from April 15, 1689, forbade both naval officers and able seamen from bringing women on to any of His Majesty's ships, either "to stay the night or for any period longer than a brief visit," the penalty being one month's suspension for officers or fifteen days in leg irons in the brig for the crew. And, strikingly, Commerson's "arrest," both in its form and in its duration, recalls the terms of punishment for infringement of this particular regulation. As a gentleman scientist on the expedition—and a royal appointee at that—Commerson was on a social and professional level with the officers, yet it was harder to suspend him from his duties for a month than it was to suspend an officer, since these duties included reporting on flora and fauna that might be encountered only once in the course of the voyage. Nor did eighteenth-century social niceties permit a gentleman traveler to be chained in leg irons like an ordinary crewman. In placing Commerson "under arrest" for a month from July 15, when the *Boudeuse* and the *Étoile* finally quit Rio, Bougainville crafted a hybrid punishment for Commerson's transgression, combining an officer's monthlong punishment with a diluted version of the imprisonment that an ordinary sailor would have suffered.

And so it becomes easy to imagine the presentation of the bougainvillea to the man it honored, and subsequent events. Visiting the *Étoile* to check on her reprovisioning and to consult with her officers, Bougainville learned that the expedition naturalist had discovered a striking new plant that he wished to name after his commander. Doubtless flattered by impending immortalization in the annals of natural history—and so soon in the voyage—Bougainville must nevertheless have wondered whether the naturalist had flouted the injunction not to go beyond the city limits of Rio. For Bougainville had enough experience of command to know that he could not be seen to condone a flagrant disregard for his own orders. His receipt of a choice bough of the ostentatious vine was therefore likely followed by close questioning of the naturalist, under the guise of learning more about the plant's habitat.

Perhaps Commerson guessed where the questions were leading and offered his leg as proof that his had been a peripheral role—Baret was the one who had disappeared into the countryside and returned with the showy climber. Meeting the naturalist's assistant to commend "him" on the new botanic discovery, Bougainville evidently ascertained in Baret's demeanor something more than tongue-tied shyness in the face of authority. Despite protestations from La Giraudais that Baret's claim to be a eunuch had seemed satisfactory, Bougainville could see that Commerson had brought a woman on board and that an entire ship's company was complicit in some sort of acceptance of the charade.

But if Bougainville knew Baret to be a woman in Rio, why would he not put her off ship immediately? Then again, we may turn this question on its head and ask, what would Bougainville gain from putting Baret off ship in Rio? Indeed, there are three very obvious reasons why Bougainville, knowing Baret to be a woman, would allow her to continue on the expedition in the role of Commerson's assistant.

To begin with, Bougainville had spent the first half of June 1767 transporting frightened and angry colonists from France's abortive settlement on the Îles Malouines back to Rio. The transportation of French settlers who did not wish to live under Spanish rule constituted the entirety of his orders with respect to the families, who now thronged the Rio dockside demanding to know what was to become of them. Physically fit men might sign on to a French ship and escape Rio, but the majority of families had already sunk their savings into provisions and equipment for the ill-fated project of colonizing the islands. (Many were originally refugees from the province of Quebec, which had been ceded to Britain at the end of the 1756–63 war.) Unless settler families had ready access to enough money for passage back to France, their prospects were poor.

In the annals of naval history, there are sadistic commanders, to be sure, but Bougainville is not among their number; his biographies testify to a humane individual with an appetite for life and a particular fondness for actresses. Having lost his mother while a child, Bougainville adored his sister who was but two years his senior. As Bougainville contemplated the fate of the women and children who crowded the Rio dockside begging for French assistance, he would have been acutely aware that putting Baret ashore was likely to condemn her to a short, hard life of poverty and probably prostitution. The French families who now pleaded with him not to leave them would have to seek employment themselves with the Portuguese masters of Rio, and no one would have any respectable use for a single woman without any friends in the port. In all likelihood, Baret would never return to France.

Humanitarian considerations aside, there was a practical reason for keeping Baret aboard. Success, for the expedition, would be defined in terms of new lands found and new scientific discoveries made. A naturalist had been appointed to the expedition in expectation of finding new plants to feed, clothe, and house the bodies of colonizers and colonized, and the Ministry of Marine had judged that this naturalist needed an assistant. To lose Baret was to lose the only person able to fulfill that role.

This may seem an extraordinary statement in respect of a party of two ships and over three hundred men, but Bougainville could not simply assign an ordinary (and probably illiterate) seaman to be Commerson's aide. Even if the naturalist could train the man from scratch in necessary procedures, Baret and Commerson each had a lifetime's exposure to French native species that would inform their work with more exotic specimens. As a child of the Enlightenment, Bougainville had his own interest in natural history, and he knew that good field botanists could not be created overnight.

If there was no chance of finding a replacement among the crew, then it was equally impossible to permanently reassign one of the more nature-loving officers to Baret's role. Seasoned career officers sought to demonstrate their nautical, not botanical, expertise. Below the ranks of the career officers were the prepubescent midshipmen sent on the voyage by wealthy and ambitious families who hoped that their boys would learn the rudiments of navigation and command, and rise to become officers themselves on some later voyage. Vivès had first been sent to sea aged seven, and apprenticed as a naval surgeon when only twelve. Were Bougainville to reassign one of the junior officers or even one of the midshipmen to work with Commerson, the chosen man—or his sponsors—would likely make a powerful enemy and vociferous critic when the expedition returned to France.

The only pool of personnel from which Bougainville could have hoped to replace Baret would have been the five other gentlemen scientists present in addition to Commerson. The surgeon on the *Boudeuse*, Louis-Claude Laporte, could clearly not be spared, nor could the *Étoile*'s surgeon, François Vivès: Both men had their hands unenviably full with the daily round of treating venereal disease and all manner of aches and pains, some symptoms requiring bloodletting, lancing, or the administration of emetics. The *Étoile* also carried the expedition astronomer, Pierre-Antoine Véron, one of the few men on the expedition who got on well with Commerson. Véron, however, was fully occupied with his own important work of developing a standardized, mechanical method for determining longitude at sea, for scholars believed that astronomy would provide an infallible method for calculating the precise position of a ship on the world's oceans.

The casual mention in Bougainville's journal that Véron would "try, during the voyage, some methods towards finding the longitude at sea" understates the magnitude of what was at stake, not just for the French but for every seafaring nation at the time. Constructing and consulting elaborate tables relating to the transit of the planet Venus across the sun, Véron was charged with nothing less than perfecting a fail-safe means for answering the question, where in the world are we?

As it turned out, Véron had been charged with the impossible. The calculation of latitude had been understood since classical times and could easily be taken by any mariner by measuring the distance of the sun, or another star, above the horizon, using an instrument called a quadrant. Longitude could be measured only if one knew a ship's distance from a meridian and the current local time. Beginning in 1727, the English watchmaker John Harrison had devoted his skills to the invention of a marine chronometer—a specially adapted clock whose moving parts would expand and contract with prevailing temperature and humidity, continuing to keep accurate time at sea and so allowing for longitude to be established. Through various refinements of his chronometer across four decades, Harrison resisted the attempt of French agents to learn his secrets. By the time of Bougainville's expedition, the French government had returned to encouraging an astronomical solution to the problem of calculating longitude at sea. But Harrison's ingenious invention was then in its fourth incarnation and would prove to be the unerring method of determining longitude that all the naval powers so desperately sought.

Given the impossibility of assigning Véron to be Commerson's assistant, it was equally impractical to consider reallocating the man with whom Véron worked most closely on the *Étoile*: Charles Routier de Romainville, the expedition engineer and cartographer. Assisting Romainville with the production of charts was Pierre Duclos-Guyot, who kept a joint journal with Commerson, but Pierre's father, Nicolas-Pierre Duclos-Guyot, the captain of the *Boudeuse*, was not about to see his son become Commerson's dogsbody. Out of 330 men, Bougainville could see only one man with sufficient knowledge and leisure to replace Baret: Charles-Nicolas Othon, Prince of Nassau-Siegen, the flamboyant scion of a German royal line that had intermarried with the Dutch House of Orange.

Always resplendent in a full dress wig and one of his extensive range of velvet suits, Nassau-Siegen was a daily vision on the *Boudeuse*. For his family, the circumnavigation was the perfect solution to an otherwise intractable problem: At twenty-two, the prince's debts and paternity suits already threatened to empty the family coffers. Three years at sea would allow scandals to subside and remove the prince from temptation—or, at least, from temptations that might have expensive consequences in European courtrooms. Yet in 1767, it was a sheer impossibility that a prince, however minor and powerless, should become the servant of a naturalist, however well connected. Eighteenth-century social etiquette simply would not allow Bougainville to request that Nassau-Siegen take over Baret's duties; nor could naval regulations require it, since Nassau-Siegen's family had paid his passage and he was not contracted to the navy. Even if the prince had expressed his willingness to assist in classifying and preserving specimens, his luxuriantly curled wig, crisp white shirts, and plush velvet breeches and waistcoats were a prime example of what not to wear in the field.

Without an assistant, Commerson's botanizing efforts would suffer and that aspect of the expedition would be judged a failure. Bougainville had already watched firsthand as other grand schemes—the French colonization of Quebec and the plan for a French outpost in the South Atlantic—had faltered. He had no desire to see his prestigious expedition also fail in one of its key goals. If Baret was a good plant collector—and the bougainvillea offered proof of this—then Bougainville had a second compelling reason to keep her aboard.

The third and final consideration that must have weighed upon Bougainville when considering Baret's fate in Rio was the question of how any revelation would reflect on La Giraudais. Bougainville and La Giraudais had already sailed together and Bougainville trusted and liked his captain; he also knew a handful of the officers on the *Étoile*. We already know from Vivès that rumors concerning the presence of a woman had begun to circulate on board within a few weeks of the *Étoile*'s departure from Rochefort, and that La Giraudais had felt compelled to interview Baret after the terrifying night she spent in the lower decks. If Bougainville had recorded his detection of a woman on the *Étoile* within days of its rendezvous with the *Boudeuse*, La Giraudais's judgment would certainly have been called into question when the expedition returned to France. How could he have failed to see what his commander intuited so readily? The officers' failure to act on observing a flagrant violation of regulations would also reflect badly on their naval records.

To put Baret ashore, then, would likely condemn her to an impoverished end in Rio; it would seriously compromise an expedition mission; and it would harm the career of at least one man—possibly more—whom Bougainville respected. Baret would be punished for Commerson's cavalier disregard of authority—all to comply with an ordinance that had been designed to prevent women from staying briefly on board while in port or cruising the coast. No one had ever thought that a woman could endure a long voyage and play a pivotal role in the fulfillment of its mission—yet if Baret had made it *this* far, surely she could complete the voyage. Bougainville chose to let Baret remain, and Baret persisted in her cross-dressing charade, relieving Bougainville—for the time being, at least—of the need to say anything about her presence in his log. As long as Baret continued to insist that she was really a man, Bougainville might have reasoned that he had no problem. But Bougainville punished Commerson—a warning shot to show that disciplinary action could and would be taken if Commerson showed any further disregard for naval regulations. As the *Étoile* and the *Boudeuse* weighed anchors and finally quit Rio on July 15, 1767, Commerson sulked, confined to his cabin. Baret was free to attend to him, to spend time reading to him or playing cards, but she was also, for the first time in the expedition, able to sit on the forecastle and drink in an ocean view that was very different from the seemingly empty expanse of the Atlantic that had come before.

Marine biologists using an imaging technology known as side-scan sonar have discovered in recent years that the coastal shelf off Brazil boasts the largest and most biologically diverse coral reef formation in the South Atlantic. The five-island volcanic archipelago at the heart of what is now the Abrolhos Marine National Park is only the most visible portion of an extensive marine ecosystem that stretches for more than one hundred miles off the Brazilian coast northeast of Rio. Along the length of the reef, corals rise from the ocean floor like gigantic organ pipes and underwater mushrooms. Thick rubbery ribbons of kelp emerge from the depths, reaching up through the current toward the light. Early data suggest that the reef harbors thirty times the quantity of life found in shallower coastal reefs, and half of the species are endemic (that is, unique to this environment and found nowhere else on earth). The groupers (Serranidae), snappers (Lutjanidae), and other fish that cruise along and among the coral and kelp attract larger predators from farther south, including pods of humpback whales. From July to December, the whales trade the frigid waters of the Antarctic for the food-rich waters of the Abrolhos bank, where they mate and nurse their young.

As Baret sat on the deck of the southward-heading *Étoile*, the waters around the ship could not have failed to reveal the barnacle-encrusted bulk of humpbacks heading north. Some experienced sailors on the voyage had likely seen whales before, but for Baret everything was new. Humpbacks are baleen whales: They feed by closing their massive jaws on gallons of seawater, trapping tiny shrimplike krill and small fish behind bony filaments known as baleen that run the length of the mouth and allow the seawater to drain. To concentrate their food, pods of hunting humpbacks will circle at depth below their chosen shoals, emitting streams of bubbles that rise to form an upwardly spiraling cylindrical wall around their prey. Swimming at speed into the midst of the dense marine meatballs they have created, humpbacks break the surface of the ocean, then crash back into the water, the massive flukes of their tails slapping on the surface with a force great enough to be heard for several miles on the open ocean. Sometimes humpbacks haul themselves out of the ocean for no reason other than their apparent wish to do so, with two-thirds of their enormous bodies typically being visible in such breaches before they roll back into their native element. Once it was apparent that these giants meant no harm to the ship, Baret must have thrilled with the happiness that still floods modern whale watchers, losing herself in the sheer unexpected joy of the moment.

The unfamiliar marine life heading north to feed and breed in the waters of the Abrolhos reef was not the only source of wonder for expedition members. Véron promised that a solar eclipse would be visible from the deck on July 25, a prospect that Bougainville wrote about with excitement in his journal. Where Commerson had the sort of mercurial temper that attracted enemies more readily than friends, Véron exuded an air of quiet good humor, making him a sought-after companion on a journey measured in years rather than weeks. As a fellow astronomer noted by way of tribute, "M. Véron was of a very gentle character, tireless in work, a good observer; he could be counted on." Though Véron did not record anything about Baret, it is safe to assume that she would have told Commerson if anything about his behavior had made her uncomfortable, and relations between the two men would have been no more than daily formalities demanded. As it is, Véron appears to have kept any suspicions about Baret to himself, accepting her at face value with courtesy and discretion. With Commerson confined to his cabin, there is no reason why Véron (lacking an assistant of his own) should not have showed his unaffected good nature by engaging Baret in explanations of his work, confident that the naturalist's assistant could follow directions well enough to help him prepare for the expected eclipse.

For ordinary seamen on the *Étoile*, it must have seemed puzzling, almost supernatural, that the young astronomer's books and instruments could predict so strange an event as the disappearance of the sun from the daytime sky. But for Baret, Véron's knowledge was simply another manifestation of the Enlightenment science she had seen practiced by Commerson since she started living with him in 1764. Between whale watching and perhaps assisting Véron in cleaning and calibrating his range of optical instruments, Baret was able to occupy her days, enjoying the respite from lugging cumbersome equipment into the field. As Commerson remained in his cabin, Baret joined those on deck who were eagerly anticipating the promised eclipse. Bougainville takes up the story:

> According to our estimation of the ship's place, the moment of immersion, as calculated by the astronomer, was to be on the 25th, at four hours nineteen minutes in the evening. At four hours and six minutes, a cloud prevented our seeing the sun, and when we got sight of him again, at four hours thirty-one minutes, about an inch and a half was already eclipsed. Clouds successively passed over the sun's disk, and let us see him only at very short intervals, so that we were not able to observe any of the phases of the eclipse, and consequently could not conclude our longitude from it. The sun set to us before the moment of apparent conjunction, and we reckoned that that of immersion had been at four hours twenty-three minutes.

Véron's success, more than that of any other member of the expedition, was hostage to meteorological conditions that he was powerless to control. But Baret and the others on deck had at least glimpsed their first solar eclipse between the clouds scudding across the coastal waters. If the start of her voyage had filled her with regret that she had ever contemplated joining the expedition, Baret was now able to drink in a world of wonders in the surrounding ocean and in the sky overhead. Like any country dweller, she was used to a familiar pattern of stars overhead, pivoting around the polestar in the Northern Hemisphere with the annual progress of the seasons. Now, from the deck of the *Étoile*, Véron could show her wholly new southern constellations; his unthreatening company was a safeguard against unwarranted attention from that portion of the crew handling the ship at any time of day or night.

On July 26, 1767, the expedition entered the shallower waters of the mouth of the Río de la Plata—a determination made by a method that had changed little since the earliest days of sail. A line attached to a lead weight with a hollow cavity in the bottom was thrown overboard. Samples of sand, shingle, or rock collected in the cavity indicated what lay underneath the hull, while the extent to which the line paid out allowed the depth to be measured in fathoms—a fathom being approximately six feet. In addition to latitude and longitude, "lead" was the final measure of a sailor's world.

For the last three days of July, the *Étoile* labored to anchor in the bay of Montevideo, the last landfall the expedition expected to make before entering the Strait of Magellan. To Bougainville's utter dismay, La Giraudais signaled the grim news that the storeship was taking on four inches of water every hour, a leak that quickly expanded to an uncontrollable seven inches an hour. They would have to empty as much water and cargo as possible from her hold, find the source—or sources—of the offending seepage, and recaulk the hull. As the crew worked in teams to pump the hold of the *Étoile*, Baret had nothing to do but tend to a much-improved Commerson (now feeling the benefit of the periodic healing of his varicose ulcers) and take his directions on organizing the collection they had amassed so far.

In Montevideo itself, Bougainville learned that the Spanish had recently arrested all Jesuits in the community and seized their effects. The cause of the tension between a Catholic order and a Catholic colonial regime was certainly of interest to a botanist, since it was a glossy-leaved native shrub called *Ilex paraguariensis*, source of one of the most lucrative crops in Spain's South American empire. Infusions of the leaves of this member of the holly family were once known as "Paraguay tea." Today, the product is best known under the synonyms of maté or yerba maté and is promoted as a health drink that packs a caffeinated punch less strident than coffee's. Brewed at its traditional strength, the tea can be more energizing than espresso. It is this stimulant effect of Paraguay tea that made it valuable to the Jesuits, and ultimately a source of friction between the religious order and the state.

Paraguay tea is a traditional drink in South America and as much a part of native culture as coffee is to Americans or tea to the British. Yet unlike these national drinks, Paraguay tea was something that had for centuries been harvested and made locally by its consumers. Seeing the Amerindians' dependence on the stimulant, which might depress the appetite as it increased the readiness for work, Jesuit missions in Uruguay and Paraguay had for years required the indigenous peoples to plant it on a commercial scale, together with cotton, tobacco, and sugar. Supplies of the native plant that they had once harvested so freely were now regulated, and indigenous peoples found themselves forced to buy the leaves that were the source of the maté they craved. Large-scale cultivation of *Ilex paraguariensis* also offered the possibility of exporting surplus leaves to other outposts of the empire, where it was hoped the dual effect of appetite suppressant and physical stimulant might be a cost-effective means of managing legions of imperial workers. Unless they bought the leaves needed to brew maté, all that the Amerindians saw of any of the products they cultivated were the rough calico shirts given to them to hide their offending nakedness as they slaved in Jesuit plantations while threatened with military action and eternal damnation if they did not comply.

In 1767, members of Spain's Council of the Indies calculated that the Jesuits' monopoly on Paraguay tea must be producing more revenue than the order accounted for in its financial returns. Claiming to be responding to complaints from indigenous peoples about the conditions they endured, the council instructed Uruguay's Spanish governor to seize all Jesuit properties and revenues. The seizure and control of botanical resources—a phenomenon that has recently become known as biopiracy—was both the source and the goal of this unprecedented dispute.

The hospitable governor of Montevideo, Don Francisco Buccarelli, promised Bougainville all possible assistance in reprovisioning and refitting the *Étoile*. (Buccarelli was a man buoyed by his newfound authority over the Jesuits, and was all pleasantries to the French now that the fate of the Îles Malouines had been decided.) And since Commerson had finally served the period of his "arrest," he and Baret were free to go ashore and learn what they could of major Spanish exports. The Jesuit-owned plantations that would have been jealously closed to French outsiders just weeks earlier were transitioning to civil ownership, and Baret and Commerson surely took advantage of the local chaos to go botanizing. As a stimulant with reputed health-giving properties, maté interested them from both a medicinal and a commercial point of view.

Spending their days ashore but their nights on board the *Étoile*, Baret and Commerson were sleeping when a freakish accident befell the ship in port. A vessel that had slipped its moorings in a night of hurricane-force winds smashed into the front of the *Étoile*, sheering off her bowsprit (the forward projecting beam beneath which the ship's figurehead nestled) and devastating everything above the bow. The captain's cabin shared by Baret and Commerson was at the opposite end of the ship, at the stern, but the collision was large enough to be felt through every timber. Indeed, the damage was so extensive that Bougainville lamented in his journal that there was not enough suitable timber available in Montevideo for repairs. The French expedition therefore requested permission to sail up the Río de la Plata to Ensenada de Barragán, a natural bay in the wide expanse of the river, southeast of Buenos Aires. Once in the shelter of the bay, the damage recently sustained by the *Étoile* was repaired and the source of her ongoing leaks finally traced: a four-foot length of hull being without any caulking and two augur holes in the hull being without bolts. It was a wonder that the *Étoile* had not sunk in the Atlantic like a cask without a stopper.

The collision gave Baret and Commerson extra time for botanizing, but it also gave Bougainville a problem. He was just over six weeks behind schedule at a time when he needed to be sure of picking up certain winds and avoiding others, on a seasonal weather pattern that cared nothing for his expedition's delay. As he fretted about the implications of the lost time, his crews certainly had other concerns. Sailors are notoriously superstitious and the run of bad luck experienced by the *Étoile* led them to speculate on its cause—as well as the implications for the rest of the voyage.

Baret and Commerson, meanwhile, took the opportunity presented by the *Étoile*'s overhaul to explore the environs of Buenos Aires, where fennel grew wild in great profusion. Though Baret was familiar with the plant from France, where herb women recommended decoctions of its leaves, seeds, and roots as both a diuretic and an antidote to poison, she nevertheless collected samples of South American fennel in case it should prove more potent than its European counterpart. More problematic for Baret, as she hauled the field press on their daily journeys, were the fleshy, pointed leaves of agaves of all sizes, and the thorny pads of cacti, especially prickly pear (*Opuntia*). All succulents have evolved to store water in their bodies, which swell with every downpour: An attempt to squash such a plant flat in the name of science is met with strong resistance and a spray of sticky juice that attracts ants and wasps. But seeds and pressed pads were not all that Baret had to obtain from the prickly pears that grew so liberally about the countryside. A still more challenging prize was her goal.

Prior to the Spanish colonization of Central and South America, both Mayan and Aztec peoples had cultivated species of *Opuntia* because it is the favored home of the cochineal beetle (*Dactylopius coccus*), whose carapace is the source of a red dye that can safely be used to color foodstuffs and clothing. In early modern Europe, the dye was in such great demand that its producers' companies were quoted on both the London and Amsterdam stock exchanges. (Cochineal dye is now enjoying something of a resurgence as a food coloring, since it can be marketed as a natural rather than an artificial colorant.) The French desperately wished to break the Spanish monopoly on the dye, yet no one outside the industry knew exactly which beetles living on the cacti were the source of the rich red color. Baret and Commerson must therefore have collected as many types of insect life as they could possibly find clinging to the elongated pads of various *Opuntia* species. A selection of these insects had to be kept alive in hopes of bringing them to a French colony where they might reproduce and form the basis of a French textile revolution. In 1777, the botanist Nicolas-Joseph Thiéry de Menonville finally succeeded in smuggling Mexican cochineal beetles to the French colony of Saint Domingue. Baret and Commerson collected both beetles and their host plants ten years in advance of Menonville, but their collection would undergo a much longer journey back to the Jardin du Roi.

As the *Étoile* was refitted, its captain's cabin filled with box after box of dried exotica—between twenty and twenty-five in all, constructed on demand by the ship's carpenter. This quantity of cases suggests that Baret and Commerson had gathered several hundred plant species from the region, represented by seeds or by dried, pressed specimens, since living specimens would be too serious a drain on the vessel's freshwater supply across time. The precious cargo must have been secured in place inside the cabin by ropes, gradually building impromptu walls and tables, encroaching upon the living space and always threatening to shift in a high sea. (To store the dried specimens in a hold that might take in water was out of the question.) Insect life made few demands on the couple; all that was needed was exposure to light and meals of the increasingly limp specimens of the greenery on which they had been found. And while it perhaps seems optimistic to suppose that any creature might survive the remainder of the journey, the destruction of many species of ants, beetles, and snails around the world by invasive nonnative competitors is a reminder of the resilience of these "passengers" from the earliest days of sail. As the carrier of all field equipment, Baret ensured that every specimen made it back to the *Étoile* in a state worth preserving. Meanwhile, Commerson pondered the nomenclature of all that was unfamiliar, won-

dering how best to classify the finds in the Linnaean taxonomy of genus
and species.

In the first week of November, as Baret busied herself with her cura-
torial duties, Bougainville made a tempting offer, inviting Commerson
and Véron to join him on the *Boudeuse* for the rest of the voyage. Two
motives likely prompted Bougainville's invitation. First, naval captains
dined in the evening with their officers and any gentlemen on board.
After months at sea, Bougainville would naturally want to introduce a
couple of new conversationalists to his depressingly familiar dinner table.
Commerson could be the definition of good company when he chose—
after all, he had charmed Voltaire into asking him to stay and work for
him in Geneva. Having punished Commerson for disregarding naval
regulations, Bougainville was now prepared to start on a fresh footing
with the man with whom he shared so many interests.

Second, Bougainville worried constantly about the *Étoile,* for though
her leaks had in theory been repaired, she was still much slower than
the *Boudeuse* and might become separated from the frigate. Bougainville
must have thought having his astronomer and botanist on board his own
ship would be the best means of ensuring that they made it home. As it
was inconceivable that an expedition scientist could have changed ships
without his assistant, the offer to Commerson certainly included Baret.
There was, however, no question of Bougainville's vacating his cabin
as La Giraudais had done on the *Étoile*. Both Commerson and Véron
could be accommodated in bunks used by the officers; Baret would be
consigned to a hammock among the servants of officers on the *Boudeuse*.

Had Commerson not had to consider Baret and the certainty of her
exposure if forced to sleep outside their cabin, he likely would have accepted Bougainville's offer. Already a man of influence, and likely to rise
still higher in the esteem of the French court and government if his expedition was successful, Bougainville was someone Commerson did not
need to displease for a second time. Recognizing a politic move when it

presented itself, Véron accepted his commander's invitation and saw his possessions transferred from the *Étoile* to the *Boudeuse* on the banks of the Río de la Plata. But Commerson declined the offer, citing the growing number of boxes of specimens in his cabin. For perhaps the first time in the voyage, Commerson saw Baret as a liability. Though the cabin suited him, he was now more isolated on the *Étoile* than at any point previously—Véron, the Prince of Nassau-Siegen, and Bougainville being the only men with whom he had connected at all on the expedition. For Baret, the departure of Véron marked the loss of the only man, other than Commerson, with whom she had felt at ease on the ship.

The expedition finally sailed out of the Río de la Plata on November 14, 1767, almost a full year since Baret had left France. At first, sailing conditions were good. The Río de la Plata is 136 miles wide at its mouth, where it disgorges mineral-rich sediments that attract a variety of marine organisms hungry for microscopic plant and animal life. This concentration of sediment and life immediately south of the Plata produces one of the most beautiful sights of the open ocean: marine bioluminescence, a milky haze on the surface of the water that may blur as far as the horizon. (It is now thought to be caused by the mechanical reaction of marine bacteria to physical stress, such as the passing of a ship or the nearby patrolling of marine predators.) Charles Darwin described the phenomenon in the area of sea through which the *Étoile* and the *Boudeuse* sailed:

> The sea presented a wonderful and most beautiful spectacle. There was a fresh breeze, and every part of the surface, which during the day is seen as foam, now glowed with a pale light. The vessel drove before her bows two billows of liquid phosphorus, and in her wake she was

followed by a milky train. As far as the eye reached, the crest of every wave was bright, and the sky above the horizon, from the reflected glare of these livid flames, was not so utterly obscure as over the vault of the heavens.

Even without leaving the safety of the cabin, Baret could sit and watch from its window, and wonder at the glow of the ocean in the wake of the ship. Commerson's science offered nothing to explain what she was seeing.

The tranquillity of the water soon gave way to much rougher seas, the ships rolling and pitching at the mercy of what Bougainville described as "contrary winds." On November 22, La Giraudais ordered a signal of distress from the *Étoile* to the *Boudeuse*, though the two vessels did not come within hailing distance of each other until the twenty-fourth. Observers from the decks of the *Boudeuse* could immediately see that the *Étoile* had lost its fore topsail (that is, the middle sail of three on the foremast), torn away by a screaming wind. La Giraudais further reported that all but two of the cattle taken aboard at Montevideo had been washed overboard as the ship was tossed from side to side.

With the chaos and loss on deck, Baret and Commerson must have believed themselves near death. The specimens for which Baret had endured days of aching muscles were mostly tucked in boxes, but if even one or two boxes escaped their moorings in the rough seas, the cabin became a lethally confined space: wooden crates sliding across the floor, ricocheting off the walls, and shattering open, sending splinters and seed pods flying. Less deadly, but still violent were the books and loose papers that cascaded from hanging shelves and tables. Bottles of India ink smashed to the floor, staining the planking with pools of dark red, blue, and green. As the ship pitched, the South Atlantic repeatedly battered the cabin's great window. Baret could scream without revealing her identity, for the mayhem belowdecks played out against a background of shouts overhead: the crew, perilously clinging to the ratlines, trying to take in the sail, and the livestock bellowing in distress as their pens broke and they careered across the decks.

Seeing as the storeship had only just been reprovisioned and was now heading away from the last known port, the loss was grave. But Bougainville, already behind schedule by nearly two months, could not turn back to Montevideo. From the little he knew of expeditions that had previously rounded Cape Horn or sailed through the Strait of Magellan, he believed that the strait had to be attempted as close as possible to the height of the southern summer. As on all long-distance expeditions in the age of sail, La Giraudais would have to jury-rig his ship—the naval slang for finding a way to achieve the desired outcome. Any spare canvas in the hold would have to be made to serve in place of the lost sail, as the ships pressed on and made for the strait.

As November became December, Bougainville recorded seals, penguins, "and a great number of whales. Some of these monstrous creatures seemed to have their skin covered with such white vermiculi which fasten upon the bottoms of old ships that are suffered to rot in the harbours." They were humpbacks again, and from Bougainville's description, obviously curious about the ships and swimming extremely close. Albatross and petrels wheeled overhead. Coleridge would not publish "The Rime of the Ancient Mariner," which equates the albatross with bad luck, until 1798, but the storm petrel was already well known as a harbinger of bad weather (as its colloquial name suggested). Finally, on December 4, 1767, the weather conditions of the South Atlantic became of less concern, as the expedition turned west into the Strait of Magellan.

FIVE

 *"HIS BEAST OF BURDEN"*

On the Shores of the
Strait of Magellan

IT WOULD NOT be an exaggeration to say that Europeans had no sooner discovered the Americas than they began looking for ways to get around or through the continents. The poet John Keats famously imagined the moment at which the Spanish succeeded in crossing the land bridge we know as the Isthmus of Panama, and the first European "stared at the Pacific." Keats attributed the eagle-eyed scouring of this new ocean to Hernán Cortés, but he had misremembered the relevant history lesson (or else needed a two-syllable surname to make a line scan): It was 1513 when Vasco Núñez de Balboa saw an unending expanse of blue on the opposite side of the land he had just crossed.

For the best part of the next three centuries, his countrymen and their imperial rivals would be plagued by the question, how best to reach it? Expeditions were lost looking for a fabled northwest passage, allowing ships an ice-free route through or around the north of the North American continent. Some visionaries dreamed of carving a canal where Balboa had stood. And in 1519, the Portuguese navigator Ferdinand Magellan worked systematically down the eastern seaboard of South America with five Spanish ships under his command, looking for a way to traverse or circumnavigate the continent. He considered a series of promising inlets, including the gigantic mouth of the Río de la Plata, which he dismissed as too shallow. On October 21, 1520, at latitude 52° south, his ships rounded a long sandbank, approximately 130 feet high, and his crews stared at a wide channel so deep that it quickly became apparent the lead could not sound the bottom. Magellan had found what he was looking for: the 330-mile navigable waterway between the tip of Patagonia and the island of Tierra del Fuego, connecting the Atlantic and Pacific oceans.

When Bougainville entered the strait on December 4, 1767, no French ship or French ally had ever sailed all the way through, and so Bougainville had no detailed charts to guide him. Volumes such as his beloved *Histoire des navigations aux terres australes* by Charles de Brosses included a map of the waterway, but a map scaled to fit on a book page made the strait appear to be a single snaking channel, cutting an obvious route through the continent. What Bougainville lacked for the strait were nautical charts indicating currents, depths, and submerged hazards for its entire length. Since the European seafaring powers were imperial rivals, hard-won, valuable information was not shared, and Bougainville's expedition operated without even the little knowledge other Europeans already held about the area.

It is natural to imagine the strait as a large river offering a clear-cut route to navigators and sheltered sailing. The reality, as Magellan himself quickly learned, is very different. A detailed map of the region shows that the southwest coast of South America has the same intricate fissures seen on Canada's northern coast, in Norway's fjord system, or on New Zealand's South Island—landscapes carved by ice. The Strait of Magellan is a sinuous 330-mile-long labyrinth, every curve of which presents a multitude of channels that vary in width from several hundred feet to fifteen miles across. The fingers of ice-scarred rock that push into each channel point out a warning: The bottom of the strait is smeared with deposits of glacial moraine, and to assume that the middle of the channel (but which channel?) will automatically give safe passage is to risk having your hull ripped open by glacial debris.

Magellan took thirty-eight days and nights to navigate the treacherous watery maze, tasting strait water for salinity and sending longboats ahead to plumb the depth. Despite his utmost caution, his expedition lost contact with its largest ship, the *San Antonio* (either by its mutinous crew's design or by accident). As others later tried to emulate Magellan's success, it is estimated that at least one thousand sailors perished on various attempts.

The route to the Pacific via Cape Horn was even more treacherous. At latitude 55°59′ south, Cape Horn is an island outcrop marking the utmost southern tip of South America. Only four hundred miles from Antarctica, it presents the most extreme challenge on earth to any vessel powered solely by sail. Whipped by gale force winds, the Southern Ocean crests into waves that can be as high as one hundred feet. In March–April 1788, Captain William Bligh in command of HMS *Bounty* tried rounding the Horn for twenty-five days, only to be repeatedly beaten back. He finally gave up and sailed east to reach the South Seas by the Cape of Good Hope.

Bougainville sailed with all the intelligence that French agents had gleaned about previous expeditions through the strait and around Cape Horn, and also knew the results of tentative French exploration of the strait when provisioning the Îles Malouines. But the extreme weather conditions experienced in the strait made recent information vital. Samuel Wallis had passed through the waterway in April 1767, but Bougainville had no word of this British expedition approximately one year ahead of him. For all practical purposes, when he entered the Strait of Magellan, his charts of the South Atlantic had ceased to be of any use.

Discussion of passage through the Strait of Magellan occupies just over one-fifth of the length of Bougainville's journal. Given that it would take his expedition from December 4, 1767, to January 25, 1768, to make passage through the strait—a full two weeks longer than Magellan had first taken—it is clear that everyone must have been in a state of nervous exhaustion as they finally sighted the Pacific. From Bougainville's determination to record every possible glacial landmark, he obviously hoped that the minutiae of his observations about the strait might be helpful to future generations of navigators. Yet because he had no means for accurately determining the longitude of what he was seeing, and also because natural landmarks along the strait are liable to great change in the harsh weather conditions, many of Bougainville's observations have not stood the test of time.

The caution necessary for the *Boudeuse* and the *Étoile* to proceed safely through the strait frequently reduced them to a standstill and, at these times, Bougainville put Baret and Commerson ashore to botanize as his men took necessary soundings. Bougainville's attention to detail during this time extended to recording the movements of those he referred to as "the botanists," and here his record is invaluable in recovering Baret's actions and experiences.

For the first three days, the ships proceeded through the wide bay that marks the Atlantic mouth of the strait. Like Magellan's fleet before them, they steered a central course between the northern shore (Patagonia) and the southern one (Tierra del Fuego). By December 8, it was apparent that they had crossed the bowl-like entrance of the strait, as the rocks of Patagonia and Tierra del Fuego now converged on each other and created a narrow passage (the Primera Angostura). On the left-hand side of the passage, the rocks jutted long and low into the strait, causing the current to break over them. Waiting for the wind to shift north-northwest, the ships tried to take advantage of the favorable breeze to pass through the narrows, but the tide confounded them, running six knots against them. With difficulty, they maneuvered north by east in the shelter of the Patagonian coast, and looked for a good anchorage in a cove now named Possession Bay. On the *Étoile,* panic set in when two successive measurements showed the depth to have decreased from twenty fathoms to five: Sailing across a steeply shelving bank of glacial moraine, the storeship was fast running out of clearance. The ships spent an uneasy night anchored offshore and tried again the next day to pass through the narrows. Bougainville describes a tense two hours sailing through the passage, with the wind blowing very hard against the ships.

Once through this constriction in the strait, they found themselves in a bay roughly half the size of the first they had encountered. Having seen about twenty men on the Fuegian shore as they passed through the narrows, they now saw Patagonians waving a white flag—a flag Bougainville believed had been left by the French when they touched at Patagonia during the provisioning of the Îles Malouines. Cheered by the care with which the flag had been preserved, and overjoyed to see it used in a manner agreeable to the French, Bougainville ordered both the *Étoile* and the *Boudeuse* to drop anchor. A longboat from each ship made for the shore, each containing ten of their ship's personnel, including officers and marines armed with muskets. Baret and Commerson made up one-fifth of the complement from the *Étoile.* As its longboat made the short journey to the shore, Baret was nearing the first tribal culture that she had ever seen.

Thirty or so Patagonians crowded around the longboats' crews, including some men who dismounted from horseback to come closer. Despite the harshness of the climate, Bougainville saw a people who did more than merely survive—they thrived.

What makes them appear gigantic, are their prodigious broad shoulders they are robust and well-fed . . . their eyes very fiery; their teeth vastly white . . . they have long black hair tied up on the top of their heads . . . they have merely a piece of leather which covers their natural parts, and a great cloak . . . notwithstanding the rigors of the climate, they are almost always naked from the girdle upwards. Habit has certainly made them insensible to cold.

While Bougainville was full of admiration for the physical prowess of the Patagonians who greeted his landing party, and though he thought them "attentive to do what might give us pleasure," he was also aware that these imposing men did not trust the French enough to bring any of their women down to the shore at this first meeting. As the officers began handing out "some trifles, valuable in their eyes," in exchange for the skins of llama-like guanacos and vicuñas, Baret and Commerson began collecting plants. Bougainville was pleasantly suprised by the response of the natives around him:

Several Patagonians immediately began to search for them too, and brought what species they saw us take up. One of them seeing the Chevalier de Bouchage occupied in this manner, came to show him his eye, which was very visibly affected; and asked him by signs, to point out to him some simple [that is, an herb], by which he could be cured. This shows that they have an idea, and make use of that sort of medicine, which requires the knowledge of simples, and applies them for the cure of mankind.

The episode initially seems puzzling: Why would Baret and Commerson immediately start collecting plants at the water's edge, with their shipmates only starting to establish cordial relations with the native Patagonians? What grows at the edge of the strait that required such urgent collection?

As the Patagonians had apparently recognized, the expedition members were gathering medicinal herbs. The flora and fauna of the strait is well documented by now, and one of the most commonly occurring plants growing beside and among the pebble beaches is a southern relative of the bilberry bush (*Vaccinium myrtillus*). Bilberry shrugs at conditions that cause other evergreen shrubs to curl up and die: It not only tolerates poor soil and unimpeded winds but seems to thrive in them, creeping close to the ground, burying it in a mat of scrubby ovoid leaves that is topped with berries in the Antarctic summer—precisely when Baret and Commerson gathered it. It strongly resembles savin (*Juniperus sabina*), an evergreen, ovoid-leaved, low-growing shrub covered in berries, which has a long history in European herbals as a treatment for venereal disease (and, as previously stated, it was an abortifacient mentioned in Baret's notebook).

The expedition's last landfall had been an extended stay in Montevideo, where the ships' crews had doubtless contracted enough cases of gonorrhea to make Vivès long for the sort of respectable French country practice Commerson had once rejected. The eagerness with which Baret and Commerson set to gathering strait bilberries may therefore be explained by the number of deckhands reporting to Vivès for treatment. The participation of the ensign, Jean-Jacques-Pierre de Gratet, chevalier de Bouchage, indicates that Bougainville ordered extra pairs of trustworthy hands to help gather herbal remedies as quickly as possible—for if something caused a loss of goodwill with the Patagonians, or if one of the ships broke free of its anchorage, the shore party would have to cease its activities immediately. If Baret and Commerson were indeed gathering a plant in hopes of treating the sailors' venereal diseases, then the knowledge they brought to bear on this problem was Baret's, not Commerson's.

To Bougainville's eye, the Patagonians appeared to be exemplary specimens of humankind. (They caused near-universal disappointment among the crew, however, since seafaring lore inexplicably represented the Patagonians as having outsized feet, and the men on the shore clearly had very ordinary feet.) Perhaps inspired by Jean-Jacques Rousseau's idea of the "noble savage" living in harmony with nature and free of civilized cares, Bougainville wrote, "They are men left entirely to nature, and supplied with food abounding in nutritive juices, by which means they are come to the full growth they are capable of: their figure is not coarse or disagreeable; on the contrary, many of them are handsome." Bougainville's conviction that the Patagonians' diet contributed to their health not only seems a strikingly modern sentiment but also reveals his interest in the "nutritive juices" of the vegetable kingdom; he seems to have taken a keen amateur interest in the plants his botanists pursued.

If identifying an herbal remedy for the relief of venereal disease was Baret's chief care on her first landing by the strait, it was only the first of many plant-gathering missions she and Commerson undertook in the days that followed. By December 11, when both wind and tide were judged favorable to weigh anchor and proceed, the immediate Patagonian shore had been extensively surveyed and judged comparable with the lost Malouines: "The soil in the place we landed at is very dry, and in that particular bears great resemblance with that of the Malouines; the botanists have likewise found almost all the same plants in both places."

It may seem obvious to us that the same rock strata exposed to the same weather conditions on roughly the same latitude would bear similar vegetation, but this was far from self-evident in 1767. (William Smith, who would make the first comprehensive map of the world's rock strata, and who may therefore be considered one of the founders of modern geology, would not be born until 1769.) As Baret and Commerson considered soil and vegetation distribution, they were therefore in the vanguard of Enlightenment science: The imperial powers of the time sought desperately to confirm that a plant might thrive if transplanted across the same latitude, and that similar growing conditions might be found on one landmass as on another.

Though Baret's fieldwork placed her at the forefront of contemporary botanical and geological investigations, to the men watching from the stationary ships, she was simply Commerson's "beast of burden"—a term that he himself coined to reflect her tireless work on his behalf. Whatever the prevailing beliefs about Jean Baret's sex, no one could deny that the botanist's assistant performed tasks that would exhaust any man. As officers and men waited for favorable sailing conditions, they lolled on their ships and stared at the expanse of rock and water around them. There was nothing to do but take in the landscape, a reverie broken by the occasional Patagonian signals from shore. On these days, the physical stress that Baret had first encountered hauling the field equipment around Rio and Montevideo was compounded by the knowledge that her every movement was being scrutinized from the ship by bored men who were instinctively attuned to the differences between male and female movement.

Commerson appeared insensible to the pressure of such scrutiny. Apparently unwilling to risk the leg that had proved the source of such anxiety around Rio, he stood on the pebbly beaches by the pearl gray water, directing Baret to boulders jutting from the ground and rock outcrops of the strait's side. Baret climbed rock faces and scrambled up and down scree slopes, bagging specimens of fern and lichen, anemone and grasses. Even Vivès expressed admiration of Baret's daily demonstrations of stamina: "In fairness to her, I should say that she surprised everyone by the work she did." His repeated use of the female pronoun, however, makes it clear that he was certainly not fooled by Baret's male clothing, and in claiming that everyone was amazed by the work undertaken, he hints at a widespread understanding that Baret was a woman, albeit one who worked herself to physical exhaustion to try to prove she was a man.

At the end of these days spent moving across the scree, clinging to boulders, and quartering the beaches of rock and shell, Baret's feet, shins, and hands must have been raw from the unyielding surfaces and the freezing temperatures. Had Vauban not left us his testament to the privations endured by the Loire peasantry of the time, Baret's ability to work through such physical hardships would seem even more incredible than it already does.

On December 11, the ships weighed anchor and began inching toward a second narrows in the strait (the Segunda Angostura). Though apparently twice the width of the first narrows, this second passage bends south-southwest round a peninsula projecting from the northern headland of Tierra del Fuego, and the *Étoile* and *Boudeuse* had to hug the Patagonian shore to avoid being torn open by submerged Fuegian rocks. When they finally cleared the narrows into the now southward-heading strait, "rain and violent squalls" soaked all on deck. The rain quickly gave way to hail, which bounced on the wooden planking, coating everything in opaque marbles of ice. The thermometer fell from 9° to 7° on the Reaumur scale then employed in France. There was nothing to do but drop anchor and ride out the storm.

From their cabin window, the weather was the least interesting thing that was visible to Baret and Commerson. Through the first and second narrows in the strait, the ships had not been alone. Their bow waves had been broken by the antics of dolphins of a type Commerson realized was unknown to European science. While he had seen dolphins in the Mediterranean and in books, Baret had no point of comparison—she had seen groupers and snappers and the improbably graceful humpbacks that had streamed north to the Abrolhos reef, but the dolphins' appearance and behavior were something that Commerson could not have prepared her for, for there was nothing recorded anywhere like this.

The species they saw was relatively small—three and a half to five feet long—blunt-headed, and it looked for all the world as though a painter had swirled black patches on its squat white body. Though Baret and Commerson could not know it, December marks the height of this species' breeding season, when its normal-sized family pods of three merge into groups one hundred strong. Known to ride bow waves, to leap in them, and often to swim upside down, it prefers strong currents;

hence it frequents the eastern entrance to the strait in the first and second narrows. Today it is called Commerson's dolphin (*Cephalorhynchus commersonii*), for Commerson was so entranced that he committed the taxonomic sin of naming something after himself.

During the course of the expedition, the number of species that Commerson named would be dwarfed by the number of species that remained unnamed: dried, preserved, and carefully stored, approximately 90 percent of the collection would return anonymously to the scientists of Paris. The exceptions, like the bougainvillea and Commerson's dolphin, tend to be the showiest discoveries. The act of naming is, of course, intended to do more than simply underscore some arresting quality in a species of flora or fauna: It classifies the living organism according to the system pioneered by Linnaeus, using a unique binomial. In the case of Commerson's dolphin, *Cephalorhyncus commersonii*, the first part of the binomial roughly translates as "beak-headed." The second part of the binomial (never capitalized, even when named after a person) identifies a unique species within the genus: Commerson's dolphin is distinct from all other "beak-headed" dolphins (and four have now been named in the Southern Hemisphere).

Inspired by the creation story of Genesis, where it is said of Adam's acts of naming that "in the names he knew the animals," Linnaeus took as his personal motto "Deus creavit, Linnaeus disposuit": God created, Linnaeus organized. For followers of the taxonomist, like Commerson, the naming of species was supposed to be an act of the utmost importance, demanding thoughtfulness and humility in the face of creation. Commerson's action displayed neither of these qualities.

Since the Linnaean system first came into being, three major rules have guided the naming of names. First, in choosing the generic classification the namer should ideally refer to some feature of the plant or animal concerned (a dolphin's head either looks like a beak or it doesn't). Second, the namer should not use his privileged position to settle scores (for example, by immortalizing personal enemies and loathed politicians in dung beetles and carrion flies). Third, the greatest taxonomic faux pas is to name something after oneself. It is assumed that a scientist with skills and opportunity enough to identify a new species should have the good grace to name it after an eminent colleague, since he will in time find the gesture reciprocated by others in the field. Having named Baret's showstopping discovery in honor of the expedition commander (and having put Bougainville center stage by commemorating him in the genus rather than the species), Commerson now celebrated himself. Today, international scientific bodies oversee the naming of new species and try to prevent christening obscenities, absurdities, and duplications, but even so, no one can stop an ebullient scientist from leaving a nomina-tive trail through the plant and animal kingdoms. Commerson must have been exceedingly pleased with himself at this time to do what almost no scientist does.

The more Bougainville recorded of the strait, the more he, too, dis-covered the satisfaction of bestowing names upon what he saw. A bay (Baie Duclos) was named for Duclos-Guyot, Bougainville's next in com-mand. Other landmarks became the French Bay and the river Gennes, the latter named in tribute to Jean-Baptiste de Gennes who led a French expe-dition to the Strait of Magellan in 1695, but who failed to make it through the strait to the Pacific. The French were therefore all too aware that they were not assured of success. But in naming topographical features on the ground, in the cartographic record, and in scientific papers, they hoped to establish a degree of international precedence. By compelling British, Portuguese, and Dutch mariners to use French names to describe physical features of the strait, Bougainville and others like him reminded France's seafaring rivals that French ships had surveyed the landscape—and that the French refused to accept others' claims of sovereignty.

While Bougainville could not be expected to name landmarks after an expedition servant like Baret, Commerson might have named something after his tireless coworker, whose knowledge and physical endurance had given him so much. Yet nothing is today named after her. Commerson's laying claim to a dolphin may therefore seem a trivial matter, simply confirming a view of personality traits already in evidence in Commerson's previous history, yet this egotistical act might well have reverberated in the relationship between Baret and her lover. In the Strait of Magellan, it must have been apparent to her that Commerson took her knowledge and diligence and labor and used it for his own ends, giving nothing in return. But there was nowhere to go, except back on the Patagonian shore when the hail stopped its deafening fall.

By December 12, the squalls had eased and Bougainville ordered the longboats to make for Elizabeth Island (Isla Isabel) in the southward-curving channel of the strait. From here on, the landscapes of the strait were like none that Baret could have imagined. The island's dust-dry soil was studded with brackish pools of freezing cold water or pockmarked with crusty patches of salt. The only plant that appeared to have colonized the island was swordleaf blue-eyed grass (*Sisyrinchium chilense*), which spotted the ground with tiny violet flowers on mats of gray green. When the landing party was caught in a downpour and unable to return to the ships until late evening, Bougainville ordered blocks of this turf to be cut in case his party should have to improvise an overnight shelter.

Baret was expected to perform the brunt of the grueling physical work; this was, after all, one of the reasons why Commerson's remuneration allowed for an assistant. As she dug a spade as far into the turf as the semifrozen ground would allow and started piling up sods with which to make a windbreak, Baret must have bitterly resented her servitude. Commerson stood and talked with the rest of the men, while Baret worked to the point of exhaustion. On Elizabeth Island, she was not only Commerson's "beast of burden" but everyone's "beast of burden"—and undoubtedly the most miserable member of the landing party.

Leaving Elizabeth Island behind the next day, the *Boudeuse* and the *Étoile* found that the island's position in the strait created a potentially deadly effect, amplifying the force of already strong winds and creating unpredictable eddies in the water. Despite desperate adjustments to the rigging, the ships were soon at the mercy of the current and found themselves swept into a great inlet in Tierra del Fuego. Finding good anchorage a short distance from the shore, the unexpected detour allowed a closer inspection of the Land of Fire than any expedition through the strait had previously recorded. Magellan had named Tierra del Fuego after his men were alarmed to see fires in the interior. Though the island was and is inhabited, the fires Magellan saw more likely originated in the dramatic lightning strikes that illuminate the glacial landscape. Covering more than twenty-eight thousand square miles, Tierra del Fuego is partially bisected by a tapering finger of frigid water, the Seno Almirantazgo, a dead end in the watery maze of the strait but a boundary between the contrasting northern and southern halves of this unique world. The larger northern portion of the island is Tierra del Fuego proper, which sweeps to its southeasterly end point out in the Atlantic at Península Mitre. If one could walk directly west from the peninsula, one would encounter the much more heavily glaciated southern half of the island, a world of deeply fissured mountains of ice and intensely blue fjords: the Cordillera Darwin.

From the decks of the *Boudeuse* and the *Étoile,* a striking range of landscape and vegetation types met the eye. On the shore of the encircling bay, to the north and east, stone beaches quickly gave way to a dense mat of ferns interspersed with small white orchids. Rolling hillsides behind them, appearing to be no more than six or seven hundred feet high, were wooded with a stunted evergreen Antarctic beech. Looking west and south, the contrast was extreme: Here the Andes reached its southernmost limit on the fractured curve of Patagonia, where mountains disappeared into clouds as they pushed skyward to heights of over seven thousand feet. Occasionally, the Patagonian sky was broken as giant condors soared on thermals rising from the tip of the Andes' southern spine. Bougainville's expedition anchored here for two days to try to observe a pattern in the currents of the strait, only to conclude that beyond the first and second narrows the number of channels of the strait made all hope of a regularly observable motion futile. In the meantime, Baret and Commerson went botanizing.

An account of the flora and fauna of Tierra del Fuego—complete with specimens of seed, rock, and soil—might seem to be of little use to government ministers in Enlightenment France. But precisely because the island presented such extreme weather conditions, it offered the tantalizing prospect that any source of timber, cloth, or food that grew under such inhospitable circumstances could be transplanted anywhere across France's empire. As he had done on the Patagonian shore, Commerson established himself on the beach and suggested to Baret what she should do. He sent her to collect a cross section of flora from the Fuegian hillside, beginning at the shoreline and working up through the beech and grass.

The vegetation Baret surveyed is beautifully described in the reminiscence of an earlier visitor to the strait. Francis Pretty, a member of Sir Francis Drake's 1578 expedition, wrote: "This Strait is extreme cold, with frost and snow continually; the trees seem to stoop with the burden of the weather, and yet are green continually, and many good and sweet herbs do very plentifully grow and increase under them." In temperatures just above freezing, Baret lugged the leather-and-wood field press from the lowest to the highest point of the shore of their temporary anchorage, often using her bare hands to uproot small specimens from the unyielding soil. Trees that were stunted by sharp Antarctic winds were obviously hardy and might attain a greater height and girth in the trial beds of the Jardin du Roi, so Baret did her best to ease saplings from the ground. In France, as in Britain, government ministers fretted about finding a quick-growing, hardy alternative to native oak trees, whose ancient stands had already been decimated by naval dockyards. (Two thousand mature oak trees were needed to make an eighteenth-century ship of the line.)

Aside from such practical considerations, and the gathering of specimens of ferns, mosses, and lichens, Baret found unexpected beauty in the wildflowers. Species of anemones, daisies, lilies, and poppies bloomed in the brief Antarctic summer, streaking the hillsides with ribbons of white and yellow. Baret's days often began in gray sleet, but at this latitude, the sun's rays were piercing when the cloud cover broke, and the landscape took on a glassy sharpness under the cold solar light.

The ships extricated themselves from their enforced harbor on December 16, edging out into the strait once more where everyone marveled at the glaciers that now seemed to dominate their field of vision. Varying in height from two hundred to five hundred feet, the glaciers presented crystalline faces of apparently blue ice—a disconcerting optical illusion caused by the reflection and scattering of light deep within the ancient masses. Progress through the strait was itself glacially slow. Bougainville wrote that the wind appeared to blow "all round the compass."

Ever since the *Étoile* and the *Boudeuse* joined up in Rio, the *Étoile* had seemed a dead weight impeding the frigate's progress, but now her boxier shape held up better to the violent squalls. As the *Étoile* bobbed responsively to La Giraudais's command, the *Boudeuse* lived up to her name and sulkily resisted her commander. Bougainville suspected damage to the *Boudeuse* below the waterline, and on December 17 ordered that they should find a sheltered harbor to the south, anchor, and effect any necessary repairs. They chose a bay close to the continent's mainland southern tip, near a point known as Cape Froward. With the Cordillera Darwin to their southeast and what is known today as the Brunswick Peninsula behind them, this would be the expedition's makeshift home for the rest of December.

Immediately after the ships moored, a camp was established on the peninsula, its perimeter defined by the steadily growing wall of wooden barrels being off-loaded from both hulls. The *Étoile*'s old leak had very obviously reopened in the strait and now, as her hull emptied, she rose in the water and was maneuvered slowly to the pebbled shore, where she was partially beached to allow access to her stern. Provisions buried in the ballast were waterlogged. (Bougainville's crews could not work in the water, even in rotation, for no one could survive longer than ten minutes in the water temperature of the strait.) Despite his ongoing frustration with his storeship, Bougainville commended "the crew of that vessel, who were almost worn out by the continual exercise of pumping."

The *Boudeuse* also received a minute inspection and was "heeled"— that is, its hull was scoured clean of marine organisms and seaweed. (One of the reasons the strait teems with marine life is that its frigid water supports giant forests of kelp, a submerged raft of which could easily ensnare the rudder and render a ship unresponsive to the helm.) The timber necessary for repairs was all around, not only in trees that grew down to the shoreline but also in neatly stacked piles of logs that Bougainville knew to be the work of his countrymen. In 1765, when Bougainville's hopes of a French colony on the Îles Malouines were still alive, he had ordered the *Aigle* (Eagle) to explore the strait for timber. It did not pass all the way through the strait, but, loaded with logs, it returned to the Îles Malouines from the icy waters, with more cargo than anyone had thought possible. Discovery of the lumber store was therefore, undoubtedly, bittersweet—the labor saved a potent reminder of the lost settlement.

As the officers supervised the men, all engaged in a hard day's work, the Prince of Nassau-Siegen hovered on the margins of the group, unwilling to distract the officers with conversation, uncertain if and how he might assist. The numbing winds and driving rain of the strait had had no impact upon his wardrobe. An eighteenth-century male fashion plate made flesh, he radiated good humor from under a wig of tight blonde ringlets and exuded impracticality from head to toe. The raised heels he wore were de rigueur for any male aristocrat who had been at the

French court and had been popularized by the late Louis XIV (proud of the royal legs and anxious that they always be shown to best advantage), although what served to display a finely turned leg at Versailles threatened to hobble a man on the pebble beaches of the peninsula. Displaying his particular fondness for jeweled hues of velvet, the prince's suit was the boldest assertion of human identity in a landscape defined by natural superlatives.

It is little wonder, then, that a party of Patagonians, curious about the activities of the French and hoping to trade local fox pelts for foreign goods, were distracted from their attempts to barter by the unique appearance of this individual, to whom all others seemed to show a degree of deference. Not having seen any Frenchwomen in the party, the Patagonians took the distinctive long hair and colorful attire of the prince as marks of gender difference. Collecting around him on the beach, Patagonian men and women began stroking his velvet jacket and pulling at the wig. As the prince tried to maintain his typical insouciance, officers moved quickly to save him from the inspection before the Patagonians started patting down his breeches.

Bougainville's journal says nothing about the prince and his interaction with the native Patagonians, but Commerson was evidently delighted to record that "the Patagonians thought the Prince was a woman, due to his youth and beauty." The fact that Commerson bothered to record the episode, even though his journal had become a sporadic series of memoranda rather than a continuous and systematic record of the voyage, indicates that it was significant to him. In the absence of any overt challenges to Baret's identity for over six months, and with Bougainville now complicit in acceptance of the charade, Commerson felt relaxed enough to double up with laughter at the sight of the Patagonians' assumption that Baret was a man while taking the prince for a woman.

For Baret herself, the episode was both reassuring and depressing: After nearly a year as Jean, rather than Jeanne, she had learned to suppress anything feminine about herself well enough to make her unremarkable to the Patagonians. (We can only guess whether the Patagonians would have scrutinized her more closely if their attention had not been captivated by the prince.) After twelve months of binding her breasts under the loosest, most nondescript shirt and breeches and pushing herself to her physical limit to prove she was a man, Baret scarcely recognized the woman in the mirror, and Commerson appeared to see only a porter and servant.

Assuming the prince to be aware of the widespread conviction that Baret was a woman, his experience at the hands of the Patagonians must have caused him to reflect. No woman had ever doubted his masculinity; indeed, his growing number of cast-aside lovers was one of the reasons his family had encouraged his joining the circumnavigation. Now he had had a glimpse of what it felt like to be the vulnerable center of attention of a group of strangers. He had known that he was not in any real danger—everything played out under the eyes of over three hundred men who would come to his assistance—but the experience was a disquieting insight into what it felt like to be a woman alone and reliant on the goodwill of male companions for protection. Perhaps inspired by this newfound sympathy for Baret's position, the prince asked to join Baret and Commerson on their daily botanizing expeditions around the bay. Like the astronomer, Véron, the prince now paid Baret the compliment of simply taking her at face value and treating her with respect.

Despite the prince's kind intentions, Baret's exasperation on setting out for a day with Commerson and the prince can easily be imagined. Both men could be charming, witty, intelligent companions, overflowing with enthusiasm, ideas, and observations. Yet neither was of any practical use in terms of a hard day's work, and work was all Baret had to take her out of the confines of the cabin. Commerson frequently reported pains in his leg, using the recurring ulcers as an excuse to sit on the beach while Baret climbed. The prince was all good humor and anxious to prove himself of some use, but even his idea of a practical outfit for a day's walking was more suited to the garden paths of Versailles than the coast of the Strait of Magellan.

Of course, it would be a disservice to Commerson to repeatedly elevate Baret to the position of sole plant collector on the expedition. Commerson still had the passion for botany he had first felt as a teenager and, when circumstances allowed, he was an enthusiastic and energetic presence in the field. But shouldering her leather field satchel, the portable press, the bug-collecting net, and the day's supplies, Baret still quickly outpaced a limping Commerson and a high-heeled Nassau-Siegen, who easily fell into conversation together regarding their shared interest in natural history. One day, striding up a small rise to read the lay of the land beyond their impromptu harbor, Baret must have stopped up short at the sight that greeted her.

Along the southwest shoreline of the Brunswick Peninsula, and visible from the arm of the strait where she stood, the smooth pebble beaches were crowded with colonies of Antarctic marine life that were still new to European science. The most arresting animal Baret saw, in size, habit, and quantity, was the southern elephant seal (*Mirounga leonina*) only recently named and classified by Linnaeus in 1758. This sixteen-foot-long, six-thousand-pound giant gets its name from the pendulous trumpetlike nose of the male, which serves to amplify its repertoire of threat calls as it throws its massive body weight into sumo-style collisions with potential rivals. Alpha males (known as "beachmasters"), bearing scars from all their past challengers, preside over vast harems of slightly smaller, indolent females that bask on the shore.

Before the elephant seal was hunted to near-extinction in the nineteenth century (for the oil that could be pressed from its blubber), it is thought that its colonies were hundreds of thousands strong. When Baret saw her first elephant seal—or her first hundred thousand elephant seals—European hunters had not begun their bloody massacre of the species. Baret stared at beach after beach of the huge, smooth, gray bodies nursing their pups and sunning themselves in utter relaxation amid a cacophony of beachmasters' calls. No place in the world today—not even the strait itself—can approximate the sheer quantity of seal flesh that greeted Baret. Like Eve, she surveyed and walked among a superabundance of animals that had no fear of man, while her male partner summoned up its name, satisfied to know what the creature should be called.

Elephant seals, which also eat squid, skates, and rays, are partial to penguin where it is available—and it was breathtakingly available along this branch of the strait. Today, the largest colony of Magellanic penguins (*Spheniscus magellanicus*) in the world can be found at Punta Tombo, a peninsula jutting from the coast of Patagonia into the southern Atlantic. The Punta Tombo colony already lay behind Bougainville's expedition, but with half a million Magellanic penguins gathering there each year for the breeding season, we can imagine how the slightly smaller colonies of the eighteenth-century strait must have appeared to Baret. The penguins named in commemoration of Magellan lack the glossy black plumage of their Emperor cousins. Rather, from a distance, their nubby feathers give them a mottled appearance, as though each were wearing a black-and-white-flecked tweed. Waddling from the beaches to nests up to a quarter of a mile inland, which they use across a period of years, Magellanic penguins are not afraid to plant themselves in the path of people, bristling their flightless wings and making noisy exhalations that dare intruders into the colony to go further.

As they skirted a guano-encrusted beach colony of tens of thousands of the birds, Baret, Commerson, and the prince likely crossed paths with one or more of the two-foot-high penguins running full tilt in its distinctive side-to-side gait as it headed back to its inshore nest. A more improbable grouping is hard to imagine, as these three eighteenth-century travelers—a woman dressed as a man, a man pretending not to know that his assistant was a woman, and a second man dressed more richly than most women—stared down at a black-and-white bird under half their height that defied them to go any further. Between the austere color palette of the penguin and the brilliant velvet of the prince, the strait has perhaps never hosted a meeting of greater contrasts.

To Bougainville, it was evident that Commerson and the prince made for a productive combination: "M. de Commerson, accompanied by the prince of Nassau, profited of such days for botanizing. He had obstacles of every kind to surmount, yet this wild soil had the merit of being new to him, and the Strait of Megellan has filled his herbals with a great number of unknown and interesting plants." These "obstacles" included the unsteadiness of Commerson's leg on the uneven terrain and the foul weather. Recording a temperature range that fluctuated from 5° to 12.5° on the Reaumur scale (that is, averaging 41.5° Fahrenheit), Bougainville credits his botanist's perseverance, though he says nothing of his botanist's assistant.

The specific mention of "herbals" (that is, Commerson's volumes of his herbarium) seems to indicate that a great many plants were collected in the hopes of ascertaining any medicinal or commercial use. Charles Darwin's account of the vegetation of the area in *The Voyage of the Beagle* allows us to infer some of the species that Baret helped collect and that Commerson subsequently displayed to his commander. Among the plants that could not be found anywhere else on earth was a striking, globular orange-yellow fungus now known as Darwin's fungus (*Cyttaria darwinii*), which sprouted like so many agglomerations of supersized popcorn from the cold, damp bark of southern beech trees. Darwin tells us that the fungus was collected by the women and children of Tierra del Fuego to be eaten raw, and that, with the exception of a few berries, it was the only "vegetable food" eaten by the natives. A fungus that appeared to sustain native peoples under harsh conditions would certainly have been of great interest to French government ministers seeking a food source for legions of imperial workers.

Baret and Commerson could not have known, as Darwin did from comparing the fungus with descriptions of a related species in Tasmania, that the fungus will only grow on beech trees. Darwin also tells us that these beech stands were so thick that it was necessary to keep checking a compass while exploring them. The gloomy, dank interior of the forest was an obstacle course of fallen, moldering tree trunks, rotting wood, and spongy vegetation that filled the fit, young Darwin with despair that he would ever emerge into the light. In this challenging environment, collecting edible fungus from the eerie forests of the strait was likely to have been Baret's job.

If Commerson and the prince could not get through the beech forests, they could get around them via hillsides covered in coarse grass that shimmered bronze in the sunlight. Above the grassline, the streaks of dwarf alpines that crept close to the peat-colored soil reminded the botanists of European alpine species, the medicinal uses of which were familiar to them. These elevated areas with their remarkable range of vegetation underfoot also provided vantage points for appreciating the scale of the landscape. Francis Pretty, of the 1578 Drake expedition, tried to describe the mountains, glaciers, and fjords at this part of the strait, but the vastness of what he saw clearly overwhelmed him: "The land on both sides is very huge and mountainous; the lower mountains whereof, although they be monstrous and wonderful to look upon for their height, yet there are others which in height exceed them in a strange manner, reaching themselves above their fellows so high, that between them did appear three regions of clouds."

All of this was laid before Baret on Antarctic summer days that stretched out under twenty hours of sunlight. If the latitude lengthened the time available for botanizing, it severely curtailed the opportunities for the botanists' friend, Véron, to collect astronomical data. As Baret, Commerson, and the prince walked back into camp each evening, Véron was cursing the sky. Even when darkness fell, great gray clouds typically scudded across his field of view, rendering pointless all his efforts in setting up his instruments. As Bougainville noted with remarkable understatement (given that the accurate determination of longitude at sea was a major goal of the expedition), "The sky of this country, which is very bad for astronomers, prevented his making any observation for the longitude."

With repairs concluded to both the *Étoile* and the *Boudeuse*, and reconnaissance of all promising inlets having been made in the longboats, the ships weighed anchors from Cape Froward on December 29, 1767. The large islands on the southwest of the strait are heavily fissured, being a geological extension of the Cordillera Darwin. Keeping a northwest course, with the Brunswick Peninsula to starboard, the ships rounded the Charles Islands, a group of small landmasses in the strait, only to be confronted with a choice of channels. On a modern map, the way through the glacial labyrinth seems so obvious that one wonders at any ship's hesitation. But as 1767 turned to 1768, Bougainville was once more anchored—this time at Fortescue Bay farther north on the Brunswick Peninsula—trying to decide whether to continue northwest or take an abrupt turn southwest, through a channel snaking between vast granite cliffs. The celebration of the New Year had no sooner passed than snow began to fall, accumulating on deck to a depth of four inches. When the longboat parties returned with their reports on the way ahead, it was clear that the northwest channel was the preferred route to the open ocean.

On January 25, 1768, the channel widened considerably. To starboard, a series of peninsulas to the mainland was still visible, but to port, a long low island (Desolation Island) tapered out into open water. The next day, still holding their steady northwest course, the *Étoile* and the *Boudeuse* saw Desolation Island slip behind their port stern, as the fractured outlying rocks of the coast to starboard melted into the ocean. They had reached the Pacific, nearly seven weeks after entering the Strait of Magellan, and its gunmetal waters strained the eyes as far as the blue-gray horizon.

In concluding that passage through the strait was preferable to passage around Cape Horn, Bougainville noted that the plant and animal life in the strait made it the more healthful option in the summertime,

since a crew that knew how to make use of the strait's plant resources
could avoid scurvy.

> Notwithstanding the difficulties which we have met with in our pas-
> sage of the Strait of Magellan, I would always advise to prefer this
> course to that of doubling Cape Horn, from the month of September
> to the end of March. . . . Certainly there will be some obstacles
> in passing the Strait, but this retardment is not entirely time lost.
> There is water, wood, and shells in abundance, sometimes there are
> likewise very good fish; and I make no doubt but the scurvy would
> make more havoc among a crew, who should come into the South
> Seas by the way of Cape Horn, than among those who should enter
> the same Seas through the Strait of Magellan: when we left it, we had
> no sick person on board.

Baret and Commerson had done their duty, guessing which species of
plants and fish would be safe and good to eat, warding off the dreaded
disease by provisioning an expedition of 330 men in a near-freezing
environment with antiscorbutics. As he entered the waters of the Pacific,
Bougainville must have been satisfied at his decision to let Baret remain
aboard in Rio.

SIX

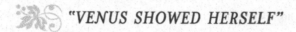 *"VENUS SHOWED HERSELF"*

Tahiti Exposed

THE FRENCH WERE not looking for Tahiti because they did not know that it was there. The first Europeans to come into contact with the island were members of a British expedition under the command of Samuel Wallis in HMS *Dolphin,* who landed on Tahitian shores in June 1767. Both the *Boudeuse* and the *Étoile* left France long before Wallis returned to England to report on his island find, so the French had no clearly defined expectations of the Pacific. They hoped to confirm the existence of a Great Southern Continent that balanced the known landmasses of the Northern Hemisphere, and also believed they might find assorted islands of strategic importance that could provide new sources of timber, food, and cash crops. When the *Étoile* and the *Boudeuse* broke through into the Pacific on January 26, 1768, their subsequent course was therefore entirely at Bougainville's discretion.

Bougainville hoped to chart a good route to the Dutch-controlled Spice Islands of Indonesia, where he might obtain some precious specimens of nutmeg in defiance of the Netherlands' monopoly on the spice. As it turned out, the challenge of getting to the Spice Islands was nearly beyond the capabilities of anyone on his expedition. For the Pacific is an ocean of superlatives, covering over one-third of the earth's total surface and just under 50 percent of the hydrosphere (the earth's water surface). The entire landmass of the planet could be fitted into the Pacific and there would still be room for a second Africa. Against this background of oceanic excess, it is a wonder that the French bumped into Tahiti at all—just one island of approximately twenty-five thousand in a vast expanse of blue. For nine weeks, from January 26 to April 2, the *Étoile* and the *Boudeuse* sailed the Pacific without any notion that such a place as Tahiti existed. Once found, it surpassed anything they had dared to imagine.

From late January to early February, the ships had kept a steady northwest course, sailing into warmer waters than those of the Strait of Magellan, and moving under kinder skies. Baret and Commerson lived at the center of their cabin, surrounded by the results of their fieldwork. Ever since the *Étoile* had been rammed by the unmoored ship back in Montevideo, the botanists had heeded the dangers of piling specimen cases three or four deep. Where they could not be secured behind ropes, expertly knotted by the crew, the crates had become impromptu tables and benches. Drying plants recently picked alongside the Strait of Magellan hung upside down from the overhead beams and had to be inspected for signs of mold or insect infestation. Ripe seed pods needed to be carefully prized open, their contents poured into paper cones. Thoroughly desiccated leaves and flowers could finally be interleaved with sheets of absorbent paper and layered in the boxes. Everything had to be checked and double-checked for weevil infestations. Shells and geological specimens required labeling with their point of origin, or else they would be useless to those in France who sought to construct a mineralogical map of the strait. The work required a skillful touch and methodical approach and Baret lost herself in it.

From time to time, a sailor would report that the ships were passing through a school of fish or a pod of dolphins. Sometimes the sightings were more exotic, and Commerson took Baret with him on deck to puzzle at the undulating manta rays (*Manta birostris*) whose fifteen- to twenty-foot cartilaginous wings pulsated slowly under the water. To the deckhands, the fish was so unearthly in its appearance and movement that they called it a devil, and with terror they realized that such devils seemed drawn toward them. Manta rays display great curiosity around stationary ships and divers, but even today they are too large for most aquariums. Much as Commerson would have loved to catch one, the manta ray proved an elusive species and so remained unnamed and unclassified until the 1790s. Sailors did manage to catch bonito (a relative of the tuna) and flying fish on their fishing lines, turning a handful of these into bait for larger prey. Commerson brought fish back to the cabin to sketch and dissect, as he had done with Atlantic species.

Smaller fish were dispensed with quickly enough, but as the *Étoile* and *Boudeuse* sailed into warmer waters in February and March 1768, the bonito on the lines attracted sharks. The specimen crates of the cabin were then covered with oilcloth and doubled as a dissection table. Baret had always been Commerson's equal in the care of plants and had become his equal in the preparation of dried specimens for herbaria, but she lacked the medical and anatomical training that Commerson brought to his consideration of all dead animal specimens. With the Prince of Nassau-Siegen and Véron traveling on the *Boudeuse,* the only man on board who might have been interested in Commerson's findings was his nemesis, the surgeon Vivès—so Commerson turned to Baret as a sounding board. But whatever Baret thought of a cabin reeking of raw flesh and the contents of a shark's stomach, she had no choice but to keep it to herself.

On February 10, 1768, at latitude 28° south, the ships adopted a more westerly course, crossing the Tropic of Capricorn on a gentle diagonal. From the decks, it appeared as though the lapis-colored waters rolled to infinity. A month went by and more, and Baret's life could not have been more different from her experience of the Strait of Magellan. She had traded frigid temperatures and grueling work for the sweat of the tropics and shimmering blue days, with nothing to do but to read and watch the horizon. In the privacy of the cabin, Baret could at least remove the linen bandages that flattened her breasts and caused angry eruptions of dermatitis on her torso. Without fresh water to keep the raised red welts clean, Baret surely applied her herb woman's knowledge to self-medicate. The cabin was effectively one large exotic medicine cabinet, and her experience of gathering bougainvillea bracts and seed pods to make a poultice for Commerson's ulcerated leg had interested her in the properties of unfamiliar plants. And then, just when everyone had begun to despair of finding anything on the water worth colonizing, conquering, or cultivating, land came into view on March 21.

The atoll chain that is known today as the Tuamotus was more inviting than anything the expedition had yet encountered. Baret watched with Commerson as the *Étoile* came close enough to the island of Akiaki to see a group of near-naked men marshaling wooden staves in unison. The natives' gestures led those on the *Boudeuse* to call this the Island of the Lance Bearers, but Baret and Commerson found the men less interesting than the wall of tropical vegetation that rose from the island's heart, and they privately called this the Plentiful Island. The ships threaded a course between islands they named for French saints, for topographical features—even for the *Étoile* itself. Today no trace of this colonial nomenclature remains and the islands bear their centuries-old Polynesian names of Vahitahi, Hikueru, Reitoru. Commerson had become bored with his journal on the open ocean, relinquishing control of it to an irritated Pierre Duclos-Guyot, but he now resumed his writing. He pointed out to Baret how the white tops of the breakers rolling on the shores of the atolls made patterns indicative of submerged coral reefs. These reefs, which seemed a standard feature of the subcoastal zone of all islands in the chain, discouraged any thought of sending landing parties ashore. Sending a longboat would only expose its occupants to native encounters at a distance from the waiting ships. But on April 2, 1768, a different prospect presented itself.

The islands behind them had all appeared relatively small, inviting speculation as to how they could sustain the native populations glimpsed through the officers' pocket perspectives. But the landmass now visible on the port bow was clearly more substantial. Bougainville at first thought it "a high and very steep mountain, seemingly surrounded by the sea." Heading northward to try to round the "mountain," it became apparent that a lower-lying area of land lay to its northwest. It was impossible to tell whether the two were joined without getting much closer to shore.

A very simple watercolor from the expedition shows a stylized appearance of the two landmasses, as the ships sailed north and west around them trying to ascertain what they were looking at. (It is possibly the work of Charles Routier de Romainville, expedition engineer and chief cartographer sailing on the *Étoile*.) The illustration is unique, being the only known representation of both the *Étoile* and the *Boudeuse*, and though neither ship is represented in great detail, the artist was careful to distinguish Bougainville's frigate with an exaggerated pennant (longer than that accorded to an admiral) streaming from its main (or central) mast. (Bougainville was clearly in high spirits at the French discovery of Tahiti.) Over the crude ink outlines of Tahiti and its stylized palm trees, placed at regular intervals along the shore, the artist laid a light green wash that blends the island with the sea. In this eye-catching illustration, we see the basic topography of the island, Bougainville's delight at the find, and the overwhelming impression made by the hues of the Tahitian coast.

During the night of April 3–4, lookouts on both the *Étoile* and *Boudeuse* reported seeing fires onshore. By daybreak, it was apparent that the higher and lower areas were joined by a low-lying ribbon of land "bent like a bow," forming a great bay. The water was the color of light green glass, and the shore was, improbably, a crescent of black sand. (Tahiti is volcanic in origin and the beaches on the northeast coast are composed of eroded laval deposits.) Within twenty or so yards of the shore, the treeline began. From out of the riot of tropical foliage, the occasional wayward palm tree had forgotten its vertical habit, and hung, precariously, at a forty-five-degree angle, waving its fronds low over the basalt beach. Like the deckhands, Baret and Commerson crowded the port rails, disbelieving the colors and the reality of what was before them. From the botanists' perspective, the land looked incalculably rich.

As the ships' senior officers debated whether to move closer to shore, a dugout canoe, or *pirogue,* came alongside, manned by twelve naked men who held boughs of ripe bananas up to the ships. With the sweet rich smell of the fruit perfuming the air, the sailors needed no encouragement to throw a hastily tied slipknot over the side. The bananas were successfully brought aboard, together with a squealing piglet. In exchange, the men threw down caps and handkerchiefs, noticing, as they had in Patagonia, that red items seemed particularly prized. Soon both ships were surrounded by a flotilla of *pirogues,* all occupied by strong, healthy, naked men; no women were in evidence. This island armada encircled the French ships until nightfall, when it melted away under an evening sky of such starry brilliance that Véron was overwhelmed. At daybreak, as the ships puzzled over where to drop anchor—repeated soundings revealed a bottom of rocks, of no practical use—the dugouts returned. Unlike the previous day, they now contained women as well as men.

Unlike the women of Patagonia, whom officers and men alike had found unattractive, and who had showed no interest in the French, the Tahitian women had lustrous black hair and radiant brown skin thrown into sharp relief by the vibrantly colored garlands that swung over their otherwise naked breasts. They flashed perfect white smiles at the sailors, who grinned back with mouths of gapped and rotting teeth, gesturing to the women to come aboard. Even in the wildest tales told by rum-sodden sailors in port taverns and brothels, no one had heard of anywhere like this. Unaware that Wallis in the *Dolphin* had landed there a year earlier, Bougainville thought his expedition the first to stumble on this second Eden. He called it Nouvelle Cythere (New Cythera): In Greek mythology, Cythera is one of the reputed birthplaces of the goddess of love (and lust), Aphrodite.

Now frantic to find a way to shore, the crew navigated a passage through the outlying reef of the bay that finally put the men achingly close to the black sand. Baret, not sharing the men's sense of urgency as they prepared to drop anchor and hoist the longboats over the side, kept to the cabin. She may have wondered how much botanizing she could accomplish onshore given that over three hundred Frenchmen were planning on making the most of what the island had to offer.

As for Bougainville, if he could not maintain naval discipline on the ground, he could at least maintain it on the printed page. When he came to write his journal—for an intended audience of male and female readers—it was inconceivable that he should represent the French as lustful instigators and grateful participants in an orgiastic shore leave. Bougainville chose instead to represent the sexual climate of Tahiti through two separate incidents in which he repeatedly characterizes the French as onlookers rather than actors, as blushing innocents rather than rapacious predators.

The first sexually charged episode that Bougainville describes occurred on board one of the ships (Bougainville does not specify which one) as it was settling into its intended moorings, with teams of men turning the capstan (belowdeck winch) to raise the anchor cable and

allow the anchor to be repositioned in deep sandy soundings. Bougainville says that the Tahitian men in the dugouts

> pressed us to choose a woman, and to come on shore with her; and
> their gestures, which were nothing less than equivocal, denoted in
> what manner we should form an acquaintance with her. It was very
> difficult, amidst such a sight, to keep at their work four hundred
> young French sailors, who had seen no women for six months. In spite
> of all our precautions, a young girl came on board, and placed herself
> upon the quarter-deck, near one of the hatchways, which was open,
> in order to give air to those who were heaving at the capstan below it.
> The girl carelessly dropt a cloth, which covered her, and appeared to
> the eyes of all beholders, such as Venus showed herself to the Phry-
> gian shepherd, having, indeed, the celestial form of that goddess.
> Both sailors and soldiers endeavoured to come to the hatchway; and
> the capstan was never hove with more alacrity than on this occasion.

Inflating his crew by seventy men or so, Bougainville manages a
rhetorical sleight of hand by which four hundred Frenchmen are directed by their Tahitian counterparts to choose whichever women they
prefer. The French have no agency, other than in displacing their sexual
energies by groaning round the tightening capstan. Without explicitly
judging the Tahitian men immoral and unnatural, Bougainville shows
enough to allow the reader to make such an extrapolation. As for the
young Tahitian woman, she is as uncomprehending and untouchable as
a classical nude. The suggestive episode climaxes with a predictable joke
and a knowing wink to the reader, without any explanation of how and
when the young woman left the ship—but no Frenchman is described as
doing anything other than looking.

In the second account Bougainville gives his polite readers of sexually charged encounters between the Tahitians and the French, he fol-
lows the same narrative strategy: The Tahitians act and the French react.

This time, Bougainville represents a lone Frenchman as the terrified and unconsenting object of a forcible stripping and probing at the hands of a group of Tahitians.

> One single Frenchman, who was my cook, having found means to escape against my orders, soon returned more dead than alive. He had hardly set his feet on shore, with the fair whom he had chosen, when he was immediately surrounded by a crowd of Indians, who undressed him from head to foot. He thought he was utterly lost, not knowing where the exclamations of those people would end, who were tumultuously examining every part of his body. After having considered him well, they returned him his clothes, put into his pockets whatever they had taken out of them, and brought the girl to him, desiring him to content those desires which had brought him on shore with her. All their persuasive arguments had no effect; they were obliged to bring the poor cook on board, who told me, that I might reprimand him as much as I pleased, but that I could never frighten him so much, as he had just now been frightened on shore.

Like the previous episode, which ends with a weak joke about the motivational effect of a naked young woman on four hundred sex-starved men, this incident also invites its contemporary readers to smile and be reassured: Despite the temptations Tahiti offers, French cupidity goes no further than a look or a thought. While it is entirely credible that the ship's cook might have been rendered temporarily impotent by being forcibly stripped and then invited to have sex in front of a group of Tahitian onlookers, his concluding seriocomic plea to Bougainville hints that he feared anything might have happened, from a homosexual gang rape to a murder. The episode establishes the Tahitians as sexually predatory, or at least animalistic, with neither awareness of, nor concern for, the effect of their behavior on the French. These successive episodes in Bougainville's journal are built of the same narrative elements: The

French look, in longing or in fear; the Tahitians act with complete disregard for their effect on the French; and the palpable sexual tension is ultimately deflated through a lame attempt at humor, because Bougainville does not know how else to change the subject.

Eighty published journal pages further on from the first sexually charged encounters between the French and the Tahitians, and buried between an account of Véron's ongoing attempts to establish longitude at sea and a report on soundings of the bottom, we find two pages devoted to Baret. They are dated May 28 and 29, when Tahiti was at least six weeks in the past, and the ships were charting a course through the island grouping now known as Vanuatu (but which Bougainville refers to as the New Cyclades).

Some business called me on board the Étoile, and I had an opportunity of verifying a very singular fact. For some time there was a report in both ships, that the servant of M. de Commerson, named Baret, was a woman. His shape, voice, beardless chin, and scrupulous attention of not changing his linen, or making the natural discharges in the presence of any one, besides several other signs, had given rise to, and kept up this suspicion. But how was it possible to discover the woman in the indefatigable Baret, who was already an expert botanist, had followed his master in all his botanical walks, amidst the snows and frozen mountains of the Strait of Magellan, and had even on such troublesome excursions carried provisions, arms, and herbals, with so much courage and strength, that the naturalist had called him his beast of burden? A scene which passed at Tahiti changed this suspicion into certainty. M. de Commerson went on shore to botanize there; Baret had hardly set his feet on shore with the herbal under his arm, when the men of Tahiti surrounded him, cried out, It is a woman, and wanted to give her the honors customary in the isle. The Chevalier de Bournand [first lieutenant of the *Boudeuse*], who was upon guard on shore, was obliged to come to her assistance, and escort her to the boat. After that period it was difficult to prevent the sailors from alarming her modesty. When I came on board the Étoile, Baret, with her face bathed in tears, owned to me that she was a woman; she said that she had deceived her master at Rochefort, by offering to serve him in men's clothes at the very moment when he was embarking; that she had already before served a Genevan gentleman at Paris, in quality of a valet; that being born in Burgundy, and become an orphan, the loss of a law-suit had brought her to a distressed situation, and inspired her with the resolution to disguise her sex; that she well knew when she embarked that we were going round the world, and that such a voyage had raised her curiosity. She will be the first woman that ever made it, and I must do her the justice to affirm that she has always behaved on board with the most scrupulous modesty. She is neither ugly nor pretty and is not yet twenty-five. It must be owned, that if the two ships had been wrecked on any desert isle in the ocean, Baret's fate would have been a singular one.

This passage is the only source for the prevalent belief, still repeated today, that Baret's true identity was first revealed on Tahiti. As Bougainville tells it, she had no sooner put her foot on Tahitian soil than a group of male islanders "surrounded" her, shouting their conviction that she was a woman. Fearing herself in imminent danger of a gang rape, Baret presumably screamed for assistance, and apparently loudly and urgently enough to cause the scales to fall from Bournand's eyes as he gallantly ran to protect his countrywoman. We know from Commerson himself that Baret and Commerson first went ashore on Tahiti on April 7, so we might reasonably expect to find some reference to this episode in Commerson's journal, at least, but Commerson says nothing about it, either in his own writings or in the notebook he shared with Duclos-Guyot. Indeed, Duclos-Guyot, the Prince of Nassau-Siegen, and Vivès all fail to mention anything odd about Baret and a group of Tahitian men on the beach, while they do refer to a climatic—and revelatory—confrontation between Baret and some of the crew in New Ireland in July, over three months later. No officer or gentleman, then, corroborates Bougainville's version of events on Tahiti. And this is not the only disturbing and singular aspect of Bougainville's account.

In its published form, Bougainville's journal sandwiches this story about Baret between unremarkable observations about the impossibility of determining longitude at sea and the quality of the sea floor. Yet in the manuscript notebooks on which the published journal is based, the entry for May 28–29, 1768, occupies the last leaf in a notebook—the bottom half of the front of the page, to be exact. The back of that page consists of seven lines about the good weather of May 29–30, followed by four more lines about the weather for May 30–31. So Bougainville no sooner states his discovery that Commerson's assistant is a woman than he turns to observations about the agreeable Tahitian climate.

Looking at the manuscript, it is impossible to escape the conclusion that Bougainville was determined to fit Baret's story into this single side of a page, for Bougainville's lines of handwriting become closer together as he progresses down the page. Having concluded that "Baret is neither ugly nor pretty and is not yet twenty-five," Bougainville draws a line right at the bottom of the page to signify that the entry is complete. The published journal concludes in a different way from the manuscript. In its published state, the entry has been expanded upon to conclude in exactly the same way as previous accounts of sexually charged encounters between the French and the Tahitians: with a weak joke (here speculating on Baret's fate had the expedition been shipwrecked).

Given the nature of the revelations in this entry, it is simply extraordinary that Bougainville never says anything more about Baret being a woman. He does not comment on the effect of her admission on Commerson or indeed anyone else. He does not tell us whether she dressed differently following her confession. All he says is that after Baret admitted to being a woman, "it was difficult to prevent the sailors from alarming her modesty." At a stroke, a woman who has spent over a year in the company of three hundred men, enduring their rites of passage and acting as her lover's "beast of burden" is reduced to a skittish ingenue, embarrassed and affronted by the male sex at every turn.

Where Bougainville seems determined to discuss Baret as quickly as possible, Baret herself had clearly spent some time thinking about what she would say if her sex was discovered. At some point in her dealings with Bougainville—perhaps as early as Rio when Commerson was placed "under arrest," or perhaps after the brutal end to her charade on New Ireland—Baret accounted for her presence on the expedition in a way that did not implicate Commerson in her deceit. Bougainville makes her prepared story part of this account of the supposed interview after Tahiti.

Intriguingly, Baret claimed "she had already before served a Genevan gentleman at Paris, in quality of a valet." To the philosophes, the independent Swiss city of Geneva was a byword for political and religious tolerance and therefore a model of what they hoped autocratic France might aspire to. (The entry on Geneva in the *Encyclopédie* is one of the longest and most famous, since Diderot implicitly attacked repressive French institutions as he lavished praise on their Genevan equivalents.) Rousseau's conservative critics thought they summed up his freethinking character when they referred to him as simply "the Genevan." For Baret to claim that she had previously worked as a valet—and by implication, presented herself as a man—for a "Genevan gentleman" was a deft move, hinting at a background spent, in part, in a more tolerant society. Perhaps this detail was deliberately contrived by Commerson to tantalize Bougainville with a remote connection to the most (in)famous Genevan in Paris—Rousseau himself.

Adding pathos to intrigue, Baret then said "that being born in Burgundy, and become an orphan, the loss of a law-suit had brought her to a distressed situation." The orphaned heiress cheated out of her fortune was a staple of sentimental literature at the time, and this part of Baret's story was, like her pseudonym "de Bonnefoy" mentioned in Commerson's will, intended to suggest that she came from a family of means. Indeed, while Bougainville emphatically refers to Commerson's assistant as "named Baret," this detail regarding the loss of family property may be the reason why a number of scholars claim—without foundation— that Baret gave her name as "de Bonnefoy" in her interview with Bougainville.

But why is Bougainville outnumbered three to one among his own crew in his assertion that Baret revealed her true identity on Tahiti? And why was Bougainville determined that the entry should fit on the penultimate page of one of his notebooks?

If, as everyone but Bougainville insists, something traumatic happened to Baret on New Ireland, and if the aggressors were French, Bougainville would be forced to explain why the officers had not shared the men's recognition that there was a woman on the expedition and acted to protect her. Bougainville would also have had to account for the complete breakdown in order implied by a group of Frenchmen attacking a lone Frenchwoman—barbarism that no French publisher or reader would have wished to countenance. In placing the scene of Baret's unmasking on Tahiti, Bougainville could make it part of a series of stories about sexually predatory and uninhibited Tahitian men who have already been seen to offer their women to the French (in the capstan story) and to strip and molest French crewmen (rendering the cook impotent). In Bougainville's story, Baret reveals herself on the beach of Tahiti because she fears a gang rape: The Frenchwoman abroad preserves her honor, or rather, it is preserved for her by her countrymen. The French of Bougainville's construction (who have only ever looked at Tahitian women, never acting on their longings) have only to hear their own countrywoman in distress and the chevalier de Bournand, first lieutenant of the *Boudeuse*, strides to her aid.

So Bougainville was fabricating his diary entry for May 28–29 to avoid having to address more embarrassing revelations at a later date, which means that this entry was written with full knowledge of what had happened on New Ireland and added to the journal after this time. How could this be?

Like all books—both private journals and printed books—in the eighteenth century, Bougainville's notebooks would have been bought as gatherings of loose, blank paper that would have been taken by their owner to a bookbinder for custom binding (hence the remarkable uniformity of spines in gentlemen's libraries from the period). Notebook or book pages made from the same large sheets of handmade paper would be sewn together as gatherings, and multiple gatherings hand-stitched together to form a complete text. If Bougainville wrote the entry for May 28–29 at a later date, he either added it in the only place where he had room (the last blank leaf of a notebook, perhaps, in which the constructed episode does not look out of place, given the context of stories already told about the Tahitians) or opened up the gatherings of the notebook and disturbed its physical form.

The notebook in question has certainly been tampered with. The front cover shows three holes where binding thread used to be, until at some point Bougainville needed to spring his notebook from its cover in order to insert at least one leaf. In between the facing pages covering the events of April 10–11, a half-size leaf jumps out at the reader: a letter from the surgeon on board the *Boudeuse,* Louis-Claude Laporte. Explaining who he is and his role on the expedition, Laporte certifies that he has been asked to examine the body of a Tahitian killed by a gun. Whether the islander was fired on by the French or was playing with a French weapon is not clear: Laporte simply confirms the fact of a dead body and that he has been asked to write this confirmation by his commander. Apparently not trusting that the letter would necessarily remain with the notebook if loosely inserted, Bougainville clearly caused the notebook to be restitched to incorporate Laporte's letter.

So Bougainville's notebook is compromised in more ways than one: Its account of Baret's confession on Tahiti is flatly contradicted by three expedition members; Bougainville's account of Baret's self-revelation is determinedly squeezed onto the penultimate page of the notebook; and the notebook's gatherings have clearly been taken apart and restitched to facilitate the insertion of at least one leaf. Taken individually, each of these things is strange; taken together, they suggest the need for a healthy dose of skepticism in accepting Bougainville's story at face value. But this is not all that calls into question the accuracy of Bougainville's journal. A fourth man now emerges to give the lie to Bougainville's version of events.

In literature and history written from the perspective of the world's colonizing powers, the colonized are typically either silent or made to ventriloquize sentiments that ultimately say more about colonizing writers than their subjects. The islander Aotourou who joined Bougainville's expedition is one of two Tahitians who would make the journey from his Pacific home to the imperial capitals of the eighteenth century. (The other was Omai, who returned to London in 1774 on HMS *Adventure*, one of two ships that had accompanied Captain James Cook on his ill-fated second voyage to the Pacific. Presumably the British establishment, galled by Aotourou's appearance in Paris in 1769, wanted its own Tahitian visitor to celebrate and stare at.)

Since Aotourou learned French and saw enough of eighteenth-century Paris to learn something of its culture, his recorded views offer that rarest of things: an explanation of the actions of the colonized in terms that the colonizer can understand. Aotourou's actions on the ships were described by Vivès. His time in the French capital inspired Denis Diderot to make him a speaking character in Diderot's *Supplément au voyage de Bougainville*, and his fame while in Paris also secured him a place in

Nicolas Bricaire de la Dixmerie's *Le Sauvage de Taïti aux Français*. His last interview with a French writer was with Jacques-Henri Bernardin de Saint-Pierre for the latter's *Voyage à l'Île de France*.

Aotourou had been one of the first Tahitians to clamber aboard the *Étoile*, but he was neither cowed nor naive in his exploration of the ship. As the anthropologist Steven Hooper reminds us, the 100- to 120-foot length of European sailing ships was matched by the dimensions of the great ceremonial canoes of Pacific peoples, and we unwittingly patronize them if we assume that they approached European vessels in utter awe of their size. Aotourou readily descended belowdecks when invited, and eagerly indicated his interest in seeing the men and everything at their disposal. The islanders of the Pacific—including those whose survival on tiny islands had so puzzled the French—had developed complex sea-going trade networks over millennia, and European ships promised new cargoes.

According to Vivès, the Tahitian had no sooner descended to the middle deck (a deck in the middle of all those running the length of the hold), where a tight knot of the crew crowded to see him, than he picked out Baret, shouting "ayenene" repeatedly, which was understood to mean "girl." Since Baret was standing next to a soft-featured gunsmith called Labare, the wits in the party started nudging Labare and insisting that the inquisitive islander had singled him out. Unable to think of a creative response, and clearly a little disturbed by what the strange Tahitian might do, Labare hastily pointed to Baret. To the laughter of the crowd and the puzzlement of Aotourou, Baret pushed her way through the crowd to the safety of her cabin, leaving a visibly fuming Commerson to stare down the men.

After Bougainville's journal of the expedition was published, with its account of Baret's identification the instant she set foot on the black lava beaches, the scientist Charles de La Condamine would conclude that the Tahitians had "a highly developed sense of smell, which is such that they can distinguish a man from a woman by the smell alone." His fellow

Frenchman Charles de Brosses, dividing the world into "the Americas" and "Europe," came to the same conclusion in more bluntly animal terms: "Americans have the advantage over Europeans when it comes to the sense of smell, as scent hounds are better than sight hounds." But as Aotourou subsequently made clear in this first meeting with Baret below the decks of the *Étoile*, a bloodhound's sense of smell played no part.

When Baret forced her way out of the crowd, Aotourou sought an explanation. He was heard to use a word that Vivès transcribed as "maou," but which anthropologists are now able to understand as *mahu:* a Tahitian word denoting a transvestite. In the Tahitian culture encountered by eighteenth-century European explorers, male transvestism caused no concern: Young men wishing to dress and behave as women would, after puberty, be integrated into the households of married women (other than their mothers) where they would assist with tasks typically undertaken by women, such as the care of children and the preparation of food. To the disgust of nineteenth-century missionaries and the recorded discomfort of some European sailors, *mahu* proved to be a constant of Polynesian cultures from Hawaii to New Zealand. Thought to combine the best of both sexes, these young men were valued members of their own and their adopted families. (The tradition continues to this day in Tahiti, where it is perfectly acceptable to find first-born sons who have been raised as *mahu*.)

Accustomed to a society in which men dressed and behaved as women without trying to convince anyone that they really were women, Aotourou saw Baret as the French equivalent of *mahu*: a person of one sex dressed and behaving as another, and apparently accepted in this role by the crew. That Aotourou could identify Baret as anomalous within minutes of seeing her among the sailors only serves to add weight to the suggestion that Baret's true sex was an open secret on the *Étoile*. It may also have been Bougainville's inspiration for the story of instantaneous recognition on the beach, if Bougainville heard about it as the French enjoyed their shore leave. As the incident occurred on the *Étoile*, its absence from Bougainville's journal is not surprising. We would expect to find the episode mentioned in La Giraudais's log from the *Étoile* but, as already mentioned, that document appears never to have been submitted to the French authorities.

Though Aotourou's public identification of Baret as a woman was an explosive start to their relationship, it did not sour it beyond repair. Rather, Aotourou appears to have made conciliatory gestures to Baret, both on board and onshore. Eager to attempt French words, and willing to slowly enunciate Tahitian ones, Aotourou put himself literally in Baret's hands—sitting in front of her and miming his wish that she might style his hair as the French officers wore theirs. (Even while circumnavigating the globe, tens of thousands of miles from the nearest French wig maker, the officers displayed a range of powdered wigs that gave them the appearance of a shoulder-length ponytail. Bougainville's own preference was for the blond color popularized in France at the turn of the century, with powdered cornstarch being the preferred means of keeping such a wig looking clean on the voyage.)

Seeing that Baret used clothes to try to appear what she was not, Aotourou indicated his desire to join her in presenting a different appearance to the world. Baret and Aotourou could often be seen together when Baret was not botanizing: Aotourou alternately admiring and laughing at all the stylish accoutrements of a gentleman of Enlightenment France; Baret undoubtedly marveling at the dense black tattoos that signified Aotourou's acceptance into adult male Tahitian society. When he finally signaled his wish to return to France with the expedition, he turned to Baret for instructions in dressing like a Frenchman. When Commerson was absent from the cabin, Baret and Aotourou experimented with clothes, hairstyles, and the imitation of upper-class French male behaviors (walking with a dress sword, bowing). The linguistic barriers that prevented complex conversations about Baret's situation were likely liberating to her rather than problematic. Baret and Aotourou could have fun.

Unfortunately for Aotourou, he attempted to replicate his informal relationship with Baret with aristocratic women he met on his arrival in France. There his interest in fashion was—hypocritically and unfairly—taken to be evidence of a superficial personality, and his inquiries about a lack of visible tattooing on both men and women caused offense.

But it is from Aotourou that we learn that Baret was never in danger of being gang-raped by a group of Tahitian men. Confident in his identification of Baret as *mahu*, Aotourou had shared this information with the Tahitians who welcomed expedition members ashore. Like all Polynesian peoples, the Tahitians believed that any visit by their gods would come from across the ocean. Divine power, or *mana*, was to be propitiated and, if possible, put to use for good rather than ill. Believing that women, with their seemingly "magical" reproductive powers, played a special role in mediating between the divine and the earthly, the Tahitians offered their wives and daughters to the French in hopes that the women could contain and channel divine power. Baret must have seemed marvelous to the Tahitians—a lone *mahu* who moved among three hundred Frenchmen, possessed of the knowledge of medicinal plants. Bougainville could not have known that an understanding of the sociology and anthropology of Tahitian culture at the time would expose his story as false. Baret had nothing to fear on Tahiti because she was *mahu* and therefore revered.

So what was Baret's experience of Tahiti really like? The journals of both Commerson and the Prince of Nassau-Siegen indicate that the French—and the strikingly dressed officers in particular—could not move about the island without being assailed by groups of Tahitians proffering women of all ages, from teenage girls to generously built matriarchs. Nassau-Siegen cryptically confides that his decline of a beautiful but obviously young girl caused consternation, leading a Tahitian accompanying the girl to attempt manual stimulation of his velvet-clad body. Commerson rhapsodizes about Jean-Jacques Rousseau's theories of the noble savage, and eulogizes the Tahitians' veneration of sex as "a sacred act" to such an extent that it is impossible to imagine that he refused a "hospitable invitation" to join in the "shared pleasure." Baret was no fool, and she had surely begun to see her lover for what he was— from his inability to protect her from the ceremony of Crossing the Line to his egotistical urge to name species after himself and his readiness to give her the hardest, coldest work along the Strait of Magellan. Her willingness to share her knowledge with Commerson and to work ceaselessly for him received no public acknowledgment other than a cruelly joking reference to her as his "beast of burden." Now he was among the men accepting the Tahitians' repeated offers of sex. Baret let herself be swallowed by the dense tropical vegetation of the island, hoping that her botanizing would not be interrupted by French-Tahitian couples looking for somewhere more private.

Bougainville had charged Baret and Commerson with identifying Tahitian plants that could be used as antiscorbutics. Scurvy was not in evidence among the crews, but given the expedition's lack of knowledge about what lay ahead, Bougainville wanted to be prepared for the appearance of the disease. No one in 1768 understood the disease to be caused by a deficiency of vitamin C—since no one had yet formulated the concept of vitamins—but Bougainville expected his botanists to find some herbal remedy for the mysterious disease once it had struck.

Baret and Commerson also continued to seek out plants with the potential for commercial development and did not fail to see the Tahitian breadfruit (*Artocarpus altilis*), which Samuel Wallis was already sure the British government would be interested in. Commerson tentatively sketched the breadfruit in his notebook. The breadfruit tree, a member of the mulberry family, grows up to sixty feet tall, with glossy, deeply divided leaves that wave like gigantic seven-fingered hands around its basketball-sized fruit. And since the white-fleshed, doughy fruit is 25 percent carbohydrate and a mature breadfruit tree might produce between one hundred and two hundred of these globes in a year, the French and British governments were fascinated by their potential to feed both empires' slaves. The famous 1789 mutiny on HMS *Bounty* commanded by William Bligh was made possible by the ship's adaptation to accommodate over one thousand breadfruit seedlings collected on Tahiti: The breadfruit's anticipated needs caused the *Bounty* to be divested of everything perceived as unnecessary for a simple plant-collecting expedition, including a complement of marines who would have stopped the mutiny as soon as it began.

In addition to breadfruit to feed France's legions of slaves, Tahiti also seemed to offer a source of fibers with which to clothe them. Baret and Commerson noticed an unfamiliar material used for both skirts and ceremonial hangings: tapa cloth, which was then made from the bark of the now rare dye fig (*Ficus tinctoria*). They collected several pieces of tapa cloth, but rigorous inspection back in France revealed that the process of removing the bark from the tree and sizing it (that is, soaking and smoothing it to prepare it for painting) lends it all the properties of tissue paper. Like the paper dresses that enjoyed a brief vogue in the 1960s, tapa clothing would dissolve in the rain, leaving its increasingly naked wearer streaked with streams of dye. What was worn judiciously in Tahiti could not be worn at all in France or the rainier outposts of its empire.

Considering that Tahiti is a fecund tropical island and the Strait of Magellan a frigid wasteland, it may seem strange that the expedition's stay on Tahiti from April 2 to 14 yielded fewer botanical and mineralogical specimens than the voyage through the strait. But after attempting to botanize for the first few days of their stay, Baret had to give up her earnest exploration of the Tahitian interior. Officers and crewmen were too frequently encountered for her liking, Commerson too often absent and secretive. According to Vivès, Baret retreated to the *Étoile*, which was manned by only a skeleton crew, where she could enjoy the relative calm in the ship now that virtually everyone was on land. Having lived his whole life on Tahiti, Aotourou preferred to explore the *Étoile* and seemed happiest in Baret's company; his presence provided her with an additional safeguard against unwanted attention from the few remaining deckhands.

Never one to hide his feelings, Commerson's irritation at Baret's retreat to the ship was noticeable. Without the strength and botanical skills of his "beast of burden" in the field, Commerson's journal records only one lackluster day of botanizing on April 11. Around this time, he sulkily joined officers attempting to chart something of Tahitian topography. If Baret had intended to make Commerson understand her worth, she succeeded. When the ships weighed anchor and sailed from Tahiti, their relationship was more fragile than it had been at any time since its beginning.

S EVEN

"THE LOCATION OF HELL"

Baret on New Ireland

BY APRIL 20, 1768, four days after leaving Tahiti, the westernmost of what would become known as the Society Islands were slipping out of view on the ships' port sides and an unbroken expanse of ocean again lay ahead. Relations between Baret and Commerson had been strained to the breaking point by events on Tahiti and might have broken down irrevocably had an accident not forced Commerson to be more solicitous of Baret's feelings.

On April 18, Commerson's presence had been requested on board the *Boudeuse*, where Bougainville appeared to be seriously ill. Summoning

the *Étolie*'s botanist in preference to its surgeon, Laporte clearly wanted
to consult about herbal remedies for a recognizable condition rather than
to puzzle over diagnoses with his opposite number. Since the symptoms
of gonorrhea were widespread among the crew after the expedition left
Tahiti, and since Bougainville would remain confined to his cabin for
two weeks, consistent with the standard treatment of gonorrhea at the
time, it seems reasonable to conclude that he, too, might have been af-
flicted by venereal disease, though no biography of Bougainville dares
to make this suggestion. (When the expedition returned to France and it
was learned that the British commander Samuel Wallis had landed with
his men on Tahiti in 1767, the French were quick to blame the British for
contaminating this second Eden. Aotourou, however, insisted that this
disease was known to his people long before the British arrived.)

The transfer of Commerson from the *Étoile* to the *Boudeuse* took place
on the open ocean; one of the longboats from the *Boudeuse* was lowered
and rowed across to the storeship, from which Commerson climbed down
a rope ladder and dropped into the waiting vessel. He struggled to keep
his composure as the longboat bumped against the side of the *Étoile,* and
the longboat's rowers were doubtless amused to see one of the gentlemen
(and one of the more arrogant, less popular gentlemen at that) swaying
about at the bottom of the ladder.

After a day of descending from the *Étoile*, climbing onto the *Boudeuse*, descending from the *Boudeuse*, and finally returning to the *Étoile*,
the weaker of his legs was in agony. Ever since Baret had moved into
his house, she had nursed him when he was sick. Now they fell into that
familiar routine, with Commerson reiterating his need of her and Baret
able to focus on a clearly defined physical problem rather than a messy
emotional one. Recuperating from his exertions on the ships' rope lad-
ders, Commerson spent a few days resting in the cabin, sketching and
dissecting dead marine life positioned on the specimen crates. Baret
began her mornings on deck, watching with the men for another island

like Tahiti, until the prospect of another day of unbroken sea and sky sent her back to the cabin to help Commerson in whatever way she could.

As April became May, the expedition threaded its way through the Samoan islands. In the absence of any charts to guide his navigation, Bougainville decided to give these island shores a wide berth: To plot the reefs and currents surrounding each one would have taken weeks, if not months, for no discernible gain in terms of the expedition's goals. Holding a steady course along the line of 15° south latitude—with small maneuverings north and south around the islands directly in their way— Bougainville was confident that the specimens from Tahiti would serve to represent the island flora and fauna of the region. But two weeks into May, the water in the barrels began to give off a musty, fetid odor.

By the end of the eighteenth century, there was widespread recognition that freshwater would not keep in wooden barrels for the duration of a Pacific voyage, and nineteenth-century sailing vessels began to experiment with metal canisters. Perhaps because there was no disputing the unhealthy state of the potable water on board, additional grumblings about the weevil-infested biscuits and the salted, preserved meats in the *Étoile*'s hold became commonplace. With the robust exception of coconuts, fresh fruit taken on board in Tahiti had started to putrefy under the unblinking stare of the sun, while the Tahitians' gifts of poultry and pigs had been devoured too quickly in the certain belief that bigger and better gardens of plenty lay just over the horizon. The expedition would have to make a landing, ideally where an island river disgorged into the sea and freshwater could be collected. Bougainville and his officers agreed to drop anchor off the next acceptable shore that presented itself, whereupon a longboat from each ship would undertake some basic reconnaissance before trying to establish a beachhead.

On May 22, still hugging the line of latitude 15° south, the westward-sailing ships saw an archipelago strung north to south across the sea in front of them. The group is today known as Vanuatu, though older maps will show the New Hebrides, and Bougainville called them the New Cyclades (thereby equating them with islands of the Aegean). In 1606, the Portuguese explorer Pedro Fernandes de Queirós had explored the region, and accounts of his voyage detailed his discovery of the same archipelago, the largest island of which he had named La Australia del Espiritu Santo. Bougainville was confident that his expedition was now staring at the shore of Espiritu Santo, and he was right. The *Boudeuse* lowered two boats with a total complement of twenty-six armed men, two officers, and the Prince of Nassau-Siegen; they were joined by a third boat from the *Étoile*. Within minutes after the boats landed, those watching from the safety of the *Étoile* and the *Boudeuse* could see that their countrymen were outnumbered by a growing crowd of islanders that was soon estimated at over five hundred strong.

With the lordly air that resulted from being welcomed and generally deferred to wherever he went, the Prince of Nassau-Siegen stepped forward from the landing party and extended his hands, which three islanders ventured to approach and then touch. The Melanesians appeared to recognize him as someone of great rank, and the prince capitalized on this to mime his desire for food and drink. When it became apparent that the islanders were bringing fresh fruit to the beach for the landing party, Bougainville decided he should join those expedition members onshore and he requested that Aotourou accompany him as translator. Only if the French could be certain of a continued welcome would Baret and Commerson be required to make the journey and begin looking for additional sources of vegetable matter for the crew.

To Bougainville's immense frustration, Aotourou could make nothing of the Melanesian language he heard, preventing Bougainville from making negotiations for a more systematic French landing. Language was not the only obstacle to communication however: Aotourou could scarcely hide his disgust at the Melanesian warriors who clustered a few feet away from him. Their nostrils were pierced with bones that passed through the septum at its widest point, and the animal teeth and shells that adorned their bodies did little to hide the obvious signs of widespread skin disease in the community. (This was likely the result of yaws, a bacterial disease once found throughout the tropics, which causes the skin to erupt in lesions. In an isolated, close-knit population, it could run rampant.) Whatever had ravaged them, Bougainville's journal reference to a "colony of lepers" provides a sobering indication of the islanders' appearance. Their muted reception on Espiritu Santo made the French uneasy about sending men into the interior to take what they wanted, and the unhealthy appearance of the native population made some question the wisdom of taking any provisions at all.

The French course of action was finally dictated to them by two separate incidents that turned a cautious native population into an openly hostile one. A warning musket shot intended to scatter a dense group of Melanesians examining the beached longboats caused all the islanders on the beach to disappear rapidly into the adjoining forest. The nervous landing party then judged it best to head back to the *Étoile* and the *Boudeuse*, even though they had no barrels of freshwater to show for the day's trouble. Now jumpy from the awkward interactions between the French and the islanders, Ensign Pierre Landais, the officer in charge of the *Étoile*'s longboat, assumed the worst when he saw native canoes approaching his retreating vessel. He needed no provocation other than the sight of bows and arrows among the Melanesians for him to order the French to fire.

The number of Melanesian dead and wounded is unknown, but whereas musket fire had previously scattered the native population, the action taken by Landais now enraged them. It became evident to all those watching from the decks of the *Étoile* and the *Boudeuse* that many more canoes were being brought onto the beach in preparation for what had suddenly become a Franco-Melanesian naval war.

As French oarsmen in the longboats pulled themselves within range of covering musket fire from the decks of the ships, Bougainville ordered the gun crews on the *Boudeuse* to ready her cannon. Once the longboats and their crews were aboard, the *Étoile* and the *Boudeuse* made sail, although the Melanesians puzzled the French by showing no desire to pursue their hastily departing guests. Reasoning that these seafaring islanders might alert neighboring peoples to the foreign presence in the area and might characterize the French as aggressors, Bougainville decided that the expedition would make no further landings until they had put several days' distance between them and Espiritu Santo, or until the mythical Great Southern Continent was found. Whichever happened first, he was confident that supplies in the hold of his storeship would see the expedition through in the meantime, and that the inky millpond of the Pacific had to yield land, tractable people, and abundant supplies before May was out. He was wrong.

Leaving Vanuatu behind, the ships passed through the strait between Espiritu Santo and Malekula, and sailed out into the north of the Coral Sea on May 28, 1768—just when Bougainville's journal tells us that he had finally found the time to investigate rumors about Baret's identity. This would have been a bizarre time indeed for Bougainville to address rumors emanating from his storeship concerning his botanist's assistant, since Bougainville's overriding concerns at the end of May 1768 were fleeing Vanuatu and finding a safe source of food and water. The expedition was clearly in a serious predicament as Malekula receded from sight; the ordinary hands started receiving boiled leather to gnaw on with their weevil-ridden biscuit, while the officers' messes on both the *Boudeuse* and the *Étoile* started serving rat. Bougainville hardly had time to undergo the perilous transfer to the *Étoile* simply to investigate personnel issues.

Absurd though it is to imagine a roomful of officers in their dress uniforms feigning delight as the silver lid was whisked off a serving platter to reveal the unmistakable form of a roasted rodent, in reality they were soberingly close to starvation. Chronicling the expedition from the *Boudeuse*, Louis-Antoine Starot de Saint-Germain thought he would not be able to stomach the rats, but once he had tried the leather strips made from South American grain sacks, he was ready to concede that rat might be preferable. (Although, Saint-Germain's designated role on the expedition was as its historian, his account was not published until the twentieth century, and then only in partial form.) Ever concerned with the appearance of gentlemanly behavior, the Prince of Nassau-Siegen offered to share a rat with Saint-Germain. Treating the dining experience as though they were sampling the finest cuisine the French court had to offer, Nassau-Siegen's good humor quickly overcame Saint-Germain's revulsion. As the men caught rats in the hold for the benefit of the officers, Saint-Germain decided he was lucky to at least have meat and noted in his journal "for dinner, we were served three rats, and devoured them with pleasure."

Nassau-Siegen may have livened the officers' mess on the *Boudeuse* with his infectious goodwill, but the captain's table on the *Étoile* had an altogether different dynamic. As Commerson and Vivès glared at each other, La Giraudais and others took every opportunity to remind Ensign Landais that his order to fire on the Melanesians had likely cost the expedition fresh food and water. Given the scarcity of food, even at the officers' table, Commerson could not request additional rations to take back to his cabin for Baret. To obtain her share of infested ship's biscuit and pungent water, she had to join the men as they stood in line on the deck and waited for their daily allotment. Baret had grown used to carrying one of Commerson's pistols with her when she moved about the ship, and now more than ever, she felt grateful for the cumbersome apparatus, tucked into a belt at the top of her wide-cut linen trousers. As she joined all those on deck who were scanning the horizon for land, the anger among the hungry crew was palpable. With Tahiti four thousand miles and two months behind them, the vastness of the Pacific was more isolating than anyone could have imagined.

Then, on June 5, the *Boudeuse* fired warning shots to alert the *Étoile* that the faster, lighter frigate, traveling ahead of the storeship, perceived danger in the water. Without understanding what had happened, the expedition had run up against one of the natural wonders of the world.

The Great Barrier Reef stretches 1,260 miles along the northeast coast of Australia, forming a wall of coral limestone along virtually the whole of the Queensland coast. Many expeditions charted sections of the 100,000 square miles covered by the reef and its outlying formations before a safe route could be established through the apparently solid barrier of coral into shallower coastal waters beyond. Though many topographical features have been renamed since the time of Bougainville's expedition, Bougainville Reef continues to mark the spot approximately 120 miles from the Australian coast (just northeast of Cairns and directly east of Cooktown) where the ships stopped and all aboard gazed uncomprehendingly at what lay before them; Captain James Cook would later describe it as "a wall of coral rock rising perpendicular out of the unfathomable ocean."

Looking at the Bougainville Reef, Baret could see what appeared to be a beach in the middle of the ocean. Radiating out from the sand, submerged fingers of an almost luminous green pushed their way through the water—the tops of coral formations growing up from the coastal shelf below. Waves broke over the branching emerald structures, hiding them for a moment before the ebb of the water revealed the rough surface of the coral. Sailing across the coral to land on the pristine island at the center of the Bougainville Reef would be impossible; the coral would gut any ship's hull. Bougainville decided he had sailed as far west at this latitude as he dared. If the fabled Great Southern Continent lay beyond the reef, it was unreachable. On June 6, the ships turned north, heading directly for New Guinea.

As they moved north, squalls became an almost daily occurrence. Squinting through the warm driving rain for sight of land, the men

Dall'Acqua inc.

MAD.^{LLA} BARÉ.

Lazaretti colori

Baret is unlikely to have sat for this intriguing image, which dates from 1816. It shows her dressed in striped fabric not popular with sailors until the 1790s, cut in a loose style to help conceal her shape. Wearing the red liberty cap of the French revolutionaries, she is portrayed as a symbol of the Republic. As for the sheaf of flowering plants in her hands, such posies were iconographic shorthand for the medicinal value of a botanical garden.

This image, thought to have been made two years after Commerson's death, is the only known likeness of him.

This page from the teenage Commerson's herbarium shows his precocious interest in botany and skill with specimens. The plants are hyssop and marshmallow and have retained their color and form remarkably well.

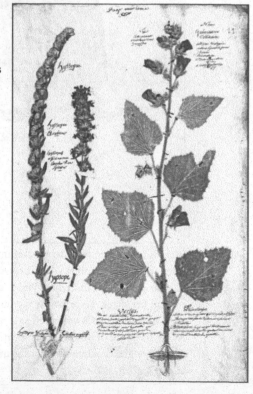

This rare engraving of an herb woman—probably from the mid-nineteenth century—is intriguing on several counts. The woman is represented as having very muscular arms, and she appears to be wearing trousers under her skirt. If both of these were typical consequences of the herb woman's life outdoors, they help explain Baret's belief that she could carry off her disguise. The female customer waiting at the counter may indicate that, well into the nineteenth century, herb women continued to be a resource for female clients embarrassed to see a male physician.

Baret's herb woman's notebook—perhaps a lover's gift to Commerson—is now cataloged as one of his papers. The *Tables des plantes medicamenteuses* is a list of herbal remedies for common ailments, using plants native to France or easily obtained there.

This nineteenth-century view of the Jardin des Plantes shows a formal layout that would have been easily recognizable to Baret and Commerson. Straight ahead of the viewer is the Grande Galerie du Muséum, over which a statue of the naturalist Buffon now presides.

This mid-nineteenth-century depiction of a mother overcome by emotion as she places her baby in a niche in the Paris Foundling Hospital wall shows the sad continuance of this tradition nearly a century after Baret relinquished her son.

Coffee, tea, and sugar cane do not grow together naturally. Placing them on a single plate, the *Encyclopédie* invited readers to consider how indispensable such plants had become—and how important economically.

Other than a single image of the *Étoile* and the *Boudeuse* anchored off the coast of Tahiti, no detailed illustrations of the *Étoile* are known. This plate from the *Encyclopédie* shows a mid-eighteenth-century French flute, fully rigged. The captain's cabin—Baret's only refuge on the *Étoile*—is prominent at the stern.

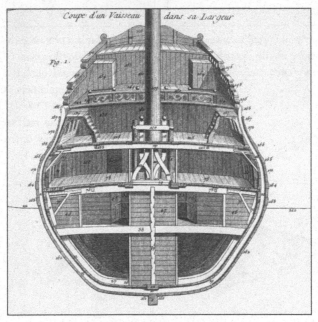

This cross section of a frigate like the *Boudeuse* invites the viewer to marvel at the decks and accommodations arranged on top of one another and shows the intricate housing of one of the ship's masts. Perhaps unintentionally, the image also suggests the claustrophobia of life at sea.

Delpech's early-nineteenth-century picture shows Bougainville at the height of his fame: a French national hero.

Sydney Parkinson produced this watercolor of a bougainvillea plant (like the ones Baret collected around Rio de Janeiro) during Captain James Cook's first Pacific voyage of 1768–71. The outer "leaves" are brick red bracts that surround swelling pistils, or fertilized seed pods, at their center.

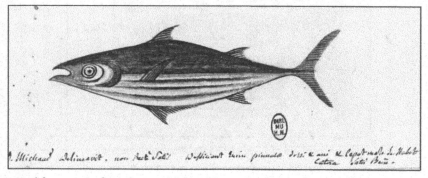

Detail from a page from the journal shared by Commerson and Pierre Duclos-Guyot dated March 17–18, 1767, shortly before the ceremony of Crossing the Line. Disappointed at the apparent emptiness of the mid-Atlantic, Commerson sketched one of the few fishes caught before dissecting it in the cabin, as he would do throughout the voyage.

This foreign engraving attempts to belittle Bougainville's achievement by showing the French colors raised on nothing more than a rock—but the fact that Bougainville's expedition was a target of British satire in the 1820s suggests both its continuing fame and a certain British unease at French maritime power.

The Prince of Nassau-Siegen's love of fashion is evident in his plum red velvet suit, heavily ornamented with gold brocade. He points to a globe to indicate his travels—perhaps in an attempt to show himself as different from the typical aristocrat.

Entry from Bougainville's journal dated May 28–29, 1768, describing events that supposedly occurred when Baret went ashore on April 7. Immediately after Bougainville acknowledges his belated discovery of Baret's true sex, his journal reverts to a discussion of the good weather of May 29–30. Remarkably, Bougainville never returns to the subject of Baret and her cross-dressing charade.

Baret spent seven years on Mauritius, most of them around Port Louis. This 1831 engraving, depicting sailing ships in port and the island's exotic plant life in the foreground, lets us imagine how small the settlement must have been when Baret lived there.

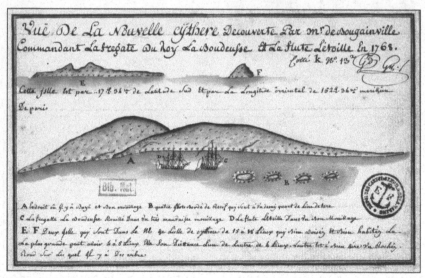

This is the only illustration from the voyage that represents both the *Étoile* and the *Boudeuse*, here seen riding at anchor off the coast of Tahiti. The artist has covered the whole image—both island and sea—in a light green wash, suggesting the brilliant hues and lushness of vegetation that struck Europeans.

noted with satisfaction that at least the spare sailcloths rigged taut across the deck were filling with freshwater. Since the expedition had left Tahiti nearly two months earlier, neither Baret nor Commerson had had even a bowl of freshwater with which to wash. The dermatitis on Baret's tightly bound torso wept continually, while Commerson's ulcerated leg had begun to ooze pus again. Twenty cases of scurvy were reported on the *Étoile* alone—its sufferers readily distinguished by their pallid complexions erupting in sores, general listlessness, and darkening, receding gums. As if the ship and her personnel were mirror images of each other, the *Étoile* appeared to be coming apart; the officers noted an alarming number of shrinking planks and rotten spars under increasingly dull sails. Claiming a share of the collected water with which to bathe Commerson's leg in their cabin, Baret must have felt it the height of luxury to soak a cloth in a bowl of rainwater and press it to her raw skin. Food was still in desperately short supply, but the presence of freshwater gave hope of better conditions.

Given the abundance of life found on New Guinea, it seems incredible that the expedition did not land there and reprovision. After Greenland, it is the second largest island in the world, and though it occupies less than 1 percent of the earth's landmass, perhaps as many as 10 percent of the earth's species call it home. (So much of its tropical flora and fauna is believed to be unnamed, unclassified, and unresearched that the true extent of New Guinea's biodiversity can only be guessed at.) The expedition knew none of this, of course, but no one sighting the land could fail to appreciate its fecundity. On June 10, 1768, as the expedition approached the southeastern shore of New Guinea, the island was still covered in virgin forest—the tropical rain forest of the lowlands giving way to midmountain and subalpine forests that in turn yielded to grassland hidden in the cloud cover above twelve thousand feet. Judging from Bougainville's charts, the ships were probably heading for the mouth of what is now known as the Kemp-Welch River. But the expedition eventually sailed past New Guinea without taking on board so much as a barrel of freshwater, rebuffed by fierce crosscurrents, rain, and fog that only seemed to intensify the nearer the ships approached to land.

As the lookouts lost sight of each other in the warm, heavy mist, the *Boudeuse* took to firing cannon to apprise the *Étoile* of its position. Belowdecks, all Baret and Commerson could do was sit in their cabin and wait. No seafaring experience was needed to understand that they were in imminent danger of being wrecked: The log of the *Boudeuse* shows that its compass "covered 18 points," meaning that the ship was so buffeted by the offshore winds that its direction reversed and reversed again. The boxier *Étoile* was in theory more stable, but La Giraudais still strained to locate the source of the *Boudeuse*'s cannon through the shroud of gray fog. Even if the *Étoile* managed to avoid being run aground, she still might easily smash into the *Boudeuse,* which was unable to hold its position from one minute to the next.

On June 10, so close to the New Guinea coast that they could smell the sweet humid scent of the forest, yet so much a victim of the wind and currents that every ship length gained was shortly lost, Bougainville ordered the ships to turn. For five days, they retraced their course, until they were far enough out in the Coral Sea to escape the fierce coastal conditions. In the intense tropical squall they had just sailed through, no one had felt remotely like eating—even seasoned sailors were queasy, and discontent was everywhere. The ships sailed east and then north-east, avoiding visible reefs and any mysterious areas of disturbance in the water. The cook on the *Étoile* had now exhausted his full repertoire of rat cuisine, and Jean-Louis Caro, first lieutenant of the *Étoile* and second in command on the vessel, confessed to his journal just how bad things had become: "We are in over our heads . . . there is not a single thing to give to the sick and no fresh food of any sort for a long time."

They tried to fish, but true to the run of bad luck they were experiencing their lines repeatedly failed to attract a bite. The reason lies in the geology of the region and in the difference between continental islands and volcanic islands. New Guinea lies on the northernmost edge of a continental shelf that stretches south to Australia. The contours of the shelf run parallel to the northern New Guinea coast, beyond which the ocean floor drops precipitously. In avoiding offshore squalls by sailing at a distance from the New Guinea coast, the ships' course placed them over deep water and away from the fish shoals they hungered for. Marine life favors the seas on continental shelves, which are relatively shallow compared to the deep water of open ocean. Away from the earth's great continental shelves, islands tend to be volcanic in origin, welling up directly from the ocean floor. Sailing past islands of volcanic origin, it is necessary to come in close to the shore to fish, because marine life does not stray very far from such landmasses. The *Étoile* and the *Boudeuse* were therefore too far from both the continental island of New Guinea and the volcanic islands of the South Pacific to stand any chance of catching anything.

The ships sailed on, through a chain of islands running parallel to the curving northeast coast of New Guinea: the Solomon Islands. The route of the expedition at this point is easy to trace on any modern map, for the volcanic islands of Bougainville and Choiseul (the naval minister who had authorized the circumnavigation) still bear the names given to them from the scurvy-ridden, cracking decks of the ships. But negotiations for food, let alone any landing, were out of the question: ten canoes launched from Choiseul proved to be full of pugnacious warriors. Over one hundred men showed their white geometrical body paintings to perfection as they flexed their bow arms, poised to shoot a phalanx of arrows at the French. Avoiding New Guinean weather and Solomon Island warriors, the ships plotted a course that unwittingly guaranteed their crews' hunger.

As the men grew incredulous that they could find no relief in the midst of obvious tropical plenty, the ships came across what appeared to be a hastily abandoned canoe. The canoe held a few baskets of fruit, which were immediately commandeered for the worst scurvy cases—though when shared between the *Étoile* and the *Boudeuse*, not even the sickest man received more than a segment of juicy flesh. Other than the fruit, all that remained in the dugout was a human jaw, described as partially cooked. Although hardly a botanical specimen, this was deemed to be something for a naturalist and medical man to handle, and Commerson was soon the recipient. Without the guidance of any islander to explain the jaw's origin—whether a battle trophy or partially cremated remains from a practice of ancestor worship—the French were quick to assume they had found the remnants of a cannibal's feast. To men who had been receiving boiled leather as part of their rations, it was an unlucky omen, graphically suggestive of the last resort of the isolated and starving. If Baret had balked at the smell of bonito and shark dissections in the cabin, the presence of the jaw must have made her wish for such relatively mundane specimens.

Worse than the presence of the jaw itself, its lurid pull was enough to bring Vivès to the cabin, where he claimed a doctor's interest in examining the grisly fragment. Eighteenth-century natural historians like Buffon included discussion of *Homo sapiens* in their work and scientific and philosophic circles speculated on the origins of the various human races. Examination of the jaw provided a rare opportunity to examine dentition and make calculations about the skull of the deceased, adding more data to European debates about physiological variation within the human species. But given that Vivès had seen through Baret's disguise within a few weeks of the *Étoile*'s setting sail, the charred jawbone was not the only thing he came to observe in the great stern cabin. Unlike the Prince of Nassau-Siegen and the astronomer Véron, who gave every appearance of accepting Baret's story, Vivès stared and smirked as though she, too, were an object for examination. When Commerson was not in the cabin with them, Baret was acutely aware that the pistol was her only safeguard—not only against Vivès but against all the men now pushed to their limit by starvation rations and months on the open ocean. In the cabin, the jawbone must have seemed a potent symbol of something predatory aboard.

Then, on July 6, 1768, the ships passed into a strait running between two long, low, fertile islands. One year previously, the English captain Philip Carteret had been brought by wind and water currents to the exact same spot, and he had already named the island whose northeast tip formed one side of the strait New Britain. Its smaller neighbor, whose southwest edge formed the other wall of the strait, was called New Ireland.

Three written accounts place the revelation of Baret's identity on New Ireland rather than in Tahiti. Their authors are Pierre Duclos-Guyot, Nassau-Siegen, and Vivès. Most modern commentators either ignore this or assert that the three men must be in error, even though they all corroborate one another's stories. Taken individually, any man's account could reasonably be questioned; taken together, the three journals of Duclos-Guyot, Nassau-Siegen, and Vivès provide a powerful challenge to Bougainville's version of events.

Duclos-Guyot's narrative is a masterpiece of concision when one considers what is being related: "They have discovered that the servant of Mr. Commerson, the doctor, was a girl who until now has been taken for a boy." Duclos-Guyot does not elaborate upon how "they" had discovered this, or exactly who "they" were. The Prince of Nassau-Siegen is a little more expansive than Duclos-Guyot on the page (though admittedly it is hard to imagine anyone being less expansive), and he begins to hint at darker issues raised by Baret's situation.

The men discovered they had a girl on board the Étoile, who disguised herself in men's clothing to work as a servant to M. Commerson.

Without casting any aspersions on the naturalist for having retained her for such an arduous voyage, I want to give her all the credit for her bravery, a far cry from the gentle pastimes afforded her sex. She dared confront the stress, the dangers, and everything that happened that one could realistically expect on such a voyage. Her adventure should, I think, be included in a history of famous women.

The most striking part of Nassau-Siegen's narrative is its enigmatic allusion to "everything . . . that one could realistically expect on such a voyage." What did Nassau-Siegen think that a lone woman traveling among over three hundred men might "realistically expect" to happen? He lets the reader be the judge, according to his faith, or lack thereof, in human nature.

Where Duclos-Guyot's prose reveals a determination to present only the facts, and Nassau-Siegen's journal displays a gentleman's avoidance of anything that might be regarded as unsavory according to the sensibilities of the time, Vivès writes according to a different set of criteria. Like Bougainville, he has left us not one journal, but two. (Navy precedent dictated the spartan style of Bougainville's commander's log, and it is therefore understandable that Bougainville allowed himself a little more descriptive freedom when he prepared his journal for publication.) Vivès appears to have fancied himself something of a prose stylist and wrote two accounts of the expedition in order to try different literary effects. His two journals are known by the names of their sometime resting places—the Rochefort and the Versailles manuscripts. Where they differ from each other, it is in matters of style only, not substance. And both insist in locating a group assault on Baret on New Ireland. The Rochefort manuscript lingers longest over Baret's trauma:

The reader will remember all that I described as occurring on Tahiti [with Aotourou calling Baret a *mahu*], and will conclude that no real doubt remained about the sex of our self-styled "eunuch." But finding it was impossible to agree on the matter, some offered to get the evidence necessary to settle the argument. The servants had an animated discussion that caused widespread unease, which led to preparations being made for an inspection at the next port of call. As has been detailed, this was the first landing after Tahiti. Our "eunuch" went collecting plants and shells every day and always made sure to take a brace of pistols with her and show them when she got into the longboat, aiming to keep all assaults on her modesty at bay, but her precautions failed to achieve the desired result.

One fine day, the eleventh of the current month, the servants were ashore doing the laundry. She made the error of trying to do her laundry with them. It was—I should say—a sorry day when, having seized her pistols, the gun was examined, the lock plate was drawn back, and light was shed, putting an end to all doubts.

But really it was a service they did this girl, whom I shall now call Jeanneton, because the cloths she had wound round her had caused her to sweat so much since we entered the tropics that she was covered with spots. After the inspection, she didn't have to bind herself, though she continued dressing as a man.

"Jeanneton," it should be explained, is a traditional French folk song, first mentioned in written records as early as 1614 and still known today—indeed, modern performances of it can readily be viewed online. Like all folk songs, it has a number of variants, but all tell the same basic story of a peasant named Jeanne ("Jeanneton" in the diminutive) who takes her sickle to go to cut the corn. In the field, Jeanne encounters four men. The first man is shy and steals only a kiss. The second is less timid and lifts her skirt. The third, bolder still, is said to lie on the ground. The lyrics then declare that the actions of the fourth man cannot be detailed in the song. The curious female listener is instructed that she will have to go to cut the corn herself ("Si vous le saviez, Madame / Vous iriez couper les joncs"), if she wants to understand what happened to Jeanne.

The lyrics then insist that the first moral we should draw is that three of the four men mentioned were "couillons," a word that any standard French-English dictionary will typically define as a prissy "idiot" or "cretin," but which is best compared to the American insult "asshole." The second moral that the lyrics ask us to take away is that men are pigs. Yet the final verse of the folk song concludes that the "moral of this fable is that women love pigs" (La morale de cette morale / C'est que les femmes aiment les cochons!), perpetuating the misogynistic notion that when women say no to sex they really mean yes.

This traditional harvest song, often sung during the *vendage,* or cutting of grapes from the vine, asks its hearers to contemplate a woman's rape by at least three participants, before building to a rousing declaration that women really love such behavior. In the suggestion that any woman who wants to get the full picture should go into the harvest fields herself, the song conjures a world of sexual violence routinely meted out to women laborers, who were physically, economically, and socially powerless to protest their routine brutalization. When Vivès says that he should start calling Baret "Jeanneton," it is a winking, leering admission that Baret was gang-raped—which he expects us to condone, since women protest too much and really like their aggressors.

In the Versailles manuscript, Vivès can be seen trying the effect of a metaphor other than that of inspecting a gun: "One sorry day—when I have no idea what happened to the pistols—her master left her looking for shells after they had been botanizing. The servants who were doing the laundry seized their advantage and found in her concha veneris the precious shell they had been seeking for so long. This inspection was mortifying to her but ultimately made her more comfortable since she no longer had to pretend, binding herself with linen."

"Concha veneris" translates as "Venus's shell," a term for any member of the family of cowrie shells, which have appeared since ancient times in a range of symbolic ways throughout art and literature. All cowries present a curved, frequently patterned upper surface and a smooth, typically white, flat undersurface that bears a lateral fissure, the edges of which are ridged rather than smooth. Among early pictographs carved on rock and inked on papyrus the image of the cowrie shell has been used to distinguish women from men and the possibility of growth, as opposed to sterility. However much he plays with the affect of different metaphors and references, Vivès consistently points us to the same brutal truth; historians of the expedition who argue that these passages imply only an inspection and not a rape are projecting onto Baret's story what they wish had happened, as opposed to what so clearly did happen.

The reality of what happened to Jeanne Baret on New Ireland was a human trauma that screams for recognition. Ultimately, the subject of the narrative is a lone, powerless, terrified woman, who was violated emotionally, psychologically, and physically, and this can hardly be conveyed by any amount of academic research. The psychology of what occurred on New Ireland can perhaps be described in terms of the anger and resentment of a group of men who had observed Baret for eighteen months and who believed that she needed to be put in what they considered to be her place. But the ability to make such an analysis should never desensitize us to the misery resulting from their actions. By studying these manuscripts, we are at least allowing the fullest account of her experiences to be given and, when sexual violence is added to the catalog of conditions within which she lived and worked, only enhancing the nature of her achievement.

Baret's rape was in theory a crime punishable by hanging, and after it had occurred everyone on the expedition must have paused to reflect on what might happen. Word of the rape likely stopped all journal keeping for a period; since no one knew what was to be recorded officially, those writing their unofficial accounts thought it wise to pause until they were sure what the prevailing sentiments aboard might be. Vivès insists in both versions of his journal that the crime was perpetrated by servants, not sailors—and certainly not gentlemen. But how would Vivès have known that Baret's linen strips had caused her skin to erupt in dermatitis unless he had been told this—or seen it for himself? What possible set of circumstances might have caused the usually cautious Baret to drop her guard and become separated from one—or both—of Commerson's pistols? And Vivès's conclusion in both versions of his text that Baret's attackers had done her a favor by relieving her of the necessity of binding herself so uncomfortably gives the appearance of a man trying to justify the indefensible.

Is it possible that the only way Baret would feel secure without her pistols would be if one of the expedition's officers or gentlemen—like Vivès—were nearby? Freshwater had been in such short supply in the preceding weeks that every raindrop and bead of condensation collected in the sailcloth had been drunk or used to wash the sick (Commerson included). If Baret was tempted to kneel by a New Ireland stream to splash its clean cold water over her face and neck, she would have been uncomfortable to see Vivès and some of the crew nearby, but would likely have thought that his rank guaranteed her safety. His looks had made her uneasy before, but he had never offered more than this. The ordinary hands had so far been the only men on board to frighten her, in the Crossing the Line ceremony and when she was forced to sling her hammock between decks. Baret may have disliked Vivès because of the animosity between him and Commerson, but she nevertheless associated rank with decency and civilized behavior: Véron and Nassau-Siegen were always courteous and easy in her presence, and La Giraudais and Bougainville had declined to enforce naval regulations against her.

We cannot prove that Vivès was among those who gang-raped Baret on New Ireland, and it is problematic to accuse a man of being a rapist across two and a half centuries, since he is unable to refute the charge. But considering his description of Baret's naked torso covered in dermatitis, and the amusement he seems to derive from recasting Jeanne Baret as the Jeanneton of folk song, Vivès can at least be charged as the sadistic voyeur of a woman's misery. Of this he is unmistakably guilty.

Though Bougainville's journal makes no mention of Baret on New Ireland, his entries for this time period are not without incident. On July 11, Bougainville tells us that a crew member was bitten in the water by a creature that was assumed to be a snake. Experiencing violent convulsions and drifting in and out of consciousness, the unidentified crew member was treated by Commerson, who administered an opiate that finally allowed the patient to sleep. Given that Vivès places Baret's rape on this date, the medical emergency and solution described by Bougainville suggest the procedures that would have been followed when a traumatized Baret staggered into full view on the New Ireland shore and collapsed before the majority of the shore party.

For his part, Commerson conspicuously allowed Pierre Duclos-Guyot to write up the portion of their joint journal pertaining to New Ireland. All that is recorded of Commerson's reaction to events on New Ireland is his insistence that he was as surprised as anyone by the revelation that Baret was really a woman—a claim that could indeed be true if no one was surprised at all.

As Baret lay in an opium-induced sleep in the cabin, with Commerson tending to her, Bougainville had to decide what should be done to the perpetrators. In his 1980 novel *Rites of Passage,* William Golding imagined a similar situation, albeit one that leads to a man's death. Yet the novel's dramatic climax has so much in common with the situation aboard the *Étoile* in 1768 that it is illuminating to consider how Golding's fictional protagonists navigate the social and moral complexities in which they find themselves ensnared. Like Golding's best-known work, *Lord of the Flies,* which shows how murderously tribal instincts emerge among a group of schoolboys wrecked on an island, *Rites of Passage* also examines the propensity of *Homo sapiens* to display pack behavior, bonding in shared antagonism toward a targeted individual.

Rites of Passage is set on an eighteenth-century ship sailing from England to Australia, whose passengers and crew begin to share a near-universal dislike of one man aboard—the unfortunate Reverend James Colley. When Colley is found dead, Captain Anderson convenes a hearing to establish the facts—or a convenient version of them. But Anderson has not allowed for the investigatory zeal of the novel's principal narrator, Edmund Talbot, who believes that he can solve the crime by determining which of the men on the ship are known to engage in the punishable offense of "sodomy." When Talbot refuses to drop his line of questioning and demands that a crew member tell the tribunal which men are guilty "of this particular form of, of interest, of assault," the wily crewman extricates himself by a stroke of rhetorical genius: "Shall I begin with the officers, sir?" The sailor knows that any legal investigation will expose the leaders' complicity in allowing an untenable situation to fester, and he signals that the men are not going to take the rap for the officers' earlier failure to act decisively. In Golding's fictional floating courtroom, everyone hangs on the captain's first words after the crewman's implicit challenge: "Very well, Rogers. That will be all. You may return to your duties."

The dynamics of this fictional scene seem pitch-perfect for the situation that confronted Bougainville. No ordinary sailor or naval servant convicted of raping Baret was going to face the gallows without insisting that Bougainville and his officers had long known Baret's true sex and had done nothing about the breach of naval regulations. Vivès's involvement in the rape complicated matters further, for Vivès was a naval surgeon, an educated man whose version of events—that it was merely an inspection of Baret, not a rape—would be hard to disprove in a court of law, where a man's word counted for more than a woman's. And as modern studies of rape and trauma victims show, a woman in Baret's situation, forced to stand before a summarily convened naval court and to give evidence within feet of all her attackers, would likely break down. More rarely, a victim might seem to disengage from the process completely in a struggle to suppress the recollection of what had occurred. Either way, Baret would be rendered speechless.

As if this were not enough, having lied about her identity in order to work as Commerson's assistant, Baret had made it all too easy for someone like Vivès to question her truthfulness. The prevailing morality of the time did not countenance the possibility that a respectable woman would choose to isolate herself among over three hundred men on a journey around the world. It did not even allow that any imagined "normal" female sensibility could contemplate Linnaean taxonomy, based as it was upon observation of the reproductive organs of plants, without being overcome by embarrassment. Through her words, actions, and intellectual curiosity—indeed in her very being—Baret would have been a pariah in an eighteenth-century courtroom.

Understanding all this, Bougainville decided that the easiest, most logical course of action was to remain silent about Baret's rape. Since all the officers had behaved as though they saw nothing odd about Commerson's assistant, the fictions that Baret told about herself would be allowed to stand. Bougainville could not, however, be certain that the presence of a woman on the expedition would not slip out after the ships returned to France. The story of Baret's discovery on Tahiti was therefore the most economical and convenient way of alerting those interested in the expedition that a woman had been found in disguise among the crew, while forestalling difficult questions about who knew what and when. His journal was guaranteed publication on his return to France, so Bougainville could be confident that his version of events would assume primacy in the minds of the French reading public. Bougainville's only oversight was not realizing that three of his own personnel would contradict him, and in doing so would make possible the discovery of Baret's true story.

The expedition sailed from New Ireland on July 26. In theory the *Étoile*'s hold should have been groaning with fresh produce. Certainly, they had taken assorted fruits and vegetables on board, but in the tropical heat, freshly cut leaves wilted on deck as surely as if they had been steam-cooked. What the crew craved most was fresh meat, but New Ireland had disappointed in that respect. In New Ireland and many other tropical islands in the Pacific, the number and range of native fauna and avifauna appear to have been decreasing even before the arrival of European explorers, whose crews exacerbated island extinctions. Today the science of island biogeography can explain the minimum size an island landmass needs to be in order to develop and sustain a rich cross section of life, including a quantity of mammals (for example, Madagascar, Mauritius, and New Guinea all meet this critical size threshold). In 1768, all that Bougainville's crews understood was that New Ireland was desperately short of plump birds and fat four-legged creatures to give to the ships' cooks. Men worn down by weeks of starvation rations blundered about within striking distance of the shore, salivating at the prospect of finding nonexistent goats and wild pigs.

As Bougainville confided to his journal, "there has been much disagreement over the location of Hell. We have found it." Baret too had found it, days before, on New Ireland.

EIGHT

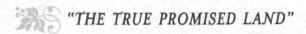 *"THE TRUE PROMISED LAND"*

*Making a Home on Mauritius
and Botanizing on Madagascar*

As Baret remained in the cabin, a prisoner of Commerson's opiates, the expedition made an arc, heading northwest around what would later be named the Bismarck Archipelago. For the first two weeks of August, Bougainville charted as best he could the positions of the sand gold, emerald green islands that hugged the rounded northeast coast of New Guinea. On August 8, perhaps in recognition of the trials of the last fortnight, Bougainville named an island after Commerson. Within this volcanic archipelago, islands have individual names, but they may also be identified by one of a number of collective names given to local groups of atolls. As a result, a westward-sailing ship will find the solitary island of Commerson lying beyond the "Hermit" group. Given how little he appears in others' journals at this time, and his lack of contributions to the notebook he shared with Duclos-Guyot, Commerson appears to have stayed by Baret's side, belowdecks, in careful watchfulness.

Bougainville knew only two certainties about what lay ahead. First, beyond New Guinea, the next major island group they would sail through—the Moluccas—was aggressively patrolled by its Dutch colonizers, who were protecting their lucrative monopoly on the temperamental nutmeg tree and their near-monopoly on cloves. For the French to botanize in the Moluccas and perhaps obtain a specimen of nutmeg or cloves was one of the goals of the expedition, but a potentially deadly one. In an age when spices were as rare and as sought after as gold, French explorers who were discovered to have landed on any Dutch possession without permission could expect to be imprisoned or summarily executed. Second, after the Moluccas, Bougainville would face at least three more months of sailing before reaching any French possession, the nearest being the island of Mauritius at the western extremity of the Indian Ocean.

Since passage through the Moluccas was inevitable, Bougainville knew he would be negligent if he did not require his botanists to land and search for seedlings or, better yet, small plantations of spices hidden in island forests. But the danger of gathering provisions and specimens on Dutch territory was the least of the difficulties Bougainville saw in requiring anything of his botanists at this time. Baret did not leave her cabin. And in a reversal of their usual roles, Commerson attended to her every need. From a command perspective, Bougainville had no botanist to explore one of the most commercially important concentrations of flora on the planet, and scarce rations to feed the men who would risk their lives in landing on Dutch possessions.

With all this weighing on Bougainville's mind, the ships sailed beyond the Bismarck Archipelago and back into New Guinea waters, attempting—for the second time in two months—to find a good anchorage so that they could reprovision. In June, violent squalls and strong currents had driven them back from the southeastern coast. Now they tried their luck and seamanship in making landfall on the long northern side of the island (coming nearest to the shore at the modern settlement of Wewak). But here the weather presented a deadly staccato pattern: terrifying thunderstorms with drenching rain and a headwind, followed in short succession by clear skies, still waters, and equatorial heat. Just when those on the becalmed ships thought that they could stand the sickeningly heavy heat no longer, another thunderstorm rose up in its place.

Locked in this cycle of storm and deadly calm, the northern coast of New Guinea appeared as unreachable as the southeast of the island. The officers had previously resisted harming a Patagonian dog that had somehow found its way on board back in the Strait of Magellan, preferring to eat rat rather than harm their canine companion. But now, seeing no alternative, the pugnacious little hunting dog was killed and served in the officers' mess, where its meat provided two days' respite from the eternity of ship's biscuit and the flaccid greens remaining from New Ireland.

Bolstered by their meal, Bougainville and his chief officers determined to hug the coast of New Guinea all the way to its western extremity, at which point the expedition would enter Dutch territory. If necessary, the French would throw themselves on the mercy of the Dutch, seeking enough rations to allow them to make it to the island of Java, three to four weeks' sailing to the west. Once on Java, where diplomats and traders lived in the port city of Batavia, Bougainville was confident that his name and the eminently respectable nature of his mission would be proof against suspicion of French aggression or subterfuge. Provided that neither the *Boudeuse* nor the *Étoile* could be found to be smuggling specimens of Dutch-controlled plants, the French would enjoy a civil reception. If Baret and Commerson were able to obtain even a few plants or seeds, Bougainville reasoned, surely it would be possible to conceal them somewhere on the ships.

On August 25, 1768, the expedition sailed past the westernmost point of New Guinea and into the seas of Ceram and Banda, home to a disparate group of volcanic landmasses that have been known collectively as the Spice Islands, or Moluccas, since the beginning of the Renaissance in Europe.

It is easy to be complacent about the availability of spices today, and a world in which they were the violently contested spoils of war for which men suffered torture and death is astonishing to contemplate. Before the development of icehouses and refrigeration, salt was used to preserve meat through the long northern winter. To mask the taste of ill-preserved or overly salted meat, sugar became a standard accompaniment to meat in the form of sweet sauces on rich European tables from the fifteenth to the eighteenth centuries. To imagine all food tasting only salty or sweet is to begin to understand the urgency with which Europe's imperial powers sought to obtain and control spices that tantalized the senses with their color palette, their tastes, and their smells. Like any valued commodity, spice quickly became a source of financial speculation. Though only one of the five ships that set out with Magellan on the first circumnavigation of the globe in 1519 limped home three years later, the 381 sacks of cloves that half filled the hold of the *Victoria* netted a substantial profit for the expedition's investors. To bring spices to Europe—or better yet, the ability to grow spices—was to fill treasuries and make fortunes.

In 1768, as the *Étoile* and the *Boudeuse* sailed into the Ceram Sea, Bougainville had a checklist of desirable spices, spice plants, and other rarities for his incapacitated botanists to obtain: cloves from the islands of Ternate, Tidore, Makian, and Amboyna; mace (the red covering, or aril, of the nutmeg seed) from the Banda islands of Run and Neira (where the region's spices were processed through the formidable Dutch

East India Company stronghold of Fort Belgica); sago from Ceram. (The sago palm, *Metroxylon sagu*, is the source of sago flour, which Moluccan islanders make into *toman*—compressed bars of energy-rich sago wrapped in palm leaves. Like Paraguay tea or breadfruit, *toman* seemed to offer an easy way to get more work out of legions of imperial workers.) The greatest prize was, however, the unprepossessing nutmeg tree, native to only a single spot on the planet: the tiny volcanic island of Run in the south of the Banda Sea. Hyperbolic western herbals credited the nutmeg with prolonging life, health, and youth; depending on one's written source, the nutmeg was the ultimate aphrodisiac or the complete cure-all. All of Europe's seafaring powers hoped to obtain their own nutmeg tree with which to start plantations outside the Dutch-controlled Moluccas. And to obtain a tree (ideally several trees) and transplant it from Run, expeditions needed good botanists.

Many trespassers into Dutch waters hoped, by some miracle, to find nutmeg trees that had germinated at some distance from Run, but the heavy weight of the nutmeg's fruit prevented the seeds from traveling any distance on the wind. To the Dutch, it seemed self-evident that Providence had placed Run in the south of the Banda Sea to help the empire protect its most precious commodity. Any rival power hoping to blunder into Run would first have to run the gauntlet of Dutch sea patrols encircling all of the more northerly islands in the region. Were Baret and Commerson to be found botanizing on any of these islands, they could be killed. This had happened to previous English adventurers seeking to break the Dutch nutmeg monopoly. Anglo-Dutch hostilities only concluded in 1667 when, under the terms of the Treaty of Breda, the English promised to stop their incursions into Dutch Indonesia in exchange for the swampy island of Manhattan on the other side of the world. Bougainville was expecting his botanists to evade and deceive Dutch authorities, when it was not clear that they were willing or able to engage in any botanizing activities at all.

Baret's rape happened on New Ireland, where the *Étoile* was anchored from July 6 to 26, 1768. By the time the expedition broke into the Ceram Sea on August 25, Baret had spent one month in the cabin. Beyond its wooden walls, ravenous men sailed two dessicated ships. If any aboard the *Étoile* were sympathetic toward her, those feelings were likely eclipsed by thoughts of self-preservation: Men were dying from scurvy and the survivors were caught in obsessive daily examinations of teeth and skin. Were Baret to leave the cabin she might well find herself in close proximity to one or more of her rapists who were protected by the veil of silence that Bougainville had tried to draw over the events on New Ireland.

Fortunately for Bougainville and his botanical goals, the islands offered Baret a welcome chance to leave the confines of the ship and the presence of her attackers. In order to minimize the chance of attracting attention from Dutch planters and overseers, only Baret and Commerson would be landed at any chosen spot. That she and Commerson risked their liberty and perhaps their lives in agreeing to go ashore on these Dutch possessions may well have been explained to her, without causing her to protest. Because Baret had endured so much and was almost certainly in a state that would today be identified as post-traumatic stress disorder, the prospect of capture and a summary trial by Dutch agents probably held little horror for her. Anywhere was better than the claustrophobic world of the *Étoile*.

Baret had no sooner agreed to resume botanizing with Commerson than a practical difficulty presented itself. In an effort to safeguard their spice-rich possessions, the Dutch had for generations strictly regulated the production and availability of navigational charts of the Moluccas. Everyone knew that nutmeg came only from Run in the Banda Sea, but *where* in the Banda Sea? Only a native Moluccan would know such information and might be willing to share it. Hoping to hire the guiding services of a local man and to reprovision stores at the same time, expedition officers designed a ruse to bring enterprising islanders to the ships. As they approached the crescent-shaped island of Ceram on August 31, where a variety of small boats bobbed by the shore, the *Étoile* and the *Boudeuse* ran Dutch colors up their masts, anticipating that locals would approach their Dutch overlords with offers of aid. To the horror of the hungry French, the flotilla quickly filled with villagers and then dispersed in every direction but the desired one. Concluding that the Dutch were feared rather than loved in the region and having once more failed to secure fresh provisions, the expedition command finally agreed to make their presence known to the only people who might conceivably help them—the Dutch themselves.

For the first week in September, the *Étoile* and the *Boudeuse* lay at anchor off the Dutch plantation island of Boeroe (modern Buru), immediately west of Ceram. Both ships were exhaustively searched by Dutch authorities looking for live specimens of locally grown spices. Baret and Commerson's cabin had been vetted more thoroughly than any other place on the two ships, and what once had a semblance of order was now turned upside down by officials going through thousands of specimens from the previous eighteen months. Once satisfied that the French had not obtained any spices, the local Dutch governor invited Bougainville and his gentlemen to dinner at his official residence. At first attributing the voracity of their French guests to cultural difference, the Dutch soon understood that they were dining with men who had, until the previous day, believed starvation to be their fate. Vivès observed one of his fellow French diners request seven consecutive helpings of greens.

Commerson was among those invited to the governor's house, where any animosities that existed between Bougainville's officers appeared to have been forgotten at the prospect of unlimited food. Certainly there is no record of any altercations among the diners at the governor's residence. If Vivès had been among Baret's rapists, either she had not told Commerson, or Commerson knew and declined to confront Vivès, or the combination of trauma and powerful sedatives had left Baret unable or (understandably) unwilling to remember those involved.

Commerson's presence among the French shore party left Baret alone in the cabin for the first time since her rape. To take anything that might numb her senses by drugging her to sleep was now out of the question and she undoubtedly preferred to stay awake, facing the cabin door, holding tight to Commerson's brace of pistols. Around her, the cabin lay in chaos from the Dutch officials' search, but it was impossible to think of dropping her guard and beginning to recrate all the disturbed specimens. Baret watched the door, measuring the hours of Commerson's absence by the burning of the candle in the lantern.

When the shore party finally returned, it was evident that the officers had eaten well. Now persuaded that the French claims of starvation were true, the governor of Boeroe gave permission for locals to trade with their unexpected visitors. The day following the officers' dinner, fresh fruit, dried fish, rice, and hens were hauled aboard the *Étoile* and the *Boudeuse*, instantly changing the mood of their crews. With permission also granted to transfer the most serious scurvy cases to a hut on the shore, Bougainville requested Baret and Commerson to accompany the sick, then strike out into the countryside in search of spices. If apprehended, the botanists were to claim that they were in search of indigenous plants to observe rather than to collect. As an excuse, it was unlikely to save Baret and Commerson from interrogation and imprisonment. But their hosts prevented matters from escalating to that point. As they attempted to go botanizing, Baret and Commerson found themselves being watched and followed by Dutch agents.

What was irksome to Commerson must have been deeply disturbing to Baret. The last time she had set foot on land had been in New Ireland, on the day of her rape. In nearly two years at sea, she had not enjoyed a single day of privacy. Now the prying eyes of Frenchmen had simply been replaced by those of the Dutch. Since she had not taken any women's clothes on the expedition, she was still dressed in the oversize linen shirt and trousers that had been her habitual costume throughout the voyage, although since her rape she had abandoned the attempt to hide her sex. Feeling unable to leave Commerson's side, she listened as he engaged their stolid Dutch observers with a barrage of questions about the minutiae of local bird life, hoping to irritate them into going away. There are no significant finds, botanical or mineralogical, from this stage of the expedition. Between the unblinking watchfulness of the Dutch and the brutality of her crewmen, Baret had been robbed of the confidence and pleasure she took in searching for and gathering plants. These were not, however, the only reasons for her distress as we shall see. In addition to being traumatized by what lay in her recent past, she now had an urgent reason to worry about the future.

Having thwarted the botanists on the island of Boeroe, the Dutch governor also did his best to ensure that no Moluccan would offer to guide the French through local seas. Lacking charts or a local pilot, and stocked with enough provisions for a month or so, the French had little choice but to sail directly west across the Molucca Sea. They skirted the large island of Celebes (modern-day Sulawesi) but did not attempt a landing. Bougainville was now resigned to making straight for the most significant port for over five thousand miles—the Dutch power base of Batavia (today's Jakarta) on the long, fertile island of Java, at the eastern rim of the Indian Ocean. Leaving Boeroe on September 8, the expedition arrived at Batavia on September 27. The French would stay in Batavia for three weeks, until mid-October. During that period, while repairs were undertaken on the *Étoile* and the hold was completely restocked, Commerson and Nassau-Siegen were frequently ashore, recording their aromatic observations of avenues lined with fruit trees and coffee plantations in the countryside, where wealthy traders had built homes that impressed even the prince. Baret did not accompany Commerson on any of these fact-finding promenades, and no specimens seem to have been collected.

Where the Batavian countryside delighted both the eye and nose, the city of Batavia itself disgusted its French visitors. A thriving center of international trade, publishing, and ship repair, Batavia sucked in thousands of Asian and European laborers, then spewed their effluent (and that of their Dutch masters) into a system of civic canals that choked on their own filth, breeding mosquitoes along with bacteria. With the dock-side taverns not scrupling to water down both ale and locally made spirits with contaminated water, Aotourou and a sizable number of officers and men suffered bouts of dysentery. Throughout all the reveling, sight-seeing, and bartering, Baret stayed on board the *Étoile*. The prospect of shore leave among rambunctious crews was simply terrifying, and the serious illness of Aotourou and others testified to the unsanitary nature of the city. More than ever, she had no wish to attract unwelcome atten-tion or invite illness: For now, two months after the violence on New Ireland, she knew beyond doubt that she was pregnant.

Since she had given birth herself to a healthy son in Paris nearly three years earlier, Baret was under no illusion about what lay ahead for her physically, with five months remaining in the voyage. Her herb woman's notebook, given to Commerson, confirms that she knew which Euro-pean plants had a history as abortifacients but, as already mentioned, these plants frequently proved acutely toxic. As an herb woman, Baret would have been sadly familiar with clients who cried out for relief when their pregnancies—or perhaps their attempted abortions—went wrong. She was not about to put herself in this position while on a voyage, with only Commerson—and Vivès—able to attend to her. The safest place she could be in relation to the malarial haven of Batavia was on board the *Étoile*, standing well out from the harbor in the roadway. Baret spent the whole of the expedition's stay on board ship, but Commerson fre-quently went ashore, and over these three weeks they lost the shared botanical activities that had provided their first and most enduring con-nection. When the *Boudeuse* and a fully stocked *Étoile* sailed from Bat-avia on October 17, Baret and Commerson had little to say to each other and no prospect of landfall for at least three more weeks.

They passed the volcanic island of Krakatoa but the expedition did not land. Since natural springs on the island produced both cold and warm water in equal measure, the Dutch were flirting with a pepper plan-

tation on Krakatoa; having been saved by Dutch hospitality, Bougainville did not wish to be found exploring a plantation island. (The massive
eruption of Krakatoa that made the island infamous did not occur until
August 1883. In 1768, the island was therefore a smoking curiosity to the
French, but neither a famous nor a feared sight.) Bougainville instead
charted a gentle southwest course across a six-thousand-mile expanse
of the Indian Ocean, aiming for one of the most strategically important
islands occupied by France: the naturalist's wonderland of the Île de
France, today known as Mauritius, which lies 1,250 miles off the east
coast of Africa and in 1768 was home to the most important French botanical garden outside Paris. Had anyone told Baret that Mauritius would
become her home for the next seven years, she would likely have had
plenty of questions for Commerson about the place and the people they
were shortly to encounter.

Mauritius: the first French-controlled land in over twenty-two months at
sea and an island—at last—whose waters were comprehensively represented on Bougainville's charts. On November 7, the *Étoile* and the *Bou-*
deuse sighted Port Louis, located on the relatively sheltered northwest
coast. After a day spent piloting the ships into harbor and securing them,
the sailors were overjoyed to find themselves in French territory. With
only one-fifth of the island's thirty-thousand-strong population being
French or Francophile, and the remainder being African slaves or Asian
laborers, even the humblest deckhand aboard the *Étoile* felt himself to be
part of a privileged group of Mauritians.

For Bougainville and Commerson, the welcome received on
Mauritius was especially warm. Bougainville had already met the
commissaire-intendant (or civil administrator) of Mauritius in Paris two
years previously, when both had been considered top-flight candidates

for administrative positions in the colonies. Commerson was known to the administrator by reputation, for he, too, was a renowned botanist who had been charged with transforming the French East India Company's botanical garden of Pamplemousses into a living storehouse of exotic commercial crops. In the process, the intendant would become known to every child across the English-speaking world, for he was Pierre Poivre, immortalized in a nursery rhyme that testifies to the importance of the spice trade:

> Peter Piper picked a peck of pickled peppers,
> A peck of pickled peppers Peter Piper picked,
> If Peter Piper picked a peck of pickled peppers,
> Where's the peck of pickled peppers Peter Piper picked?

While Poivre's surname actually translates as "pepper," the nursery rhyme (first published in Britain in John Harris's *Peter Piper's Practical Principles of Plain and Perfect Pronunciation* of 1813) plays on the Latin name for the tropical woody vine that produces peppercorns: *Piper nigrum* (literally "black pepper"). Generally used fresh at their aromatic source, peppercorns must be preserved if they are to be shipped far and wide, and the favored method of preserving them in the mid-eighteenth century was to "pickle" them in brine. Today, pepper is the most widely traded spice in the world, accounting for one-fifth of world's spice trade: In the mid-eighteenth century, pepper was perceived as less exotic than cloves or nutmeg, but its greater availability and more widespread use made it infinitely more lucrative. Open access to pecks (a unit of measure equal to 16 dry pints) of pickled peppers not only would make a man rich indeed but would make his masters anxious to track down any missing inventory. And so, bizarrely, a tongue twister that is a staple of the English language commemorates a French botanist and the desire of his backers in the French East India Company to consolidate their hold on the eighteenth-century pepper trade.

The rapport between the two botanists was strong and immediate. Indeed, previous chroniclers of the expedition have unanimously declared the men's mutual admiration for each other as the reason why Commerson—accompanied by Baret—accepted an invitation to move into Poivre's official residence. There, in the comfortable, two-story colonial mansion of Mon Plaisir, Baret and Commerson supposedly decided to stay and assist with the work of the botanists of Pamplemousses for an unspecified term, when the expedition sailed on.

But when the *Étoile* and the *Boudeuse* departed from Port Louis on December 12, 1768, Bougainville left behind not just Baret and Commerson but also the astronomer Véron. Given that the scientists' royal appointments supposed their work to be of central importance for the empire, and given that both were in the pay of the French government, they could not simply decide to quit the expedition without very compelling reasons for doing so. Against the backdrop of eighteenth-century Anglo-French imperial rivalry and the goals and needs of the French government, Bougainville would never have considered allowing two key scientists to remain behind in Mauritius simply to provide Poivre with entertaining houseguests.

Véron probably wished to avoid returning to France because he had failed to find a reliable astronomical method for determining longitude at sea. Bougainville, who counted mathematics and astronomy among his range of considerable skills, was well placed to understand his astronomer's situation. (As Véron contemplated his failure in the bustling Port Louis, it is also possible that a visiting ship brought rumors of British claims, circulating in the Royal Navy that watchmaker John Harrison was on the verge of solving the problem with his wondrous marine chronometer, which had finally shown promisingly in trials at sea.)

Commerson was certainly attracted by the prospect of an extended period of botanizing on Mauritius and in the unique island environment of Madagascar, just over five hundred miles to the west. But he, like Véron, must have been acutely aware that he had failed in his appointed mission. Commerson had named species in honor of French ministers, expedition members, and most notably himself, but he could not point to a single commercially useful plant that he had collected. Thousands of specimens sat snug and dry in their crates in his cabin, but they had not been systematically organized. Most glaringly, the expedition had managed to sail through the Spice Islands without so much as a clove or nutmeg tree to show for it. The species that Commerson had discovered and the observations he had jotted down would be of interest to fellow botanists and naturalists, but the French government was certain to be underwhelmed by his achievements, and the sinecures and fat pension Commerson had thought he would enjoy immediately upon his return to France now appeared somewhat elusive.

To be sure, Commerson's future career was not Bougainville's problem—but Baret's pregnancy would be. In 1768, a journey by sea from Mauritius to France took between three and four months, assuming favorable winds rounding Africa via the Cape of Good Hope and along the length of Africa's western coast. By the time Bougainville's expedition arrived at Mauritius, Baret was already three months pregnant. If the expedition encountered unexpected delays, or ran into bad weather, Baret could potentially go into labor at sea. A woman disguised as a man could be got off ship back in France—even a pregnant woman could be concealed as a ship docked—but a birth at sea, with any attendant difficulties or fatalities, would have to be reported, inviting an official investigation into who knew what, and when. Véron and Commerson may have had excellent reasons for wanting to stay behind, but Baret was the one member of the party for whom Bougainville would have actively negotiated an extended stay on Mauritius.

Removing Baret from the *Étoile* would remove her from daily proximity to her rapists, ensure that tensions between Commerson and Vivès would not escalate, and excise all evidence of the rule breaking that had brought a woman aboard and facilitated her assault. For Bougainville, then, the accommodating presence of Poivre on Mauritius seemed an answer to his every problem. Poivre was all too ready to assist in accommodating the botanists, hoping that their presence would shore up his prestige both on the island and with the home government. As the *commissaire-intendant* of the island, Poivre was the highest-ranking French civil administrator there, but he often clashed with Governor Daniel Dumas, the chief military commander of the colony: Each man hoped to help the other to a rebuke and recall from Paris. In Commerson, Poivre saw a well-connected ally who could tip the balance of power in his favor by making new discoveries and validating reports made by the horticulturalists of Pamplemousses.

Certainly, the manner in which Poivre framed his invitation to Commerson to stay suggests that Poivre had been well briefed by Bougainville in how to appeal to Commerson's vanity. Poivre told Commerson that the gardens of Pamplemousses needed a botanist of Commerson's caliber, and that after he had botanized on Mauritius to his heart's content he could begin a botanic survey of Madagascar, where the French maintained a coastal presence. Poivre emphasized that Commerson should bring his assistant, who would be relatively untroubled by formal duties, since Poivre also offered Commerson the dedicated services of a full-time illustrator, Paul de Jossigny. (That Poivre's staff included a spare full-time natural history illustrator suggests the scope of the French operation on Mauritius.) As if worried that this already generous offer required further sugar coating, Poivre capped it all with a promise he had neither authority nor ability to make: Commerson was assured he could continue to claim his expedition salary for the (unspecified) duration of his stay on the island.

When Commerson wrote to his estranged brother-in-law to explain the arrangement (since Father Beau continued to take care of Commerson's son), he hinted that the proposed arrangements originated with a request from Paris: "When I arrived, I discovered that the Governor had been asked by the Minister to entreat me to stay and, after a short time, to go and explore the great island of Madagascar, together with other places for which the government has significant plans. You realize that a request of this nature is the same as an order and cannot be declined." Either the involvement of "the Minister" (presumably César Gabriel de Choiseul, duc de Praslin, who had taken over the naval portfolio from his cousin Étienne at this time) was a fabrication on Commerson's part, designed to placate a disapproving brother-in-law, or it was part of the bait by which Bougainville and Poivre hoped to hook the botanist—and his assistant—into staying on Mauritius. For in 1768, the duc de Praslin had not made any request that the botanist prolong his stay on Mauritius. Indeed, the minister of marine would prove so resistant to the idea that Poivre was forced to ask Bougainville to make use of friends at court to go over Praslin's head.

The official who finally, in April 1770, granted (backdated) permission for Commerson's stay was one Monseigneur Poissonnier, royal physician and colonial inspector-general of medicine, surgery, and pharmacy. (Clearly fortune had smiled on the doctor who originally nominated Commerson to Bougainville's expedition.) In Poissonnier's direction that Commerson should assess all medicinal plants found on the island to determine which might be cultivated and sent back to France, we see how much effort Poivre and Bougainville were prepared to make to ensure that Commerson—and Baret—remained at Pamplemousses.

And so, on November 15, 1768, Bougainville signed the certificate that released Commerson from his obligations with respect to the expedition and made him a free agent able to stay on Mauritius. Since Baret was technically employed by Commerson, she had no legal obligations to the expedition and therefore required no release. The whole idea had been conceived and concluded in just one week after the ships docked in port.

In all likelihood, Baret and Commerson quit the claustrophobia-inducing confines of the *Étoile* as soon as the official paperwork was complete. Several specimen cases remained on the *Étoile* to give evidence of the botanists' work when the ship returned to France, although Commerson took the great majority of his favorite treasures with him, presumably intending to write up his thoughts at a future date. How anyone other than Baret or Commerson could be expected to make sense of the collection, when few items were labeled with their place of origin, and many species, both plant and animal, were new to eighteenth-century science, appears not to have been considered. As the couple walked down the gangplank of the *Étoile* onto the dry land of the Port Louis dockside, what was Baret's likely mental and emotional state? The thirty-by-fifteen-foot captain's cabin on the *Étoile* had been her home for almost two years. During that time she had pushed herself to her physical limit in an attempt to sustain the fiction that she was a man. Overworked, exhausted, starving, and the victim of a gang rape, she now trusted to Commerson to negotiate yet another radical change in their lifestyle.

At first glance, life on Mauritius was infinitely more appealing than continuing with the circumnavigation. Poivre's residence, Mon Plaisir, nestled in the shade of native casuarina trees that threw their tall, slender shadows on the green shutters and whitewashed walls of the colonial mansion. Madame Poivre must initially have balked at the impropriety of housing Commerson's unmarried young companion, but since she was at the center of the small French social scene in the area, she was an arbiter of local manners rather than their victim.

Baret received her own room in the servants' quarters. Though not a fraction as luxurious as the guest room given to Commerson, with its imported French furniture and overstuffed cushions, the plain walls and simple bed guaranteed her privacy for the first time in years. The incessant motion of the *Étoile* that had at first made her so ill had been exchanged for solid ground beneath her feet. The sounds of men everywhere, constantly monitoring the progress of the ship at all hours of day and night, were replaced by the sedate rhythms of a wealthy home, where shouting was a breach of decorum and where the only sounds that disturbed the night came from a tropical insect chorus. Perhaps most strikingly, the acidic stench of the vinegar-soused planking of the *Étoile,* scoured daily in an attempt to keep disease at bay, had been traded for the smells of a lush island garden. At night, the fresh air filtering through the shutters was heavy with the almond-scented sweetness of the frangipani shrubs (*Plumeria*) that grew around Mon Plaisir, as they advertised their showy presence to their nocturnal pollinators—giant sphinx moths that tapped on the windows if they detected a candle flame inside. Baret may have been accommodated in the servants' quarters, but she undoubtedly enjoyed the most calm and comfort since she had left the Paris apartment on rue des Boulangers two years ago.

Baret would spend seven years on Mauritius. To determine how those seven years were filled, we need to examine the evidence for Baret's pregnancy as a result of her rape. If Baret was pregnant as a result of a rape in July 1768, then she gave birth no later than April 1769. In that month, neither Baret nor Commerson were to be found at Poivre's home in Port Louis. Instead, they had left temporarily for a settlement called Flacq, which was surrounded by coffee plantations in the northeast part of the island. There they made a lasting connection: M. Bézac, a planter who seems also to have possessed some medical training. The origin of the connection between Baret, Commerson, and Bézac is unclear, but surely Commerson's experience with plant trials at the Jardin du Roi in Paris would have been useful to a coffee planter seeking to maximize his yield. Once the two men discovered their shared interest in plants and medicine, they struck up a warm relationship.

The names Bézac and Flacq are more than simply an incidental part of Baret's story, however. They appear in the archives of the National Library of Australia, in a manuscript which has nothing directly to say about Baret but nevertheless offers compelling evidence that she gave birth to a son in Flacq—a son whom she left to the willing care of M. Bézac.

The manuscript is part of the vast archive of papers relating to the British explorer Matthew Flinders (1774–1814), whose early experience

of reading *Robinson Crusoe* had filled him with an urge to go to sea. But
just as Defoe's protagonist found his journey interrupted by an enforced
long-term stay on a desert island, Flinders found himself a prisoner on
Mauritius from 1803 to 1810. (This was certainly not the way in which
he had intended to imitate his fictional hero.) Flinders was returning
from the first successful circumnavigation of Australia from 1801 to 1803
(proving beyond doubt that it was a separate continent) when he stopped
at Mauritius, not for a moment supposing that hostilities between Britain
and Napoleonic France had extended across the Indian Ocean. He was
dismayed to find himself arrested by French authorities on Mauritius
and charged with being a British spy. From 1803 to 1804, he was placed
under house arrest in Flacq, and his voluminous correspondence from
these months shows that his host was one M. Bézac. For many British
gentlemen of the period, knowledge of French was a mark of a good education, but Flinders's background was relatively humble and he proved
unable to communicate with his jailer hosts. The interpreter provided to
him in 1803 at the home of M. Bézac in Flacq was a man with the surname "Bonnefoy"—the very alias that Baret had been known to use. If
this is only a coincidence, it is a truly remarkable one.

Bonnefoy is a common enough French surname, but we know that
it was a name Baret sometimes gave in place of her own, when circumstances suited her to do so. And now we find a man at the house
of M. Bézac of Flacq called Bonnefoy in the first decade of the nineteenth century, when any son born to Baret in 1769 would have been in
his early thirties. But why would Baret give a child a name other than her
own? Remembering the violent circumstances of the child's conception,
Baret might understandably have wished to dissociate herself from a son
whose father she neither knew nor wanted to know. And having rejected
his own child in Paris, we can be certain that Commerson had no wish
to give his name or his affection to anyone else's child. Thus Baret chose
the surname Bonnefoy. As they escaped to Flacq in early 1769 to avoid
the notoriety of the impending birth, it is easy to imagine that a man

sharing Commerson's interests, without any children of his own, might agree to bring up Baret's son as his charge. The couple's removal to Flacq for the birth of a child would also explain why Commerson did not leave for Madagascar immediately after being released from Bougainville's expedition. Commerson had many failings, but at this time, when Baret needed him most, he was with her.

Baret felt comfortably close to home on Mauritius—the harbor was full of French ships that had recently rounded the Cape of Good Hope to do business in Indian and Indonesian waters. And after all that Baret had endured to follow her twin passions for plants and Commerson, life on Mauritius offered a potent reminder of what had originally inspired her to believe in him. On the island, Commerson became his old self, someone whose interests and enthusiasms once more appeared boundless now that they were no longer constrained by the day-to-day realities of life at sea. He scribbled plans for a university on the island that would be closely linked to the botanical work of the gardens of Pamplemousses. He kept Jossigny fully employed in illustrating some of the nearly one thousand specimens collected on Mauritius in 1768–69. With Poivre, he spent hours in the botanic gardens conducting field trials of strains of cassava, maize, millet, rice, and wheat. The scientists also scrutinized avocado and tamarind trees, but quickly deemed them unsuitable for significant commercial exploitation. They invested great hopes in crops of flax and hemp to clothe France's imperial workers, but the test beds in the Pamplemousses gardens refused to flourish, despite all the care lavished upon them.

Given that Poivre had originally tried to gain official support for Commerson's stay by insisting to the duc de Praslin that Commerson was cataloging the medicinal plants on the island, Baret must have assisted Commerson in the field. His ulcerated leg continued to trouble him; her knowledge of curative plants approached or exceeded his; and Baret and Commerson were used to working together. Indeed, at the outset of their time on Mauritius, the field would have been the only place where they interacted.

As Baret continued to occupy her room in the servants' quarters, and Commerson continued to enjoy the comforts of one of Poivre's guest rooms, the couple led separate social lives. Commerson, an educated bachelor with the cachet of royal connections, attracted island society, such as it was, as surely as the frangipani blossoms around Mon Plaisir attracted their nocturnal moth pollinators. Visiting Mauritius in 1768, the French writer Jacques-Henri Bernardin de Saint-Pierre estimated that one hundred "women of condition" (that is, of social standing) lived within the environs of Port Louis, and these ladies had long ago grown tired of their familiar companions. (Since Bernardin de Saint-Pierre traveled in the same small circles as Commerson but never mentions the botanist by name, it may be inferred that Commerson's temporary residence in Flacq and his botanizing expeditions around the region kept him out of the writer's company for the duration of his stay.) Unlike the planters, whose number Bernardin de Saint-Pierre puts at approximately four hundred, Commerson was capable of conversation on subjects beyond the management of plantation slaves. French society on Mauritius embraced the botanist, who could not be mentioned without its being recalled that he was a great friend of the intendant, and therefore close to the seat of colonial power on the island.

As Commerson whiled away his evenings revisiting social niceties he had almost forgotten, Baret was left to her own devices. Friendship with the servants in Poivre's household was made difficult by her indeterminate status—she worked exclusively with Commerson and displayed expert knowledge of a subject that no other household worker understood. Recent research has shown that communities of slaves, especially those from sub-Saharan Africa, often included individuals with extensive knowledge of plant-based medicines, and Baret might have found much to discuss with these folk healers had she encountered any. Like Baret, they must have scanned the greenery of their new lives, looking for plants that reminded them of more familiar species, with properties they understood. But the slaves who labored to put swaths of Mauritius under cultivation were confined to the plantations outside Port Louis, under conditions that prompted Bernardin de Saint-Pierre to exclaim, "Whether coffee and sugar be really essential to the comfort of Europe, is more than I can say, but I affirm—that these two vegetables have brought wretchedness and misery upon America and Africa."

If Baret ever ventured out alone, to wander the gardens of Mon Plaisir and to take in the beauties and oddities of her new island home, then only her experiences of the previous two years would have mitigated the shock of encountering native Mauritian fauna. Bernardin de Saint-Pierre describes recoiling in horror from hairy spiders with "bellies as big as a nut" that spun webs strong enough to catch small birds, and bats "as big as a small cat, very fat . . . eaten by the inhabitants as a rarity." Drawing on the courage that had sustained her throughout the voyage, and perhaps rekindling some of the natural curiosity that had inspired her to join the circumnavigation, Baret mapped her way around her immediate environs, learning what to expect from the Mauritian ecosystem. As in all stages of her life since she had left La Comelle, however, a familiar pattern was no sooner established than it was broken by forces beyond her control.

Poivre was frustrated to receive word from Paris in late 1769 that navy bureaucrats declined to send Commerson any more of his salary, since he was no longer under naval command. Baret was dependent on Commerson, and Commerson on Poivre, who now found himself the sole financial benefactor of the couple. Madame Poivre's feelings on finding that her sometime guests appeared to have become semipermanent fixtures can easily be guessed at. Commerson had always turned any living space of his into a hothouse and laboratory and presumably sought to store the overspill from his own room in Baret's servant's quarters. Fortunately for Commerson, Poivre shared his irrepressible interest in the natural world and neither man was about to let financial considerations stand in the way of a botanical survey of Madagascar, over five hundred miles to the west of Mauritius.

Poivre knew little about Madagascar, but he believed it to be a unique environment: an intuition that has since been confirmed with breathtaking force. For Madagascar, the fourth largest island in the world, is home to at least 5 percent of the world's plant and animal species, including some plants that collapse the distance between our world and that of herb women and folk healers. One of the most publicized—and controversial—of recent discoveries of a cancer-fighting agent in nature's pharmacopoeia concerns the rosy, or Madagascar, periwinkle (*Catharanthus roseus*), an evergreen shrub whose derivative vinblastine has increased survival rates of childhood leukemia from 10 percent in the 1970s to 90 percent today. Originally used by Madagascan healers as a folklore remedy to treat diabetes, the rosy periwinkle has become a cause célèbre for proponents of biodiversity and ethnobotany and for those who champion the rights of indigenous peoples to benefit from the products of their land and from centuries of accumulated tribal wisdom. We are only beginning to understand the biological riches of Madagascar (even as they disappear to logging and development), and Poivre surely deserves credit as the first appointee of any government to see the potential of Madagascan flora to benefit mankind.

Despite a lack of official funding, in October 1770, Poivre gave Commerson papers authorizing his passage from Mauritius to Madagascar in the frigate *Ambulante*, under the command of the Baron de Cluny. Commerson's letters of transit named the illustrator Jossigny as his companion, and asked all French officials whom they might encounter to assist them in their government-directed work. Baret also accompanied

Commerson, since she could not remain in the servants' quarters at the intendant's mansion as her "master" undertook what was likely to be a journey of some months.

Boarding the *Ambulante* was a very different experience to that of boarding the *Étoile* nearly four years previously. Finding the linen trousers and shirts she had worn as her disguise to be infinitely more practical for botanizing than even the plainest women's dresses of the time, Baret continued to wear male clothes, though she made no attempt to hide the fact that she was a woman. With a tiny passenger cabin to herself, just large enough for a single hanging cot, Baret was not required to explain herself to anyone. On Madagascar, the Baron de Cluny was overseeing the drawdown of French personnel at Fort Dauphin: In cases that concerned the movement of civilian personnel, the royal ordinance forbidding women on board did not apply (as it had not applied to Bougainville in transporting colonists from the Îles Malouines to Rio). Scandalous as it was for an unmarried woman to travel in the service of a single man, Baret and Commerson had long since ceased to care about notions of appropriate behavior. Cluny's assignment was to deliver Commerson and his party safely to Madagascar, not to inquire into their lifestyle, and the paperwork from Poivre guaranteed their acceptance by French authorities both on ship and in Madagascar. And it is from their time in Madagascar that we find the only taxonomical tribute that Commerson ever offered to Baret.

Baret and Commerson spent four months away from Mauritius, from October 1770 to January 1771. In the naturalist's paradise of Madagascar, familiar species take on bizarrely unfamiliar forms: a pygmy hippopotamus, a giant chameleon. More than 80 percent of its flora and fauna is, like the lemur, endemic—found nowhere else on earth. It is therefore little wonder that Baret and Commerson collected approximately five hundred specimens of flora and fauna during these four months. Energized by his time on Mauritius and now Madagascar, Commerson had started making intermittent written observations on the strange new world around him and he acknowledged the difference of Madagascan wildlife in a remarkable tribute: "I can announce to naturalists that this is the true Promised Land. Here nature created a special sanctuary where she seems to have withdrawn to experiment with designs different from those used anywhere else. At every step one finds more remarkable and marvellous forms of life."

Finding more species than he could hope to describe and catalog, Commerson commemorated a wide circle of family and friends in Linnaean binomials. Since Jossigny followed him everywhere, drawing whatever Commerson specified, he was honored in the plant genus *Jossinia* (now *Eugenia*). The commander of the *Ambulante*, the Baron de Cluny may have been a relatively recent acquaintance, but he was deemed to merit immortality in the genus *Clugnia*. (Only two species were ever named—*volopis* and *volubilis* and the genus is scarcely mentioned outside early nineteenth-century botanical textbooks.) Both genera include a range of tropical trees and shrubs that yield aromatic fruits and valuable hardwoods, and Commerson perhaps thought them appropriate embodiments of the solid, dependable men.

Charmed by the profusion of white blossoms on a ten-foot-tall shrub with dark green glossy leaves, Commerson designated another new genus *Baretia*. Believing he had distinguished three different species of *Baretia,* he named them *B. bonafidia, B. oppotisiva,* and *B. heterophylla.* (Clearly, the first name recalls Baret's pseudonym Bonnefoy—"good faith"—while *oppotisiva* and *heterophylla* attest to characteristics of the leaves and flowers that Commerson believed distinguished them as separate species.) A peculiar quality of the shrub shows why Commerson chose to commemorate Baret with this particular genus. The individual plants each carry a variety of leaves of different shapes and sizes: Some are oblanceolate (long and widening after the midpoint of the leaf); others are obovate (egg-shaped); yet others terminate in two rounded lobes. *Baretia*, in other words, resists easy identification or summation on a single glance, since any individual plant unites a range of attributes that would not typically be found together.

Commerson presumably thought this trait provided a neat botanical summary of Baret herself, who united a range of contradictions: a woman dressed as a man; a female botanist in a male-dominated field; a working-class woman who had traveled father than most aristocrats. How could the eighteenth-century mind classify someone who refused to be bound by her gender or her class, and the expectations associated with them?

Without a general knowledge of southeast African flora, Commerson could not know that the genus comprises many more species than he saw on Madagascar. Baret would surely be delighted to learn that these plants have a long-established history in folk medicine in Zimbabwe and neighboring countries. Some fifty species of this genus, which has long since been reclassified and renamed, have now been identified. While the majority of Commerson's names for flora and fauna have survived, *Baretia* has been superseded—first by *Quivisia* and then by *Turraea*. Today, not a single genus or species commemorates this remarkable botanist.

Perhaps more valuable to Baret than finally having a plant named after her was the opportunity to spend more time with Commerson. If the cramped conditions on board the *Étoile* had made time together often seem interminable, Mauritius had forced enough distance between them for Baret to fear losing anything that remained of her relationship with Commerson. On Madagascar, however, the couple were not separated by others' perceptions of social class or by the distractions of polite society. Jossigny, though ever present, occupied himself for hours at a stretch with illustrations of Madagascan flora and fauna. Away from Poivre and all other distractions, Baret and Commerson were once again two botanists in the field, rediscovering their ability to live and work together.

Aware that their five hundred specimens represented the merest fraction of Madagascan life, the couple nevertheless agreed that they should
return to Mauritius at the close of the year. Their treks through southeast Madagascar were causing a recurrence of pains in Commerson's leg
and he was limping badly. As they returned to Fort Dauphin, they were
cheered that the *Ambulante* was again in port, continuing its drawdown of
French personnel from the island's margins. Mauritius was no more than
a week's sailing away, and they anticipated a straightforward return to
Poivre's comfortable residence, which had become their de facto home.
But a violent storm at sea, possibly a typhoon, forced the ship to change
course. The story is told in a letter written by a minor French administrator, Crémont, stationed on the Île Bourbon (now Réunion), a French
territory some 120 miles southwest of Mauritius. Crémont addressed
himself to the same French government officials who had stopped Commerson's salary, and it is tempting to imagine Commerson dictating to
Crémont as he wrote:

> The Ambulante, under the command of Baron de Cluny . . . was
> forced by a storm of 4 December to put in here. Among the recovering
> passengers is M. de Commerson, doctor, of the University of Montpel-
> lier, to whom we are indebted for the discovery of many plants hitherto
> unknown, made as he participated in the circumnavigation of M. de
> Bougainville. His research has already revealed what a multitude of
> plants might be collected here, indeed, he has shown our doctors some
> plants they knew nothing about but which are in widespread medicinal
> use. A naturalist as informed and determined as M. de Commerson
> really should be encouraged in this valuable work . . . in its infancy
> here, where we are possessed of riches unsuspected until now, but
> which will be revealed thanks to M. de Commerson.

Commerson was apparently eager to demonstrate the medical uses
of several island plants to local doctors, although government officials in

Paris and modern readers alike may wonder how a man so ill from the effects of a storm at sea found the energy to start botanizing on Bourbon. The same government officials must also have picked up on the clumsy hint that Bourbon might yield botanical "riches"—if only some money could be found for Commerson's employment. Presumably tired of assuming secondary importance to Poivre's Mauritian schemes, Crémont hoped to change the status quo by poaching his star botanist. Of course, Crémont gives all the credit for these assessments of Bourbon's plant life to Commerson, saying nothing about Baret, though she must have been as quick as Commerson to see the medicinal value of the island's species. Perhaps observers saw Baret as unimportant because she was ostensibly Commerson's assistant, or perhaps they considered her unable to contribute anything because she was a woman; for whatever reason, she was repeatedly omitted from reports of Commerson's plant-gathering successes.

Though Baret had expected that they would leave Bourbon as soon as Commerson started feeling better, Commerson was enjoying himself too much to consider leaving anytime soon. Basking in the enthusiastic reception afforded by officials such as Crémont, Commerson decided to please himself by undertaking a more systematic survey of the landscape. Baret had little choice but to accompany him, since without Commerson, Baret was a single, penniless woman, four months' sailing from home. Her ability to move freely between the islands depended upon the documents Commerson held from Poivre, while her ability finally to gain passage home to France depended upon the depth of Commerson's purse and the reach of his influence. To berate him for taking his time might have been satisfying in the short term but ultimately counterproductive.

One of the chief attractions of the island for Commerson was not even botanical but geological. One of the world's most active volcanoes, Piton de la Fournaise, erupts nearly every year in the southeast of what is now Réunion. Locals would have confirmed that the volcano was active, since it had erupted most recently in 1766 and 1768; therefore, the volcano could be considered overdue for a blowout in 1771, when Commerson coaxed Baret to join him in a reconnaissance of the deeply fissured basalt rock around its base. Indeed, they were fortunate not to be overcome by the sulfurous fumes belching from the more active of two summit craters, for La Fournaise did erupt later that year (and in 1772, 1774, 1775, and 1776).

This single instance encapsulates both the rewards and the frustrations of life with Commerson. The girl who statistically should not have moved more than twenty miles from La Comelle now strode in trousers across the base of an active volcano on the edge of the Indian Ocean, accompanied by a man who could explain the latest thinking about such phenomena and who could be charming, thoughtful company when he chose. But when Commerson focused only on his own wishes, he was arrogant and reckless to the point of endangering life itself.

While Baret had little choice but to accept Commerson's whims, men who were his socioeconomic equals and superiors suffered no such compunction. Poivre had already been recalled to Paris and the new intendant, Maillard Dumesle, had no intention of indulging his predecessor's eccentricities and enthusiasms. (Véron, understanding that he had outstayed his welcome at Mon Plaisir, had already started on his way to India, where he hoped to make astronomical observations that would impress back in France.) Learning of the change in regime on Mauritius (which followed governmental changes in Paris), Commerson reluctantly saw the necessity of returning there. When Baret and Commerson finally presented themselves at the door of Mon Plaisir in February 1772, they were greeted with a roomful of packed boxes—their specimens and personal effects already stowed away and waiting simply for a new home.

For a gentleman such as Commerson to rent rooms in a city of transients like Port Louis was not, on the face of it, difficult. But Baret and Commerson presented a troubling spectacle to prospective landlords. In addition to approximately five hundred specimens from Madagascar, they had roughly twice as many from Mauritius. Dried plants were the least troublesome, since they were not a source of odor as long as they had been properly preserved. Live insects, animal pelts, and dried fish were, however, likely to reveal themselves by sound or smell. Then there were the packing cases full of specimens from the circumnavigation. A wooden crate was not, in itself, an especially threatening item for a landlord to contemplate. But Commerson had between twenty and thirty such boxes, and the upheaval of taking in all these—in addition to his inappropriately dressed female companion—was more than any landlord was willing to accept.

After days of unsuccessfully looking for accommodations to rent, Commerson counted up his remaining money and purchased a house on the rue des Pamplemousses in Port Louis. Though this could be interpreted as the act of a man resigned to living out his days within walking distance of Pamplemousses—having failed to find any commercially useful crops on the circumnavigation—Commerson never lacked self-confidence and had a history of doing what suited him in the present rather than thinking about future consequences. It is therefore likely that he saw the house as a temporary expedient, while he waited for family and friends to facilitate his passage home.

The eighteenth-century houses of the town are long gone, having been replaced by businesses, hotels, and restaurants. (Even the substantial stone residence of Mon Plaisir has been supplanted by a newer building.) A description of the type of home Baret and Commerson moved into survives, however, in Bernardin de Saint-Pierre's account of his first visit to Port Louis in 1768. Away from the airy colonial mansions of the planters, Port Louis resembled nothing so much as the first British and French settlements in North America: "The town or Camp, consists of wooden houses of one storey high; each house stands by itself and is inclosed in pallisades. The streets are regular enough, but are neither paved nor planted with trees. The ground is every where so covered, and as it were staked with rocks, that there is no stirring without danger of breaking one's neck." Residents of Port Louis clearly took their homes' security seriously, presumably because the town played host to an ever-changing cast of sailors frequenting the taverns, as well as migrant workers from all over the region.

The pallisaded houses may not have looked attractive, lining the stony shadeless streets, but for the first time since Paris, Baret and Commerson lived together in a place they could organize and furnish as they wished. With the specimen crates stacked high on top of each other and pushed up against the walls to maximize floor space, the effect must have unintentionally recalled the great cabin of the *Étoile*. And as in Paris and on the *Étoile*, Baret found herself responsible for the day-to-day maintenance of their rooms and the collection, which had grown to approximately six thousand specimens all told.

The couple remained in the house on the rue des Pamplemousses from February 1772 to February 1773. Though Commerson was as interested as ever in botanizing and making observations of Mauritian wildlife, Baret noted that as their first year in the house wore on Commerson spent increasing amounts of time writing to friends and naval ministers back in France. These letters were depressingly monotonous: begging and cajoling for money, complaining about perceived slights, detailing Commerson's worries about his own health. Any funds that might have returned Baret and Commerson to France had apparently been swallowed by the purchase of the house. Since Baret and Commerson had no income, only expenses, even the usually impractical Commerson could see their position was not sustainable. Baret was not only Commerson's housekeeper and coworker but also his caregiver, and as the year wore on he needed more and more attention. In October 1772 he wrote to his friend Lalande:

I have scarcely strength to write to you . . . after an attack of rheumatism, which has confined me to my bed for some three months. I was looking forward to convalescence when I was overtaken by an unconquerable dysentery, from which I still suffer, and which has brought me to death's door . . . If the air of our country and a diet of rice and fish do not carry me through, you will be able, as you have more than once promised, to set to work on the history of my martyrology.

The physical strength and reserves of stamina that had kept Baret going on the frozen sides of the Strait of Magellan and in the aftermath of her rape were now devoted to the care of a bedridden forty-five-year-old man weakened and irritable from dysentery that became more debilitating the longer it persisted. Commerson now became convinced that a change of air would lift him, emotionally and physically. For his projected convalescence, he chose the home of their old friend, the plantation owner and doctor M. Bézac.

To leave Port Louis for Flacq was to exchange barren streets for lush countryside, stands of orange trees, and fields of rice. Given the connection between Baret, Commerson, and Bézac, the planter accepted them into his house without hesitation in the last days of February 1773.

On March 14, 1773, Bézac wrote to M. Bompard, the comptroller at Port Louis, to notify him of Commerson's death the previous night: "He suffered from an abscess which had been forming in his chest, and burst six days ago. He did not wish anyone to attend him." On the day of Bézac's letter, Philibert Commerson was buried in the cemetery at Flacq, although no paperwork or identifying marker has yet been found that locates the precise place of his grave. (Given the provision in his will that his body was to be disposed of without ceremony, this is not surprising.)

Baret had lost the man who for a decade could have been variously described as her pupil, teacher, coworker, friend, lover. She had shared a tiny ship's cabin with him for two years and tended him when he was sick, as he had tended her after her rape. She had borne him a son. And she had given him knowledge: a notebook full of herb women's secrets, expertise that she placed at his disposal in Toulon-sur-Arroux and throughout their travels together. At the age of thirty-two Baret was now alone, on a French territory in the Indian Ocean, with no obvious means of getting home—indeed, with no real home at all.

When she finally bid farewell to Bézac, certain that she would never see him or her son again, she returned to the simple house in Port Louis, presumably intending to take stock in every sense of the word. The collection she had been so instrumental in building needed to be provided for: its approximately six thousand specimens included every stage and state of plant life (leaves, flowers, and seeds), shells and rock samples, dried fish, preserved insects, dead birds, the skins of mammals, and man-made items such as the tapa cloth from Tahiti. Together these things formed a record of the circumnavigation and represented seven years of Baret's life. Yet as Baret neared the house in the rue des Pamplemousses, she was in for an unforeseen and unpleasant development. Just as Poivre had been succeeded by Maillard Dumesle, so Poivre's nemesis Daniel Dumas had ultimately been replaced as governor and chief military commander by the officious M. de Ternay. The new men sent to administer French rule in Mauritius were loyal drones of the government intent on curbing costs and implementing a strict rule; legislative freedoms, and personal ones, were regarded with suspicion.

Under this severe new regime, Baret and Commerson's house— and everything in it—had been impounded, not because the new governor knew there was anything of value in the property, but because its contents had been amassed when Commerson was on the government payroll. Reasoning therefore that the French government owned Commerson's entire collection, the governor ordered that it was to be returned to Paris on the first suitable ship. Without the legal status that she would have enjoyed had she been Commerson's widow, Baret could not gain access through her own front door. In the eyes of the law she was a servant—and a very singular servant at that. The men who were eyeing the specimen crates for removal were not about to allow a woman into the house to ransack drawers and claim property. Baret now had nothing but the clothes she wore and the knowledge she carried.

Nine

 *"A MONUMENT MORE DURABLE THAN A PYRAMID"*

Journey's End

THE TRAUMA OF losing everything was surely compounded by the sheer frustration of knowing that Commerson's will would have alleviated all of her material distress:

> To Jeanne Baret, also known as Jeanne de Bonnefoy, my housekeeper, I leave monies to the total of six hundred livres to be paid in a single lump sum . . . I desire that all the furniture be handed over to Jeanne Baret and that there not be any difficulties made, even if she chooses to stay in the apartment for one year after news of my death, which

residence may provide time to organize the natural history specimens that are to be sent to the Royal Collection [Cabinet des estampes] as is detailed above.

But Baret would find it difficult to arrange her return to France without access to the monies remaining from Commerson's estate back home. The situation appeared impossible, yet it had to be overcome. Somehow, Baret had to find either a way of earning enough money to buy passage on a ship bound for France or another way of making the journey. And the will set a clock ticking, since it gave Baret free access to the Paris apartment "for one year after news of my death."

Many individuals placed in Baret's position would have told themselves the difficulties they faced were insurmountable and given in to despair. The docks of Port Louis were undoubtedly full of women who, like Baret, owned little or nothing. But Bougainville had spared Baret from a fate of prostitution in Rio de Janeiro, and Baret was not about to succumb to it herself. (Vivès insinuated more than once that Baret gave herself to members of the expedition, but we should remember that this was an age in which any woman who defied men's strict expectations for her sex was liable to such a charge. For example, actresses and female writers were typically assumed to be prostituting themselves with their patrons, for how could a woman support herself with any other sort of work? There is no evidence that Baret prostituted herself, either on the *Étoile* or in Port Louis following Commerson's death.) She could have returned to Flacq, to the home of M. Bézac, who would certainly have helped her find some work as a household servant. But Baret had left her son in Flacq precisely because the memories evoked by his presence were too painful, and besides, to return to Flacq and take employment there would be to accept defeat. Baret was determined to stay in Port Louis and obtain passage back to France.

In all likelihood, she was homeless for a period of weeks. The climate of Mauritius did not make this a hardship, although the ants did. (Ber-

nardin de Saint-Pierre complained that any outdoor activity was spoiled
by swarming armies of them, reflecting the fact that human activity on
Mauritius had already upset the natural ecosystem by eradicating native
species—most famously the dodo—and introducing invasive alien flora
and fauna, including nonnative ant species.) With her background as an
herb woman, her years of botanizing with Commerson, and her recent
experience of housekeeping in Port Louis, Baret was able to scrape a
living of sorts—begging scraps from stallholders she knew in town and
picking greens from the surrounding countryside. But this was no way
to generate enough savings to get home.

Her best prospect was to become a barmaid: A tavern owner would
only have to give Baret a trial to see that she was more than equal to
the task of handling the port's diverse population. After all, a woman
who had survived two years at sea with over three hundred men was
unlikely to blanch at the language or behaviors encountered in the port's
roughest watering holes. Even though sailors might have brought back
bad memories of her trauma, they were everywhere, and Baret was certainly selling alcohol in December 1773 when Mauritian records show
that she was fined for making sales on the Sabbath, though the name and
location of the tavern where she worked are not recorded.

Many of the rootless men drinking in Port Louis were French
refugees from India, unwilling to accept the ascension of British rule
there after the Seven Years' War. Bernardin de Saint-Pierre describes
the human flotsam of the docks as a plague upon Mauritius: "The late
war in India, inundated upon the Île de France the scum of Europe and
Asia; bankrupts, ruined libertines, thieves, and wretches of every kind."
The ever-changing Franco-Mauritian population also included soldiers
in transit from one French colony to another, or on their way back to
France after completing their contracted terms of service. In 1774, soldiers of the Royal Comtois regiment (named for Franche-Comté in the
east of France) passed through Mauritius on their way back to France,
and one of them, Jean Dubernat, was intrigued by Baret. Dubernat ap-

pears to have been a regimental sergeant who, like Baret herself, was from a quiet part of France (Saint-Aulaye in the Dordogne), where few of the inhabitants had ever ventured far from home. Before he became a soldier, he appears to have been a blacksmith, a skill he could continue to practice on his return to France. From their probable introduction in one of the port's taverns, they soon took their relationship beyond the squalid environs of the dockside. Little more is known about Dubernat, except this: On May 17, 1774, Baret and Dubernat were married, and the union was recorded in the parish register of Port Louis.

Setting aside the convoluted syntax of the clergyman who married them, the peculiar spelling of Baret's name should be noted:

> On 17 May 1774, the banns of marriage having been published, and an engagement having existed between Jean Dubernat, resident, son of the late Pierre Dubernat and of the late Anne Peno, his father and mother, from the parish of St Anthony in the town of St Foy, diocese of Périgord, being the party of the first part, and of Jeanne Barret, daughter of the late Jean Barret and of the late Jeanne Pochard, her father and mother, from the parish of La Comelle, diocese of Autun in Burgundy, being the party of the second part, and both of the parties being of this parish, and having found no impediment, I, the undersigned, have married them.

The name "Barret" is given in respect of Jeanne, and again of her father. Yet just as a reader might be attributing an error of transcription to the loquacious churchman who signs himself "Prefect Apostolic," the form "Barret" occurs a third time, in the bride's own signature. The register of Port Louis marks the first official paperwork that Baret had signed since the certificate of pregnancy in Digoin in 1764. In other words, Baret's marriage to Dubernat produced the first record of her signature that can be found after her rape. Given that the child resulting from the rape had been given the surname Bonnefoy, it is not incredible to suppose that Baret wished to draw a line under her former life and to adopt another name—another identity—after her rape. To be sure, the change from Baret to Barret is subtle, almost inconsequential, but the key to the change might lie in this very subtlety.

On Mauritius, Baret was no longer the same woman who had set out so full of optimism on her circumnavigation of the globe. From the grotesque rituals of Crossing the Line to her gang rape on New Ireland, Baret's faith in Commerson's promises for the voyage—indeed, her faith in human nature—had been progressively eroded. And if Baret had originally hoped that the circumnavigation might bring her closer to Commerson, perhaps even to becoming Madame Commerson, then that hope was gone too, buried even before Commerson's body was laid in the dust of Flacq. Still at heart the herb woman from La Comelle, yet profoundly changed by her experiences, Baret remade herself once more in her marriage to Dubernat.

Her new husband's army rank allowed him to claim passage on any French ship returning home with room or need for him. In Europe's early modern navies, shipboard discipline was ultimately guaranteed by the presence of a corps of marines or other military personnel reporting directly to the ship's commander. (A flogging with the cat-o'-nine-tails might have some effect on individuals, but only armed marines could prevent full-scale mutiny.) Men like Dubernat—sober, professional soldiers who wanted to work their passage back to France—were a godsend to nervous captains who feared that trouble was fomenting belowdecks. A captain who had lost members of his marine corps to scurvy or another illness at sea had to seek out trustworthy men in ports of call to replenish his depleted forces. French royal ordinances still forbade women on board navy ships, but if Dubernat could find a captain desperate enough to fill his ship's security detail, then a little creativity in the purser's register would allow M. and Mme Dubernat to secure their return.

Baret would, of course, be too late to claim residence of the Paris apartment, since Commerson had died in March 1773 and she married

Dubernat in May 1774, after which the newly married couple had to find a westward-heading French vessel in need of Dubernat's manpower. The journey back to France via the Cape of Good Hope and the South Atlantic coast of Africa would take a further three to four months, depending on the duration of any stay at the cape and in the Azores—the usual ports of call for European ships navigating the Atlantic south to north. But once back in France, Baret would at least be able to pursue a claim to monies owing from Commerson's estate, for the man who had been reduced to fretting about money in Mauritius had died in possession of the country property his father had bought so long ago, to secure the right to sign himself "de Commerson."

It is easy to be cynical about Baret's marriage to Dubernat and to suppose that she only married him to gain passage back to France. Perhaps Baret and Dubernat entered into their marriage purely as a business arrangement (with Baret asking Dubernat to get her home to France, where she would be able to pay him for his trouble). If so, they were no different from tens of thousands of their wealthier contemporaries, for whom marriages of convenience—to secure inheritances and join estates—were the norm. For the year between Commerson's death and her marriage to Dubernat, Baret's goal was to find a way of getting herself off Mauritius: her marriage to Dubernat achieved that.

And even if theirs was initially a marriage of convenience, it was a marriage that they made work: Baret would spend the rest of her life with Dubernat in his hometown of Saint-Aulaye in the Dordogne. After all Baret had been through, it is impossible to imagine her settling down in Saint-Aulaye against her will. She could have paid Dubernat off and gone her own way, although they would have remained legally married, it being practically impossible for ordinary people to obtain divorces. But Baret chose to remain with Dubernat in Saint-Aulaye. He may have lacked Commerson's education and status, but he probably also lacked Commerson's selfishness and preoccupation with work. Because Baret

and Dubernat did not condemn each other, but finally made a life together, it would be harsh for us to condemn her choice.

When Bougainville's expedition was sighted off Saint-Malo on March
15, 1769, the port's officials readied a reception for the brave officers and
men who had completed the first French circumnavigation of the world.
When Baret stepped ashore from her unknown vessel at some point in
late 1774 or early 1775, she became the first woman to have circumnavi-
gated the globe. Yet there was no welcome committee, because no one
other than Baret (and perhaps Dubernat) understood what she had done,
nor even that she had returned. Like anyone who completes a significant
task at great sacrifice of time and self, only to find others insensible to
the nature of the achievement, Baret must have experienced a peculiar
mixture of elation and disappointment upon reaching France. She was
home, but she was the only person alive who understood what it had cost
her to be able to say that. And she still had to stake her claim to all that
Commerson intended for her in his will.

Commerson's will had been made known to a handful of his close
friends in Paris. Baret had failed to come forward in the year after Commerson's death to sort through the collections in the apartment on the rue
des Boulangers, but Commerson's friends had nevertheless hesitated to
turn all monies and effects over to his brother-in-law, whose requests were
growing more and more insistent. Still in Toulon-sur-Arroux, and still
bearing all the costs of looking after Commerson's son, Father François
Beau complained bitterly that Commerson had borrowed against his
dead wife's property and interests, which were intended to be reserved
for her son. Now the thirteen-year-old found himself at the center of a
bitter legal dispute. Beau wrote to the minister of marine requesting that

the French state fund an annuity for Archambaud Commerson, whose father had died in the service of France, but like Commerson's friends, the relevant government ministers did not accept Beau's self-portrait of a disinterested priest forced into penury as he cared for his nephew. The government's position was that Commerson's death had occurred not in the service of France, but while he pursued his private interests on Mauritius. As for financial arrangements made within the Beau family, these were also a private matter.

There was, however, one legal issue concerning Commerson's estate that the French government could resolve quickly and to the satisfaction of a different claimant. For in addition to Father Beau's letters, the ministry had also received a written request from a Madame Dubernat, formerly Jeanne Baret, claiming her due under the terms of Commerson's will. Demonstrating a sure grasp of her rights under the law, Baret requested both her back wages and all proceeds generated by the sale of household effects from the rue des Boulangers apartment. Government legal advisers agreed that these were costs that could—and should—be met by Philibert Commerson's estate. And so, in April 1776, the thirty-five-year-old Baret received just over six hundred livres owed to her.

If anyone should still be puzzled by the attraction that Commerson had held for Baret, it is worth pausing on the fact that after a decade in his company, and despite all that had happened to her, Baret had become a supremely self-possessed, confident, articulate woman. From their first meeting, Commerson had not condescended to the young herb woman because he was not too embarrassed to learn from her. And as he learned from her, he also taught her—not just about botany but about anything and everything else that she cared to know. While Baret came from a background where no one dared to defy authority because they had neither the education nor the social status to do so, Commerson had never bowed to others' prohibitions and always felt certain of his rights. That Baret could claim her share of the money from Commerson's estate shows that life with Commerson gave her the confidence to know that she was capable of anything.

And what could Baret do with six hundred livres in France in 1776? A typical eighteenth-century domestic servant might earn a wage of eighty livres per annum, plus bed and board. Baret therefore came into possession of a lump sum that was over six times the average yearly wage for a servant. Neither a princely fortune nor a trivial sum, it allowed the purchase of a comfortable house and some land in Saint-Aulaye, with a little money to spare. And it was not to be Baret's only source of income. A document in the naval archives reprises the outline of Baret's story and indicates that she had powerful interests on her side within the Ministry of Marine.

Jeanne Baret, employing a disguise, undertook the circumnavigation of the globe on one of the ships commanded by M. de Bougainville. Using her time to help M. de Commerson, doctor and botanist, she shared all the work and danger that the philosophe exposed himself to, showing great bravery. That her behavior was exemplary is acknowledged by M. de Bougainville. When M. de Commerson died, this person, whose sex was known, married one Dubernat, lately a non-commissioned officer in the Royal Comtois Regiment. Now Mme Dubernat and her husband, having reached that time in life that brings infirmity with it, are not able to earn their daily bread. The Minister has therefore graciously bestowed upon this extraordinary woman a pension of 200 livres per annum, to be paid from the fund for invalid servicemen. This pension shall be payable from 1 January 1785.

Nine years after receiving the monies willed to her by Commerson, Baret and Dubernat were being described as unable to work for a living, though Baret was still only forty-five (and Dubernat presumably a similar age). Perhaps the individual or individuals who lobbied the minister on Baret's behalf aimed for a picture of maximum sentimental impact in describing the aging, faithful servant unable to work any longer. Or perhaps Baret was subject to the bodily aches and pains that might be expected in someone who had endured all that she had. Whatever the truth of Baret's physical condition, the pension was forthcoming, and in the exact sum that had previously been determined a suitable government stipend for a man of science. Baret may therefore be the first woman ever to be recognized by a state for her contribution to the furtherance of knowledge.

Equally interesting is the question of who lobbied the minister of marine on Baret's behalf?

The obvious candidate is Bougainville. (Though the order is signed by an M. Malézieu on behalf of his superiors at the Ministry of Marine, neither he nor they had any personal connection to Baret.) Bougainville's memoir had mentioned her, but no one ever sought Baret out; he could only have learned of her married name, place of residence, and physical and financial circumstances if she had written directly to him to announce her whereabouts. It is not improbable that she would do so, her confidence further bolstered by having successfully claimed the money from Commerson's estate. If Baret found herself in need upon her return to France, then Bougainville would be an obvious person to enlist in her aid, especially as they shared the knowledge of all that had really happened on the voyage.

One of only two members of the expedition to outlive Baret (the other being Vivès), Bougainville was in robust good health during the period 1776–86, when the majority of officers and gentlemen whom Baret had known on the *Étoile* and the *Boudeuse* succumbed to illness and died. Bougainville had also prospered; the expedition had delighted the king (though critics grumbled that there was little tangible to show for all the time and expense), and he had granted Bougainville an annual pension of fifty thousand livres starting in November 1769. With his finances and status as a national hero secured, Bougainville published his memoir in

1771 to great acclaim. No contemporary reviewer of *Voyage autour du monde par la frégate du Roi la* Boudeuse *et la flûte l'* Étoile *en 1766, 1767, 1768 et 1769* mentioned Baret's Tahitian episode; no one asked to hear more about the woman whose story had merited only a single paragraph in Bougainville's journal. And no one asked what had become of Baret.

Of course, Bougainville's account of the expedition was reviewed only by men, in magazines and newspapers that envisaged their readership as primarily male. Bougainville himself had insisted that Baret's example would not prove contagious, for the difficulties and privations she encountered were too great for the average woman to contemplate. Not until the French Revolution of 1789 would a mass of ordinary Frenchwomen force a recognition of their collective determination and power, when the stallholders of Les Halles marched on Versailles and forced a terrified royal family back to Paris. In 1771, the power of working-class Frenchwomen that would be demonstrated in the Revolution was inconceivable, as was the idea that women could make any real contribution to science.

Baret's contribution was not, of course, an invention or formulation of a theory. She collected plants under Commerson's direction and certainly discovered many of those she collected. The annals of science are full of fieldworkers and laboratory technicians whose only recognition has come from their immediate contemporaries, when it has come at all. Should Baret be singled out only because she was the first woman to circumnavigate the globe?

We live in an age that celebrates firsts: when women rise to hold premierships or cabinet positions previously closed to their sex; when nonwhite faces stand to represent their country in positions previously closed to their race; when those who are physically impaired compete and succeed in challenges previously the preserve of the able-bodied. We celebrate underdogs who overcome the mountainous hurdles of poverty and discrimination to make themselves heard. And we do so because such achievements remind us that the seemingly impossible is sometimes achievable. Had Baret been typical of her demographic—a woman born to day laborers in the Loire in the mid-eighteenth century—she would have died in her twenties after a life of crippling poverty, in which her physical and mental horizons would have extended no further than the nearest market town. But instead she lived to circle the globe, botanizing on the sides of the Strait of Magellan, traversing the Pacific, climbing on the slopes of an island volcano, and trekking through the rain forest of Madagascar, before finally finding a way back to France. Hers is, by any measure, a remarkable life.

Just as Baret lived in obscurity on her return to France, the collection she had helped to build sat hidden in boxes in government stores. She never saw it again, neither the part that returned to France with the *Étoile*, nor the remainder that was impounded in Mauritius on Commerson's death. Over six thousand items that Commerson had hoped she would catalog therefore remained unused and unknown to researchers, even though the expedition had been undertaken as much for scientific discovery as for territorial gain.

By a quirk of fate, however, the chaotic state of the collection may have helped its preservation. When the Revolution entered its bloodiest phase in June 1793—that twelve-month period of mass guillotinings and acts of atrocity known as "the Terror"—even leading revolutionaries were shocked at the mob's iconoclastic rampages against anything smacking of elitism. (An August 1793 decree of the revolutionary Convention that sanctioned the ransacking of the royal tombs in St. Denis prompted the Abbé Grégoire to coin the word "vandalism" to describe his fellow citizens' indiscriminate rage at anything beyond their comprehension.) Anything that had obviously been valued by the aristocracy and ruling elite was a potential target. But because no one had organized it to make sense of it for others, Baret and Commerson's collection was not on display, and it was never in danger from the iconoclasts.

With movements afoot to burn libraries and raze museums to the ground, Grégoire pressed the Committee of Public Instruction to think of promoting a Bibliothèque nationale and a Muséum national d'histoire naturelle, which all French citizens would have access to and from which all might learn. Knowledge was deemed to be the right of the citizen rather than the preserve of the gentleman, and subjects such as botany and zoology were once more promoted as they had been before the Revolution: sciences whose mastery could generate national wealth and prestige and improve the public well-being. In a move that would have surely delighted Commerson, the new Muséum national d'histoire naturelle was built on the grounds of the former Jardin du Roi, which was renamed the Jardin des Plantes with prosaic revolutionary fervor.

Today the elements of Baret and Commerson's collection are incorporated into the museum's vast archives, the dried plants nestling with others in forty-two thousand metal drawers split between three galleries that together constitute the French national herbarium. As research institutions across the planet contribute to international projects to collect, store, and preserve the diversity of earth's plant life in seed banks (which could be used in future to develop disease-resistant strains of crops or to reintroduce disappearing vegetation), the value of such resources cannot be overestimated. Baret and Commerson also contributed specimens to the departments of conchology, entomology, and mineralogy, enriching this vast database of knowledge about the earth that, like all databases, is better and more useful for being as complete as possible.

There is no record that Baret ever returned to Paris to see even the exterior of the new natural history museum that crowned the botanic gardens. Following the success of her legal suit in 1776 and her receipt of a government pension in 1785, she was swallowed by rural life in Saint-Aulaye. Any traveling she did must have been in her imagination, though there were undoubtedly places that she did not wish to revisit, even only in her thoughts. Jeanne Baret died in Saint-Aulaye on August 5, 1807, at the age of sixty-seven, her death certificate bringing an end to her most remarkable paper trail. There is no elaborate monument to mark her final resting place in the cemetery of Saint-Aulaye, but Bernardin de Saint-Pierre's observations regarding botanizing on Mauritius may offer a fitting tribute: "Most of the plants, trees and animals I am about to describe, have been brought here by order of government. Some of the inhabitants have contributed their endeavours for this purpose . . . the gift, or introducing of a useful plant being, in my opinion, of more consequence than the discovery of a gold mine, and a monument more durable than a pyramid."

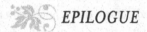

EPILOGUE

What Happened Next

THOUGH THE FIRST French circumnavigation of the world failed in its twin objectives of claiming significant new lands for France and with them commercially important natural resources, its commander, having achieved what no Frenchman had previously done, was hailed as a national hero. After the success of his published *Voyage autour du monde*, Louis-Antoine de Bougainville enjoyed a distinguished career, commanding French naval forces fighting on the side of the Americans in the War of Independence. Military obligations during the Revolutionary War did not prevent him from finding time to court a wife, and his marriage of January 1781 would produce four sons, the eldest of whom would also be a Pacific explorer. His national-hero status was not enough to shield the well-connected Bougainville from the suspicions of French revolutionaries, however, and he was briefly imprisoned in 1794, at the height of the Terror, but escaped execution. In the power vacuum left by the deaths of all the leading revolutionaries, he again rose to prominence, becoming one of the architects of Napoleon's Egyptian Campaign (1798–1801). When French naval forces were routed at the Battle of Trafalgar (1805), Bougainville presided over the official inquiry. He died in 1811, just three months before his eighty-second birthday.

The circumnavigation was a commercial failure but an ideological success, in that it inspired successive French administrations to underwrite other voyages of exploration, in hopes of finding more hidden gems such as Tahiti, which had captured the imagination of both the French and British reading public. Bougainville helped plan the expeditions of some who hoped to sail in his wake, including the ill-fated circumnavigation of Jean-François de Galaup, comte de La Pérouse, whose ships, the *Astrolabe* and the *Boussole*, left France in 1785, never to return. When Louis XVI faced the guillotine in 1793, he famously asked if there was any news of M. La Pérouse. There was none then, but since the wreck of La Pérouse's flagship, the *Boussole*, was discovered on a reef on the South Pacific island of Vanikoro in 1964, it has been the subject of ongoing marine archaeological efforts to recover and record as much as possible of this late-eighteenth-century French expedition. With every artifact recovered from the wreck site—and with a new appreciation of the truth of traditional Vanikoro stories about the white men who were once shipwrecked on the reef—the world of eighteenth-century exploration comes into sharper focus. Separated from Bougainville's expedition by only less than twenty years, La Pérouse's circumnavigation—and its deadly end—is a potent reminder of how much was risked by Baret and her companions. They suffered a variety of fates.

François Chenard de La Giraudais, whose missing captain's log from the *Étoile* has never been satisfactorily explained, went on to have a less glorious naval career than his commander. Unlike Bougainville, La Giraudais did not participate in French campaigns in the American War of Independence, preferring instead to use his seafaring experience in private service. In the six years after the *Étoile*'s return to France, he returned to Mauritius before heading for the island of Zanzibar, which is twenty miles off the coast of what is now Tanzania. In the 1770s, Zanzibar was one of the major East African hubs of the slave trade, and approximately fifty thousand slaves a year are thought to have passed through the island's port. Zanzibar was not a place where abolitionists campaigned against the evils of the slave trade, nor was it a place where Europeans chose to live unless their business was based there. The inescapable conclusion is that La Giraudais captained slave ships for private clients or oversaw the port business of slaving ships. He died in Zanzibar in 1775 at age forty-eight.

Pierre-Antoine Véron, who left the expedition, along with Baret and Commerson, on Mauritius, quit Poivre's residence with the intention of traveling to India to make astronomical observations there. But the expedition had taken its toll on him. Perhaps in an attempt to refresh himself physically and mentally, he did not take a direct passage from Mauritius to India and ended up on the island of Timor. Ravaged by fever, he died there in 1770. He was thirty-four.

Charles-Nicolas Othon, Prince of Nassau-Siegen, proved as flamboyant in his life following the expedition as he did before and during it. Delighted by his experience at sea, he maneuvered for a senior naval position on his return. Even in ancien régime France, this was greeted with a chorus of opposition from career officers, and Nassau-Siegen directed his energies to French involvement in the War of Independence. After the conclusion of the war, he pursued the lifestyle that had caused his family to encourage his participation in Bougainville's expedition. His debts began to seem insurmountable, until he charmed a Polish noblewoman, Charlotte Gorzska, the Princess Sanguszko, into marriage. Engaged in what would today be termed "shuttle diplomacy" between various European courts, he attracted the favorable attention of the Russian empress, Catherine the Great, who made him an admiral of her Black Sea Fleet. He finally retired to an estate in Nemirovo, in present-day Belarus, where he is buried.

François Vivès, surgeon of the *Étoile*, continued to work for the French navy until 1782, and saw action in some of the most significant naval conflicts of the period. In December 1782, he was forced to leave ship in Boston, self-diagnosed with scurvy and suffering intermittent deafness, probably as a result of repeated exposure to the sound of cannon firing in battle. By 1786, he had returned to France and applied for retirement on account of his ill health. Refusing his request—and payment of the pension that would have come with his retirement—the government sent him to Rochefort, where he oversaw the convict hospital, a post as far from a comfortable country practice as he had ever been. When Vivès was finally permitted to retire in 1811, he opted to stay in Rochefort, having made his life there. He married twice, and both of his wives came from naval families. Despite the ill health that had once led him to seek early retirement, he was eighty-four when he died in 1828.

Baret's home for two years, the storeship *Étoile*, served in the Caribbean in 1771, provisioning French interests on Martinique. After this, she is known to have sailed from the French port of Lorient in February 1773 for a four-year tour of duty in the Indian Ocean. Though the *Étoile* returned from this voyage, the name does not appear in naval lists after 1778—typically an indication that a ship was decommissioned and broken up for usable parts. Bougainville's frigate *Boudeuse* fared better. Refitted with her original weight and configuration of cannon, she saw service in the War of Independence and then in the Mediterranean. She was finally condemned in 1800 and, like the *Étoile* before her, broken apart.

The only non-European passenger on the ships' expedition, Aotourou, never saw his native Tahiti again. Like his fellow Tahitian Omai, who agreed to return to London with Captain James Cook, Aotourou found himself a temporary wonder as he made the social rounds in Paris. But French (and English) newspapers of the period found their readers more interested in salacious details of Polynesian men's sexual prowess than in learning about Tahitian customs and beliefs. From both Aotourou and Omai, Franco-British government ministers learned that Tahitians did not live in perfect peace with their island neighbors, and that local tribal rivalries might be exploited for European territorial and commercial gain.

After twelve months in Paris, during which he styled himself "Boutavery" (after Bougainville), Aotourou embarked for home on a voyage heading west to east. The ship transporting him called to repro-vision at Mauritius, where Bernardin de Saint-Pierre described seeing Aotourou in Port Louis proudly consulting one of his many presents—a pocket watch—and using it to think about the rhythms of a Parisian artistocrat's typical day, for "he was enchanted with the opera at Paris, and imitated the airs and dances he had heard and seen there." French navigator Marc-Joseph Marion du Fresne was supposed to take Aotourou back to Tahiti from Mauritius after completing business in the region. But Aotourou contracted smallpox and died in the Indian Ocean—possibly at Fort Dauphin, Madagascar, in November 1770. Whether he met Baret again as he passed through Port Louis is unknown.

In Port Louis, the botanical garden of Pamplemousses continued to flourish, despite changes in personnel. Renamed the Sir Seewoosagur Ramgoolam Botanical Garden in 1988 to honor the man who led Mau-ritius to independence, it is a popular tourist attraction on the island and proudly displays a range of exotica unknown in Baret's day. Many of its visitors hope to see one of the garden's most famous specimens in flower: *Victoria amazonica,* the giant water lily whose six-foot-wide leafy pads sit upon the surface of the lily pond and are capable of bearing human weight. Smiling benevolently down on this botanical giant, a bust of Pierre Poivre commemorates the man to whom the gardens owe so much.

Poivre's return to France in 1773 marked the end of his long experience of living outside its borders. He retired to a charming château, La Freta, in Saint-Romain-au-Mont-d'Or, near Lyon, where a third daughter soon joined two sisters who had never known what it was to live in France. A contemporary illustration of La Freta shows the beginnings of a formal garden—complete with water feature—that allowed Poivre to indulge the botanical interests that would immortalize his name. He died in 1786, at the age of sixty-six.

The decade in which the Poivre family returned to France marked an intellectual and political watershed for the country. In 1772, the last of twenty-eight volumes of Diderot and d'Alembert's monumental *Encyclopédie* rolled off the presses, heavy with the latest scientific knowledge. Its core group of contributors, the self-styled philosophes, had not missed an opportunity to challenge the authority of church and state, and in 1774 the state felt a political tremor when Louis XVI and his young queen, Marie-Antoinette, ascended the throne. Their coronation took place against a backdrop of riots over poor wheat harvests and the increasing price of bread. As the political order shifted, so did the intellectual one. Linnaeus, Rousseau, and Voltaire all died in 1778. Of all the men whose ideas had shaped Commerson's life, and to whom he had been especially close, only Buffon survived. From 1749 to 1804, the forty-four volumes of his *Histoire naturelle* complemented and completed the *Encyclopédie*'s redrawing of the natural world; the last nine volumes appearing posthumously after Buffon's death in 1788.

No matter how far the bounds of knowledge expanded in the late eighteenth century, and no matter how much individual countries changed politically and socially, one thing remained constant: Bougainville thought that Baret's example was unlikely to be "contagious"—that is, unlikely to prompt a wave of female imitators—and it is certainly true that the eighteenth and nineteenth centuries saw only a handful of women follow in Baret's footsteps. Occasionally, tales of an idiosyncratic woman traveler captured the reading public's imagination; for example, Lady Hester Stanhope (1776–1839) adopted Turkish male dress to ride into Damascus and the forbidden city of Palmyra. But Lady Stanhope did not attempt to deceive anyone that she was anything other than a woman who found it more practical to wear local male attire, and she was essentially a tourist rather than a woman pursuing professional goals.

There were female botanical *illustrators* before Baret and among her contemporaries, to be sure: The Dutchwoman Maria Sibylla Merian (1647–1717) lived in the South American slave colony of Suriname for two years during which she drew and colored some of the most visually striking botanical and entomological images ever produced, and the Englishwoman Mary Delany (1700–1788) never left Britain but worked in collage to produce over seventeen hundred "paper mosaicks" of plants so accurate that Sir Joseph Banks thought them the only botanical illustrations from which he could accurately identify species. These women's achievements are remarkable, but they are different both from Baret's and from each other's, making any claims for a "tradition" or a "movement" tenuous at best. Indeed, it would be just under a century after Baret's return to France before another woman is known to have come close to her experience of travel in pursuit of botany: The indefatigable Marianne North (1830–90) spent fifteen years crossing five continents to illustrate the world's flora, and her watercolors are now proudly displayed in a dedicated gallery at Kew Gardens.

But Merian, Delany, and North had one thing in common that Baret did not share: They were independently wealthy. And so the ending of Baret's story seems to provide the first—and so far, the last—example of an early-modern working-class woman who, refusing to be defined by her sex and her class, traveled the world in pursuit of what she loved.

AFTERWORD TO THE
PAPERBACK EDITION

One of the stories told in this book is that of the naming of places, animals, and plants by European explorers who wished to commemorate themselves and their countrymen in the cartographic and scientific record. Even though Jeanne Baret helped Commerson collect over 6,000 specimens, he proposed to name only one plant after her, the genus *Baretia*.

Many of the names that Commerson proposed were later published by notable botanists including Jussieu, Lamarck, and De Candolle, but *Baretia* was not included in these names. Instead, the three species that Commerson called *Baretia* were recognized by later botanists as belonging to the genus *Turraea:* a genus first published in 1771 (when Commerson and Baret were on the Île Bourbon). Baret therefore was left without anything in the natural world to commemorate her name. That is now to change.

Shortly after this book was first published, I was contacted by Eric Tepe of the Department of Biology at the University of Utah. Eric had discovered a new species of *Solanum* in southern Ecuador and northern Peru and he proposed naming it in honor of Jeanne Baret: *Solanum baretiae*.

Solanum is one of the largest genera of plants in the world, with an estimated 1,500 species, including the tomato, potato, and eggplant. It is therefore not only one of the largest genera, but also one of the most economically important. Its newest proposed species, *Solanum baretiae*, is a vine, trailing along the ground or climbing other vegetation to a height of ten feet or more. Its flower petals have been seen in shades of violet, yellow, or white. And, like the three plant species that Commerson originally grouped together in the genus *Baretia*, a single specimen of *Solanum baretiae* may exhibit highly variable leaves.

As this paperback edition of Jeanne Baret's story goes to press, Tepe and colleagues are submitting a scientific paper on *Solanum baretiae*, introducing this new species to the international community of plant biologists and seeking proper approval for the name to be entered in the taxonomic record. I would like to thank Eric Tepe for honoring Jeanne Baret in this way. And I would also like to thank his project collaborators: Lynn Bohs, Bobbi Angell, and Segundo Leiva. *Solanum baretiae* may be a relatively unassuming plant, but its name is the product of an extraordinary history.

NOTES AND REFERENCES

In many places in the text I preface a quotation by referring to the writer (typically Bougainville, Commerson, or Vivès) and the precise date of a particular journal entry. Where this information is readily apparent in the text, I have not duplicated it in the following notes. The notes clarify which books, journal articles, and Web sites will most readily allow the reader to verify information given in the preceding text.

❧ INTRODUCTION

The starkly factual "they have discovered that the servant of Mr. Commerson, the doctor, was a girl who until now has been taken for a boy" is taken from the journal kept jointly by Commerson and Pierre Duclos-Guyot. This entry, for July 18, 1768, was written by Duclos-Guyot. It is often quoted as a complement to Bougainville's account of Baret's unmasking on Tahiti. It is discussed in its proper chronological place in chapter 7. Bougainville's version of events on Tahiti is found in his journal entry for May 28–29, 1768. It is discussed in detail in chapter 6.

The journal keepers referred to are Louis-Antoine de Bougainville (sailing on the *Boudeuse*); Pierre Duclos-Guyot and Philibert Commerson (sharing a journal and both sailing on the *Étoile*); Charles-Nicolas Othon, Prince of Nassau-Siegen (paying gentleman passenger on the *Boudeuse*); François Vivès (surgeon of the *Étoile*); Jean-Louis Caro (first lieutenant of the *Étoile*); Charles-Pierre-Félix Fesche (volunteer, sailing on the *Boudeuse*); Joseph Hervel (pilot, joining the *Boudeuse* in Mauritius); and the chevalier Walsh. The authenticity of Walsh's sixteen-page notebook is debated among scholars of the expedition. It was first described and published in 1901. Bougainville scholar Étienne Taillemite has found no member of the French marine corps with the Anglophile surname "Walsh" in the period 1766–69.

Nassau-Siegen's experience of the expedition has been imaginatively re-created by Peter Brooks in the novel *World Elsewhere* (New York: Simon and Schuster, 1999).

Vivès speculates frequently on the reasons why Baret spent so much time shut in the *Étoile*'s great cabin—sometimes with Commerson, sometimes without him. His journals are the only source for the insistence of some modern writers that Baret prostituted herself on the expedition. The most recent example is the baffling assertion of Andy Martin that, following the expedition's landing on Tahiti, Baret was "required to perform sexual favors for the crew"; see "Bougainville, Tahiti, and the Duty of Desire," *Eighteenth-Century Studies* 41, no. 2 (Winter 2008): 214.

Aotourou's experience with Bougainville's French expedition has a parallel in the experience of his fellow Tahitian Omai (now properly referred to as Mai) with Captain James Cook's British expedition on the *Endeavour* (1768–71). This is discussed in *Cook and Omai: The Cult of the South Seas* (National Library of Australia in association with the Humanities Research Centre, the Australian National University, Canberra, 2001). Aotourou arrived in Paris in March 1769 and spent one year as the toast of high society. He intended to return to Tahiti and sailed with Marc-Joseph Marion du Fresne in March 1770, but died (probably of smallpox) in the Indian Ocean in November 1770.

Commerson has been the subject of dedicated biographies, though Baret's role in these biographies is tailored to the sensibilities of the age. For example, she becomes Mme Commerson in S. Pasfield Oliver's *The Life of Philibert Commerson* (London: John Murray, 1909).

Denis Diderot's *Supplément au voyage de Bougainville* has a complex publication history and two different versions exist. What is important for Baret's story is that Bougainville's account of Tahiti had such an impact on Diderot that he summarized Baret's story (as told by Bougainville) in the *Supplément*, where Aotourou is also made one of the speakers. For the relevant passage and discussion of the issues, see Diderot, *Contes et romans* (Paris: Gallimard, 2004), 552, 1098.

On the exclusion of women from taxonomic discussion, see Ann B. Shteir, *Cultivating Women, Cultivating Science: Flora's Daughters and Botany in England, 1760 to 1860* (Baltimore: Johns Hopkins, 1996). William Smellie's horror of women's involvement in taxonomy is discussed by Sam George in "Linnaeus in Letters and the Cultivation of the Female Mind: Botany in an English Dress," *British Journal for Eighteenth-Century Studies* 28, no. 1 (Spring 2005): 1–18.

Mary Wollstonecraft's views on the importance of women's botanical education may be found in *A Vindication of the Rights of Woman*, edited by Carol H. Poston (New York and London: Norton, 1975), 123.

The range of species bearing the name *commersonii* is most easily seen in the incomparable online database, the *Encyclopedia of Life* (www.eol.org). Aiming for an eventual completeness of which Enlightenment writers would be proud, the database may be searched by genera or species for any proper name.

Bougainville's judgment that Baret would be "the only one of her sex" to attempt a circumnavigation is given in his journal entry for May 28–29, 1768.

The circumscribed lives and expectations of the typical eighteenth-century French peasant are discussed by Colin Jones, *The Great Nation: France from Louis XV to Napoleon* (New York: Columbia University Press, 2002), 148–59.

⬥ CHAPTER ONE. "A LIST OF MEDICINAL PLANTS":
THE BOTANIST AND THE HERB WOMAN

Vauban's account of the conditions of the Loire peasantry is found in Pierre
Goubert, *The Ancien Régime: French Society 1600–1750*, translated by Steve
Cox (London: Weidenfeld and Nicolson, 1973), 118.

The underresearched history of herb women is outlined in Agnes Robertson
Arber, *Herbals: Their Origin and Evolution* (Cambridge: Cambridge Univer-
sity Press, 1912), 319. The development of European university botanical
gardens is discussed in Anna Pavord, *The Naming of Names: The Search for
Order in the World of Plants* (New York: Bloomsbury, 2005). On Joseph
Banks's payments to herb women, see Patrick O'Brian, *Joseph Banks: A Life*
(Boston: Godine, 1993), 25.

Lalande's tribute to Commerson, delivered in 1773, was printed in 1775 as
"Éloge de M. Commerson par M. de Lalande, de l'Académie royale des sciences," *Journal de physique* 5, no. 2: 99–120.

The jokes played by undergraduates on University of Montpellier professors
are described by James Livesey in "Botany and Provincial Enlightenment in
Montpellier: Antoine Banal Père and Fils 1750–1800," *History of Science* 43
(2005): 57–76. The tenure of Sauvages is examined by Elizabeth Ann Williams in *A Cultural History of Medical Vitalism in Enlightenment Montpellier* (Aldershot: Ashgate, 2003), 66–72.

Commerson's description of Antoinette is found in a letter dated October 25,
1758, to his friend Gérard, and is quoted in Paul Antoine Cap, *Philibert Commerson, naturaliste voyageur* (Paris: Victor Masson, 1861), 76.

Commerson's writings originally held at the Bibliothèque de Jussieu are all
found in the *Catalogue de la bibliothèque scientifique de M.M. de Jussieu* (Paris:
Henri Labitte, 1857). Baret's herb woman's notebook is item no. 3902 in the
Catalogue: "Tables des plantes medicamanteuses." The notebook is currently MS 884 among Commerson's papers at the Muséum national d'historie
naturelle.

Huguenot practices concerning marriage and baptism are discussed by Philip Benedict in *The Huguenot Population of France, 1600–1685: The Demographic Fate and Customs of a Religious Minority* (Philadelphia:American Philosophical Society, 1991).

Baret's certificate of pregnancy, signed by her in Digoin, is in the Archives départementales 3E 22802.

❧ CHAPTER TWO. "TO JEANNE BARET, ALSO KNOWN AS JEANNE DE BONNEFOY": A CHANGED IDENTITY IN PARIS

Diderot's determination that his *Encyclopédie* would act as a corrective to previous botanical misinformation is discussed in Philipp Blom, *Encyclopédie: The Triumph of Reason in an Unreasonable Age* (London: Fourth Estate, 2004), 91. Buffon's menagerie at Montbard is described by Jacques Roger in *Buffon*, translated by Sarah Lucille Bonnefoi (Ithaca, NY: Cornell University Press, 1997), 210. On the worldwide network of amateur gardeners managed from the Jardin du Roi, see Emma Spary, *Utopia's Garden: French Natural History from Old Regime to Revolution* (Chicago: University of Chicago Press, 2000), 58. On a modern-day equivalent of this, see Michael Pollan, *The Botany of Desire* (New York: Random House, 2002), 54.

Commerson's letter to Father Beau denying a marriage to Baret is quoted in Hélène Dussourd, *Jeanne Baret (1740–1816): Première femme autour du monde* (Moulins: Imprimerie Pottier, 1987), 23–25.

Commerson's belief that the circumnavigation would open all doors for him is expressed in a letter to his friend Jean Bernard, quoted in Cap, *Philibert Commerson*, 81.

Norah Vincent's account of breast binding to try to appear more masculine is in *Self-Made Man: One Woman's Journey into Manhood and Back Again* (New York: Viking Penguin, 2006): 12–13.

Commerson's will is kept at the Archives nationales, Minutier central, Et/LXXXIV/5434/Regnault.

✦ CHAPTER THREE. "A MASQUERADE—OF DEVILS":
   CROSSING THE LINE

All eyewitness accounts in this chapter are from the accounts of either Commerson or Vivès. Both men's manuscripts present their own set of challenges. Commerson began the voyage intending to keep a daily journal, but tired of this by the time the *Étoile* reached Montevideo, with only thirty-four pages written. Even though he had been unable to sustain his diary, he evidently still hoped to publish a significant work on his return to France, and five notebooks exist of his *Mémories*—intermittent reflections on anything that took his interest on the voyage, kept jointly with Pierre Duclos-Guyot. In addition to ordered entries, the five notebooks contain a variety of marginal jottings, amendments, and additions. All quotations from Commerson are from the *Mémories,* unless otherwise stated.

Vivès wrote two accounts of the voyage. The first is a fifty-two-page manuscript held by the Rochefort Société de géographie. It contains a much higher proportion of factual navigational data than his second manuscript: a notebook of just over sixty pages now found in the library of Versailles. An introduction to the notebook written by Vivès says that the publication of Bougainville's own journal has made any other account of the voyage worthless. This statement may explain why modern scholars have been united in their assumption that Vivès writes his journal long after the events described took place. But it would certainly be strange if Vivès had written a statement to the effect that Bougainville's publication made other accounts worthless—and then proceeded to "waste" his time by writing such an account. His acknowledgment of the popularity of Bougainville's account seems more like the last rueful addition made to the Versailles manuscript, rather than a statement written at the start of its composition.

✦ CHAPTER FOUR. "PLACING ME UNDER ARREST":
   THE BOUGAINVILLEA AND THE SOUTH ATLANTIC

Bougainville's words are quoted from *A Voyage Round the World. Performed by Order of His Most Christian Majesty, in the Years 1766, 1767, 1768, and 1769. By Lewis de Bougainville. Colonel of Foot, and Commander of the Expedition, in the Frigate* La Boudeuse, *and the Store-ship* L'Étoile, *trans-*

lated from the French by John Reinhold Forster (London: J. Nourse and T. Davies, 1772). Forster's spelling of names and place-names is sometimes eccentric (for example, "Straits of Magalhaens" for "Strait of Magellan") and has been standardized to be consistent throughout. Forster's footnotes and prefatory matter rarely miss the opportunity to indulge in anti-French and anti-Spanish sentiment. (As a German immigrant to England, Forster was clearly concerned to prove his Anglophile credentials.) In the essentials of his translation, however, he offers a faithful rendition of Bougainville's original. All quotations are from Forster's translation of Bougainville's *Voyage*, unless it is specifically stated that Bougainville's handwritten manuscript is being discussed.

Episodes from Bougainville's *Voyage* referred to in this chapter are, in order: discussion of the build of the *Boudeuse* and the weight of her cannon, 2–4; the introduction of Véron, 86; discussion of the abortive attempt to observe a solar eclipse, 86–87; the Jesuits' alleged manipulation of the Paraguay tea crop, 119–20; the damage earlier sustained to the *Étoile*, 90.

Charles Darwin's account of the richness of flora and fauna around Rio is taken from *The Voyage of the Beagle*, introduced by David Quammen (Washington, DC: National Geographic, 2004), 28. Darwin's account of marine phosphorescence around the Río de la Plata is on p. 143 of the same edition.

For the history of man's struggle to establish longitude at sea, and the eventual success of watchmaker John Harrison in solving the problem, see Dava Sobel, *Longitude* (London: Fourth Estate, 1996).

☙ CHAPTER FIVE. "HIS BEAST OF BURDEN": ON THE SHORES OF THE STRAIT OF MAGELLAN

John Keats is quoted from the sonnet "On First Looking into Chapman's Homer" (1816). The loss of over one thousand sailors across various attempted navigations of the strait is detailed by Michael A. Morris in *The Strait of Magellan* (Dordrecht: Martinus Nijhoff, 1988), 6.

The best account of Magellan's attempt to find the strait is Laurence Bergreen, *Over the Edge of the World: Magellan's Terrifying Circumnavigation of the Globe*

(New York: Harper Perennial, 2004), 118–80. Bergreen quotes Elizabethan adventurer Francis Pretty on the landscape of the strait, 181, and Charles Darwin on the density of vegetation, 185.

In Bougainville's *Voyage*, the following episodes occur: the exchange of French "trifles" for Patagonian animal skins, and the gathering of "simples," 140; reflections on the healthy appearance of the Patagonians, 142; "the botanists" and their findings, 145; the abrupt weather change on Elizabeth Island and the decision that Baret should cut turfs, 149; Bougainville reflects on Commerson's and the Prince of Nassau-Siegen's plant-collecting expeditions, 161; Véron's lack of success in making observations and the general condition of the weather, 160–61 and 171–72. Bougainville concludes his recollection of the passage through the Strait of Magellan, 197–98.

❧ CHAPTER SIX. "VENUS SHOWED HERSELF": TAHITI EXPOSED

In Bougainville's *Voyage*, the first sighting of Tahiti is on April 2, 1768, and begins on 211; for "Venus showed herself" and the frightened cook, see 218–19; for the discovery that Baret is a woman, 300–301.

Tahitian seafaring and trading culture is examined in Steven Hooper, *Pacific Encounters: Art and Divinity in Polynesia 1760–1860* (Honolulu: University of Hawaii Press, 2006). He explains Tahitians' beliefs in women's special powers to placate the gods on 37–38; the necessity for Europeans to trade for food on long Pacific voyages on 49–51; and the problems Europeans had in classifying and understanding objects from Pacific voyages on 67–69.

❧ CHAPTER SEVEN. "THE LOCATION OF HELL": BARET ON NEW IRELAND

Nassau-Siegen's journal, "Voyage de la frigate *La Boudeuse*, et de la flûte *L'Étoile*, au Paraguay et sur les Côtes de la Californie," exists in three different original copies. Two of the manuscripts are preserved at the Archives nationales in Paris; a third is held at the ministry of Affaires étrangères, Mémoires et documents de France. Scholars of the expedition refer to these as Nassau-Siegen's manuscripts A, C, and B, respectively. (And though both manuscripts A and C are held at the Archives nationales, they are not held in the same place within the archives.) The account of Baret on New Ireland is taken from manuscript A in the Archives nationales, held in the collection de la Maison du Roi, 0 569 7 No. 28.

CHAPTER EIGHT. "THE TRUE PROMISED LAND": MAKING A HOME ON MAURITIUS AND BOTANIZING ON MADAGASCAR

The history of the spice trade is explained in Charles Corn, *The Scents of Eden: A History of the Spice Trade* (New York: Kodansha, 1999). The lengths to which men went to obtain nutmeg is chronicled in Giles Milton, *Nathaniel's Nutmeg: How One Man's Courage Changed the Course of History* (London: Sceptre, 1999). Poivre's history can be found in Pierre Poivre, *Mémoires d'un botaniste et explorateur* (La Rochelle: La Découvrance, 2006). Matthew Flinders's travels are detailed in Miriam Estensen, *Matthew Flinders: The Life of Matthew Flinders* (Crows Nest, NSW: Allen and Unwin, 2002).

All quotes from Bernardin de Saint-Pierre are taken from the anonymously translated *A Voyage to the Isle of France, the Isle of Bourbon, and the Cape of Good Hope; with Observations and Reflections Upon Nature and Mankind. By J.H.B de Saint Pierre, author of "Studies of Nature"* (London: Cundee, Vernor, Hood, Cuthell and Walker, 1800). Bernardin de Saint-Pierre discusses the following: the fortified wooden houses of Port Louis, 61; unfamiliar Mauritian wildlife, 78 and 82; planters and "women of condition," 110; the use of slave labor bringing "wretchedness and misery," 119.

CHAPTER NINE. "A MONUMENT MORE DURABLE THAN A PYRAMID": JOURNEY'S END

Bernardin de Saint-Pierre provides descriptions of the following: the ant infestation, 79; "the scum of Europe and Asia" on Mauritius, 102; the usefulness of botany, 124.

Baret's marriage to Dubernat is recorded in the Archives of Port Louis, Mauritius, K.A. 61/D, f21: 75. The signed government order awarding her a pension is in the Archives of the Ministère de la marine, C7 17.

A NOTE ON TEXTS, TRANSLATIONS, NAVAL TIME, AND NAMES

The primary source materials for this book are the handwritten journals and published works of a group of eighteenth-century French naval officers and natural historians. Since Bougainville's expedition was the first French circumnavigation of the globe, and one of the great voyages of maritime history, the majority of the papers associated with the expedition have been transcribed and published—in their original French—by twentieth-century French and Francophile scholars. In 2002, Bougainville's journal was also made available to an English-language audience through the work of John Dunmore, a great New Zealand scholar of Pacific exploration. All manuscripts and standard published versions of them, and all translations, are listed in the bibliography.

But *The Discovery of Jeanne Baret* challenges existing histories of the circumnavigation. The basis for this is made clear in the notes and frequently involves close consideration of the original journals upon which modern scholars have based their published editions. Because I have gone back to original sources, key passages have been translated afresh for this book, saving a range of scholars from seeing their existing translations used to reconstruct an unfamiliar version of history, one that they might wish to dispute. There are two exceptions to this production and use of new translations. The eighteenth-century reading public's interest in Bougainville's expedition was so great that an English language translation of Bougainville's *Voyage Round the World* appeared in 1772, translated by John Reinhold Forster. In 1800, an anonymous English translation of Bernardin de Saint-Pierre's *Voyage to the Isle of France* was published in London. These two eighteenth-century translations have been checked against the originals for accuracy, and then happily used: Their cadences are effortlessly those of the period, saving the modern interpreter from the translator's perpetual dilemma of whether to prefer strict fidelity to the text or a freer rendering that seeks to capture the elusive "feel" of the original.

All of the naval journal keepers quoted write according to the naval convention whereby a day runs from noon to noon (rather than midnight to midnight). But since no part of the argument of this book hangs upon understanding the difference between nautical time and its shore-based counterpart, the dates given throughout are those used by the journal keepers themselves.

Finally, a word about names. Throughout the book, I have used English terms for the parts of a ship and English naval ranks to define ships' personnel, even though the ships and personnel concerned are French. I acknowledge that differences existed between the British and French navies in the eighteenth century, but these differences were essentially minor. Similarly, I have preferred forms of names—including personal names and place-names—that will allow an English reader and Internet user the speediest location of further information. The book contains only one exception to this rule: In the South Atlantic there is a group of islands known to the British as the Falkland Islands and to Spanish speakers the world over as the Malvinas. Baret knew them as the Îles Malouines, and this is how I have chosen to identify them.

SOURCES AND SELECT BIBLIOGRAPHY

This list is divided into two sections: manuscripts (and their location in the French archives) and published works. The latter contains published versions of journals written by members of the expedition, including eighteenth-century translations and adaptations of these journals, in addition to works consulted. Some books in the bibliography (for example, Darwin's *Voyage of the Beagle*) have been published in many different editions, some of which are regarded as more authoritative than others. Where multiple versions of a book are in circulation, I have listed the edition that I have used, which is the edition for which page references are given in the notes.

◆◈ MANUSCRIPTS

Archives nationales (Paris)

Archives départementales 3E 22802: Baret's certificate of pregnancy, signed by her in Digoin

Collection de la Maison du Roi, 0 569 7 No. 28: journal of Nassau-Siegen (manuscript A)

Marine 4JJ 142/17: journal of Bougainville

Marine 4JJ 1/5: journal of Caro

Marine C7 63: personnel file for La Giraudais

Minutier central Et/LXXXIV/5434/Regnault: Commerson's will

Bibliothèque centrale de la marine (Vincennes)

SH 216: notebooks of Bougainville

C7 17: government order awarding pension to Baret

Bibliothèque municipale de Versailles

Lebaudy In-4° 126: journal of Vivès (manuscript B)

Bibliothèque nationale (Paris)

Département des cartes et plans, Pf. 176, div. 7, p. 1D: Vue de la Nouvelle-Cythère découverte par M. de Bougainville commandant la frégate du Roy la *Boudeuse* et la flûte l'*Étoile* en 1786 (view of Tahiti with accompanying notes, assumed to be by Romainville)

Ministère des Affaires étrangères, A. diplomatiques (Paris)

Mémoires et documents de France, v. 2113: Journal of Nassau Siegen (manuscript B)

Muséum national d'histoire naturelle (Paris)

MS 200: notebooks and herbaria of the teenage Commerson

MS 301, 680, 884–93: notebooks and *Mémoires* of the adult Commerson; MS 884 is the "Tables des plantes medicamanteuses" here assigned to Baret for the first time

MS 1896–98: journal of Fesche

Société de géographie de Rochefort

Journal of Vivès (manuscript A)

PUBLISHED SOURCES

Alexander, Caroline. *The Bounty: The True Story of the Mutiny on the Bounty.* New York: Penguin, 2004.

Arber, Agnes Robertson. *Herbals: Their Origin and Evolution.* Cambridge: Cambridge University Press, 1912.

Benedict, Philip. *The Huguenot Population of France, 1600–1685: The Demographic Fate and Customs of a Religious Minority.* Philadelphia: American Philosophical Society, 1991.

Bergreen, Laurence. *Over the Edge of the World: Magellan's Terrifying Circumnavigation of the Globe.* New York: Harper Perennial, 2004.

Bernardin de Saint-Pierre, Jacques-Henri. *Voyage à l'Île de France: Un officier du roi à l'île Maurice 1768–1770.* Paris: La Découverte/Maspero, 1983.

————.*A Voyage to the Isle of France, the Isle of Bourbon, and the Cape of Good Hope; with Observations and Reflections Upon Nature and Mankind. By J.H.B de Saint Pierre, author of "Studies of Nature."* Translated from the French. London: Cundee, Vernor, Hood, Cuthell and Walker, 1800.

Blom, Philipp. *Encyclopédie: The Triumph of Reason in an Unreasonable Age.* London: Fourth Estate, 2004.

Bougainville, Louis-Antoine de. *Voyage autour du monde par la frégate du Roi la* Boudeuse *et la flûte l'*Étoile *en 1766, 1767, 1768 et 1769.* Paris: Saillant et Nyon, 1771.

————.*A Voyage Round the World. Performed by Order of His Most Christian Majesty, in the Years 1766, 1767, 1768, and 1769. By Lewis de Bougainville, Colonel of Foot, and Commander of the Expedition, in the Frigate La* Boudeuse, *and the Store-ship L'*Étoile. Translated from the French by John Reinhold Forster. London: J. Nourse and T. Davies, 1772.

Brooks, Peter. *World Elsewhere.* New York: Simon and Schuster, 1999.

Cap, Paul Antoine. *Philibert Commerson, naturaliste voyageur.* Paris: Victor Masson, 1861.

Cassid, Jill. "Inhuming Empire: Islands as Colonial Nurseries and Graves." In *The Global Eighteenth Century*, edited by Felicity A. Nussbaum, 279–95. Baltimore and London: Johns Hopkins, 2003.

Catalogue de la bibliothèque scientifique de M.M. de Jussieu. Paris: Henri Labitte, 1857.

Chadwick, Derek, and Joan Marsh, eds. *Ethnobotany and the Search for New Drugs*. Chichester: J. Wiley, 1994.

Colley, Linda. *Captives: Britain, Empire and the World 1600–1850*. London: Pimlico, 2003.

Cook and Omai: The Cult of the South Seas. Canberra: National Library of Australia in association with the Humanities Research Centre, the Australian National University, 2001.

Corn, Charles. *The Scents of Eden: A History of the Spice Trade*. New York: Kodansha, 1999.

Culpeper, Nicholas. *The English Physician Enlarged*. London: J. Barker, 1653.

Damrosch, Leo. *Jean-Jacques Rousseau: Restless Genius*. Boston and New York: Houghton Mifflin, 2005.

Darwin, Charles. *The Voyage of the Beagle*. Introduced by David Quammen. Washington, DC: National Geographic, 2004.

Daugeron, Bertrand. *Collections naturalistes entre science et empire (1763–1804)*. Paris: Muséum national d'histoire naturelle, 2009.

Diderot, Denis. "Supplément au Voyage de Bougainville." *Contes et romans*. Paris: Gallimard, 2004.

Duchet, Michèle. *Anthropologie et histoire au siècle des lumières: Buffon, Voltaire, Rousseau, Helvétius, Diderot*. Paris: A. Michel, 1971.

Dunmore, John. *Monsieur Baret: First Woman Around the World 1766–68*. Auckland, NZ: Heritage Press, 2002.

———. *The Pacific Journal of Louis-Antoine de Bougainville 1767–1768*. London: Hakluyt Society, 2002.

Dussourd, Hélène. *Jeanne Baret (1740–1816): Première femme autour du monde.* Moulins: Imprimerie Pottier, 1987.

Edmond, Rod. "Island Transactions: Encounter and Disease in the South Pacific." In *The Global Eighteenth Century,* edited by Felicity A. Nussbaum, 251–62. Baltimore and London: Johns Hopkins, 2003.

Ellis, William. *Polynesian Researches, During a Residence of Nearly Six Years in the South Sea Islands.* 2 vols. London: Dawsons of Pall Mall, 1829.

Estensen, Miriam. *Matthew Flinders: The Life of Matthew Flinders.* Crows Nest, NSW: Allen and Unwin, 2002.

Evenden, Doreen. *The Midwives of Seventeenth-Century London.* Cambridge: Cambridge University Press, 2000.

Fortey, Richard. *Dry Storeroom No. 1: The Secret Life of the Natural History Museum.* New York: Knopf, 2008.

Gascoigne, John. *Science in the Service of Empire: Joseph Banks, the British State and the Uses of Science in the Age of Revolution.* Cambridge: Cambridge University Press, 1998.

George, Sam. "Linnaeus in Letters and the Cultivation of the Female Mind: Botany in an English Dress." *British Journal for Eighteenth-Century Studies* 28, no. 1 (Spring 2005): 1–18.

Goubert, Pierre. *The Ancien Régime: French Society 1600–1750.* Translated by Steve Cox. London: Weidenfeld and Nicolson, 1973.

Grove, Richard. *Green Imperialism: Colonial Expansion, Tropical Island Edens and the Origins of Environmentalism, 1600–1860.* Cambridge: Cambridge University Press, 1995.

Hawksworth, D. L., ed. *Improving the Stability of Names: Needs and Options.* Königstein: Koeltz, 1991.

Hooper, Steven. *Pacific Encounters: Art and Divinity in Polynesia 1760–1860.* Honolulu: University of Hawaii Press, 2006.

Hunter, Lynette, and Sarah Hutton, eds. *Women, Science and Medicine, 1500–1700.* Stroud, Gloucestershire: Sutton, 1997.

Jones, Colin. *The Great Nation: France from Louis XV to Napoleon.* New York: Columbia University Press, 2002.

Koerner, Lisbet. *Linnaeus: Nature and Nation.* Cambridge, MA: Harvard University Press, 1999.

Lalande, Joseph Jérôme Le François de. "Éloge de M. Commerson par M. de Lalande, de l'Académie royale des sciences." *Journal de physique* 5, no. 2 (1775): 99–120.

Lamb, Jonathan. *Preserving the Self in the South Seas 1680–1840.* Chicago: University of Chicago Press, 2001.

Lincoln, Margarette, ed. *Science and Exploration in the Pacific: European Voyages to the Southern Oceans in the 18th Century.* Woodbridge: Boydell in association with the National Maritime Museum, 1998.

Livesey, James. "Botany and Provincial Enlightenment in Montpellier: Antoine Banal Père and Fils 1750–1800." *History of Science* 43 (2005): 57–76.

Macleod, Roy, ed. *Nature and Empire: Science and the Colonial Enterprise.* Special issue of *Osiris* 15 (2000).

Malleret, Louis. *Pierre Poivre.* Paris: Maisonneuve, 1974.

Martin, Andy. "Bougainville, Tahiti, and the Duty of Desire." *Eighteenth-Century Studies* 41, no. 2 (Winter 2008): 203–16.

Martin-Allanic, Jean Etienne. *Bougainville, navigateur et les découvertes de son temps.* 2 vols. Paris: Presses universitaires de France, 1964.

Miller, David Phillip, and Peter Hans Reill, eds. *Visions of Empire: Voyages, Botany, and Representations of Nature.* Cambridge: Cambridge University Press, 1996.

Milton, Giles. *Nathaniel's Nutmeg: How One Man's Courage Changed the Course of History.* London: Sceptre, 1999.

Monnier, Jeannine, Jean-Claude Jolinon, Anne Lavondes, and Pierre Elouard. *Philibert Commerson: Le découvreur de bougainvillier.* Châtillon-sur-Chalaronne: Association Saint-Guignefort, 1993.

Morris, Michael A. *The Strait of Magellan*. Dordrecht: Martinus Nijhoff, 1988.

Murphy, Dallas. *Rounding the Horn: Being the Story of Williwaws and Windjammers, Drake, Darwin, Murdered Missionaries and Naked Natives—A Deck's-Eye View of Cape Horn*. New York: Basic Books, 2004.

O'Brian, Patrick. *Joseph Banks: A Life*. Boston: Godine, 1993.

Oliver, Douglas. *Ancient Tahitian Society*. 3 vols. Honolulu: University of Hawaii Press, 1974.

Oliver, S. Pasfield. *The Life of Philibert Commerson*. London: John Murray, 1909.

Pavord, Anna. *The Naming of Names: The Search for Order in the World of Plants*. New York: Bloomsbury, 2005.

Philbrick, Nathaniel. *Mayflower: A Story of Courage, Community, and War*. New York: Penguin, 2006.

Poivre, Pierre. *Mémoires d'un botaniste et explorateur*. La Rochelle: La Découvrance, 2006.

————.*Oeuvres Complettes de P. Poivre, intendant des Isles de France et de Bourbon, correspondant de l'académie des sciences, etc.; Précédées de sa vie, et accompagnées de notes*. Paris: Fuchs, 1797.

Pollan, Michael. *The Botany of Desire: A Plant's-Eye View of the World*. New York: Random House, 2001.

Quammen, David. *The Song of the Dodo: Island Biogeography in an Age of Extinction*. New York: Scribner, 2004.

Rice, Anthony. *Voyages of Discovery*. London: Scriptum, 2000.

Roche, Daniel. *France in the Enlightenment*. Translated by Arthur Goldhammer. Cambridge, MA: Harvard University Press, 2000.

Roger, Jacques. *Buffon*. Translated by Sarah Lucille Bonnefoi. Ithaca, NY: Cornell University Press, 1997.

Roger, N. A. M. *The Wooden World: An Anatomy of the Georgian Navy*. New York: Norton, 1996.

Schiebinger, Londa. *Plants and Empire: Colonial Bioprospecting in the Atlantic World*. Cambridge, MA: Harvard University Press, 2004.

Schiebinger, Londa, and Claudia Swan, eds. *Colonial Botany: Science, Commerce, and Politics in the Early Modern World*. Philadelphia: University of Pennsylvania Press, 2004.

Shteir, Ann B. *Cultivating Women, Cultivating Science: Flora's Daughters and Botany in England, 1760 to 1860*. Baltimore: Johns Hopkins, 1996.

Smith, Bernard. *European Vision and the South Pacific*. New Haven and London: Yale University Press, 1985.

Sobel, Dava. *Longitude: The True Story of a Lone Genius Who Solved the Greatest Scientific Problem of His Time*. London: Fourth Estate, 1996.

Spary, Emma. *Utopia's Garden: French Natural History from Old Regime to Revolution*. Chicago: University of Chicago Press, 2000.

Stafleu, Frans. *Linnaeus and the Linnaeans: The Spreading of Their Ideas in Systematic Botany, 1735–1789*. Utrecht: A. Oosthoek's Uitgeversmaatschappij, 1971.

Taillemite, Étienne. *Bougainville et ses compagnons autour du monde, 1766–1769*. 2 vols. Paris: Imprimerie nationale, 1977.

————. "Du journal de voyage au livre imprimé: Concordances et dissonances dans le *Voyage autour du monde* de Bougainville." *Revue d'histoire du livre* 94–95 (2ème trimestre 1997): 187–202.

————. *Le Séjour de Bougainville à Tahiti: Essai d'étude critique des témoignages*. Paris: Musée de l'homme, 1968.

Vincent, Norah. *Self-Made Man: One Woman's Journey into Manhood and Back Again*. New York: Viking Penguin, 2006.

Vivès, François. "Voyage autour du monde par la frégate et la flûte du Roy la *Boudeuse* et l'*Étoile*, sous les ordres de Bougainville, pendant les années 1766, 1767, 1768 et 1769." *Bulletin de la société de la géographie de Rochefort* (1983).

Williams, Elizabeth Ann. *A Cultural History of Medical Vitalism in Enlightenment Montpellier*. Aldershot: Ashgate, 2003.

Williams, Roger Lawrence. *French Botany in the Enlightenment: The Ill-fated Voyages of* La Pérouse *and His Rescuers*. Dordrecht: Kluwer Academic Publishers, 2003.

Wollstonecraft, Mary. *A Vindication of the Rights of Woman*. Edited by Carol H. Poston. New York and London: Norton, 1975.

Woolley, Benjamin. *The Herbalist: Nicholas Culpeper and the Fight for Medical Freedom*. London: HarperCollins, 2004.

ILLUSTRATION CREDITS

Mad_lla Baré. Engraving. Artist unknown. From *Navigazioni de Cook pel grande oceano e itorno al globo.* Vol. 2, 1816, Sonzogono e Comp, Milano. *Reproduced courtesy The Mitchell Library, The State Library of New South Wales.*

Philibert Commerson. Engraving c.1775. Artist unknown. © *Hutton Archive / Getty Images.*

Herbarium page. *Le Muséum national d'histoire naturelle, Paris. MS 200 p. 11.*

Mid-nineteenth-century engraving of an herb woman. Original publication details unknown. Single sheet engraving. *Copyright Glynis Ridley.*

Herb woman's notebook page. *Le Muséum national d'histoire naturelle, Paris. MS 884 p. 1.*

View of the Jardin des Plantes, Paris (colour litho) by Charles Riviere (19th century). *Bibliotheque du Museum d'Histoire Naturelle, Paris, France / Archives Charmet / The Bridgeman Art Library.*

Mother Depositing Her Child in the Foundling Hospital in Paris, c.1855–60 (oil on wood) by Henry Nelson O'Neil (1817–80). © *Coram in the care of the Foundling Museum, London / The Bridgeman Art Library.*

Plate depicting coffee, tea, and sugar. Denis Diderot and Jean Le Rond d'Alembert. *Encyclopédie, ou Dictionnaire Raisonné des Sciences, des Arts et des Métiers.* Paris, Le Breton, 1750–1776. Planches Tom. VI. Histoire Naturelle. Pl. C. Fig. 1 Le Café. Fig 2 La Canne a Sucre. Fig 3 Le Thé. *Special Collections, University of Louisville.*

Mid-eighteenth-century French flute. Denis Diderot and Jean Le Rond d'Alembert. *Encyclopédie, ou Dictionnaire Raisonné des Sciences, des Arts et des Métiers.* Paris, Le Breton, 1750–1776. Planches Tom. VII. Marine Pl. XV. Batiment appellé Flûte. *Special Collections, University of Louisville.*

Cross section of a frigate. Denis Diderot and Jean Le Rond d'Alembert. *Encyclopédie, ou Dictionnaire Raisonné des Sciences, des Arts et des Métiers.* Paris, Le Breton, 1750–1776. Planches Tom. VII. Marine Pl. V. Coupe d'un vaisseau dans sa largeur. *Special Collections, University of Louisville.*

Portrait of Louis-Antoine de Bougainville, by François-Seraphin Delpech. *National Library of Australia. Rex Nan Kivell Collection. PIC U6365 NK6559 LOC7321-7330.*

Bougainvillaea spectabilis, paper flower, by Sydney Parkinson. *Natural History Museum, London.*

Journal page. *Le Muséum national d'histoire naturelle, Paris. MS 301 p. 27.*

Monsieur Bougainville hoisting the French colours on a small rock near Cape Froward in the Streights of Magellan. Artist unknown. London. 1820–29. *National Library of Australia. Rex Nan Kivell Collection. PIC U3042 NK2829 LOC7322.*

The Prince of Nassau, 1776, by Elisabeth Vigée le Brun. Oil on canvas. *Indianapolis Museum of Art. Gift of Mrs. Ralph W. Showalter.*

Journal de la campagne commencée le 15 septembre 1766 sur la frégate du Roi La Boudeuse que je commandois comme capitaine de vaisseau avec lettres de service (Journal de M. de Bougainville). *Archives Nationales, Paris. MAR/4JJ 142/ journal 17 bis/page 181d.*

"Port Louis" from *Views in the Mauritius* by T. Bradshaw, engraved by William Rider, 1831 (engraving) (b/w photo) by T. Bradshaw (fl.1830) (after). *Private Collection/ The Bridgeman Art Library.*

Vue de la Nouvelle-Cythère découverte par M. de Bougainville. Artist unknown, possibly Romainville. *Bibliothèque national de France, Paris. Département des cartes et plans. Pf. 176 div.7 p. 1D.*

ACKNOWLEDGMENTS

Though I did not realize it at the time, this book owes its existence and something of its contents to the events of March 2001. At that time, my husband and I were both lucky enough to be awarded Conference Visitorships that made possible our attendance at the Eleventh David Nichol Smith Conference on "The Exotic in the Eighteenth Century"—a conference taking place at the National Library of Australia in Canberra. The conference provided an unrivaled opportunity to hear eminent scholars of Pacific history talk about eighteenth-century European perceptions of the region, and also gave conference goers from around the world a chance to begin to appreciate the extent of the early archive holdings of the National Library of Australia. To get to the conference, we flew from London to Singapore and then on to Sydney over waters that Baret herself sailed, and my husband, who was going to deliver a paper on the French Pacific explorers Bougainville and La Pérouse, asked me if I knew that there had been a woman on Bougainville's French circumnavigation of the globe. Knowing my love of gardens and interest in garden history, my husband thought I might have heard of the female circumnavigator, about whom only one fact seemed to be known—that she was a botanist. I had not even heard of Baret at the time and was surprised to be able to find next to nothing written about her. From such seeds, large research projects grow. So thanks are first due to all those at the Humanities Research Centre of the Australian National University, Canberra, who made our attendance at the Eleventh David Nichol Smith Conference possible, especially conference organizers Christa Knellwolf and Iain McCalman.

Only one previous English-language biography of Jeanne Baret has been written: John Dunmore's *Monsieur Baret: First Woman Around the World 1766–68*. When my interest in Baret first began, I found it impossible to obtain a copy of Professor Dunmore's book and so I wrote to him directly. He kindly sent me a copy, for which I thank him. Professor Dunmore and I construct very different accounts of Baret's life and of the motivations of her fellow mariners. Acknowledging Professor Dunmore's assistance in sending me a copy of his biography of Baret, I am happy to accept any errors subsequently discovered in my account of Baret's life as my own.

For their assistance with research in France, and their willingness to share the fruits of their own research with me, I would like to thank Pascal Ansquer, Jean Bousson, Prof. Pamela Cheek of the University of New Mexico, Prof. Odile Gannier of the Université de Nice, and Michel Laffon. Margaret Carlyle at McGill University kindly let me see her thesis work on Aotourou. And for their generosity in allowing access to original materials and making helpful suggestions about their use, I would like to thank the following individuals at a variety of French institutions. At the Archives nationales: Anne Pérotin-Dumon, conservateur en chef. At the Bibliothèque nationale de France: Hélène Richard, directrice du Département des cartes et plans; Madeleine Barnoud, conservatrice au Département des cartes et plans; and Stephanie Billet, also of the Département des cartes et plans, who kindly digitized requested materials. At the Muséum national d'histoire naturelle: Mme Michelle Lenoir, directrice de la Bibliothèque centrale, Service des manuscrits et archives; Maïké Hurel; Pascale Heurtel; and Alice Lemaire. At the Biblothèque centrale de la marine: Alain Morgat, conservateur de la Bibliothèque centrale de la marine service historique de la défense.

In fall 2009, I was invited to talk about my research at Western Carolina University in Cullowhee, North Carolina. At WCU, I would like to thank Profs. Michelle Clonch, Laura Cruz, and Mimi Fenton for the opportunities they gave me. When my drive from Louisville, Kentucky, to Cullowhee was longer than anticipated after a rockfall closed I-40E, faculty and students alike waited at the Women's Center for my embarrassingly late and disheveled arrival to lecture in the "Women Who Dare" series. They engaged with my presentation of Baret's story and asked incisive, nuanced questions, which I hope have made this a better book than it would otherwise have been. For their interest in my work and for their superb hospitality, I am very grateful.

Friends and family listened to all my observations about Baret and unfailingly made smart, encouraging suggestions. For their patience, advice, and practical help, I thank Tom Byers, Karen Hadley, Augusta Brown-Holland and Gill Holland, Mary Marcy, Monica Orr, Mary Brydon-Miller, and Bronwyn Williams. My final edits of this book were completed at the same time as I was editing the work of eighteenth-century colleagues for a special issue of the *Journal of Eighteenth-Century Studies* on "Representing Animals." Thanks to *JECS* regular editor Chris Mounsey for his patience and good humor, and to all my fifteen contributors to that volume. At the University of Louisville, Delinda Buie of Library Special Collections provided enthusiastic assistance in securing appropriate illustrations, as she has done in the past, and I feel lucky to benefit from her knowledge and goodwill. Bill Carner brought images to an appropriate resolution, and I thank him for taking the time.

At Fletcher and Company, New York, I would like to thank Christy Fletcher and Emma Parry for their involvement at different stages. Special mention should be made of my wonderful agent, Melissa Chinchillo, and of my expert editors at Random House, Lucinda Bartley and Stephanie Chan, whose engagement with Baret's story and my manuscript has been exemplary.

Finally, Baret's age was one in which writers still referred to the Muses, those daughters of Zeus who were thought to preside over the arts and sciences, bestowing inspiration and grace. But eighteenth-century artists were already moving away from picturing their muse as a classically draped woman— replacing her, in their self-portraits, with an artist's family member or two, shown as a source of light in the artist's study. In this tradition, this book has muses both canine and human, having been begun under the ever-present gaze of one pair of soulful canine eyes and completed under the intense scrutiny of two more. But it exists because my husband introduced me to Jeanne Baret and provided all the help and encouragement that I needed. For this—including all the time he spent with a digital camera in front of the relevant manuscripts—I am ever indebted to John Patrick Greene.

READER'S GUIDE

🖎ABOUT THIS BOOK

The Discovery of Jeanne Baret, by Glynis Ridley, tells the remarkable story of the first woman to circumnavigate the globe—who did so disguised as a man. In 1766, a French peasant named Jeanne Baret disguised herself as a teenage boy in order to work as principal assistant to the naturalist Philibert Commerson, royal appointee to the first French circumnavigation. The expedition commander, Louis-Antoine de Bougainville, had no idea that the two shared more than simply a passion for botany—they were in fact lovers. In his memoirs, Bougainville reported that Baret was finally exposed by the natives of Tahiti, who recognized a woman where her countrymen had not: a version of events that went largely unchallenged for more than two hundred years. But three members of Bougainville's crew provide a very different version of Baret's exposure. Their unpublished accounts suggest that the truth of what happened to her is more brutal than official chroniclers cared to admit.

This guide is intended as a starting point for your conversation about *The Discovery of Jeanne Baret*. You can also join the discussion online at www.facebook.com/authorglynisridley.

DISCUSSION QUESTIONS

1. Baret's family, typical of eighteenth-century peasants, did not expect to travel farther in their lifetimes than their nearest market town. Imagine that this was your experience. How would you feel about traveling in your own country? How would you feel about traveling overseas? What would "overseas" mean to you? Without access to newspapers, books, or television, where would you get your ideas from?

2. How many herbs, or plants of any kind, can you identify in their natural, growing state? Would you trust your ability to recognize different medicinal plant species if your life depended on it?

3. One of the epigraphs to the book is an excerpt from a poem by Susan Donnelly that reimagines the biblical account of the naming of creation from Eve's perspective. Why do you think Ridley chose to begin her book with this quotation?

4. If you were an eighteenth-century middle- or upper-class woman, what obstacles would hinder your pursuit of an interest in science? Why might you try to overcome those obstacles? Do you find it surprising that the first woman to complete a journey around the world was not wealthy, but rather was a peasant of limited means? Why, or why not?

5. Do you find it hard to understand why Baret gave her son to the Paris foundling hospital? How did you feel about her choice at this point in the book? Do you think this experience affected her later choices, and if so, how?

6. If La Giraudais, captain of the *Étoile*, had not offered Commerson and Baret his cabin, do you think that Baret would have jumped ship at Aix? Why, or why not?

7. Measure out the size of the *Étoile*—approximately 100 feet by 30 feet—and compare it to the size of your reading group's regular meeting place. If you were one of 116 men living in that space, how quickly do you think you would recognize something different about Baret?

8. Vivès was first sent to sea when he was seven and apprenticed as a ship's surgeon at age twelve. How do you think this helped shape his character, social skills, and particularly his relationship with Commerson?

9. The brutal ceremonies surrounding Crossing the Line seem to have been an equivalent to modern hazing practices performed everywhere from fraternities to the military. Why do these practices continue, and are they impossible to eradicate? Do your answers help you to understand what went on when the *Étoile* crossed the equator? How so?

10. Supporting characters in the book include Aotourou, Bougainville, Nassau-Siegen, Véron, and Vivès. Which one of these men interests you most, and why?

11. Sailing the Pacific, expedition members frequently went weeks without sight of land. The ships were therefore self-contained floating worlds. Modern research has shown that men press-ganged (that is, tricked or forced) into naval service were in the minority. The majority of the ratings, or ordinary seamen, were volunteers.

    What factors do you think motivated most of the crew to sign on for a circumnavigation of the globe, entailing at least three years away from home? How much do you think Baret's motivations resembled or differed from the men's motivations? In your view, do any jobs exist today to fulfill the needs of people in similar situations, with similar motivations? If so, what are they?

12. Were you surprised that a group of men finally raped Baret on New Ireland, or did you have a horrible feeling that this was likely? What influenced your expectations of how her life on board ship might

conclude? Do you think that this possibility entered the minds of Commerson and Bougainville, and if so, should they have done more to discourage her from participating in the expedition?

13. Are there any reasons to believe that Baret's marriage to Dubernat was anything other than a marriage of convenience? What might he have offered her that would be appealing after her experiences and past relationship?

14. When she returned to France in 1775, Baret had been away for nearly a decade. What do you imagine were the biggest readjustments Baret had to make to life back in her native country?

15. Out of all the places that Baret went ashore and visited happily (Rio de Janeiro, the shores of the Strait of Magellan, Tahiti, Mauritius, Madagascar), which one would you most like to go to, and why?

ABOUT THE AUTHOR

GLYNIS RIDLEY is the author of *Clara's Grand Tour: Travels with a Rhinoceros in Eighteenth-Century Europe*, which won the Institute of Historical Research (University of London) Prize. A British citizen, she is now a professor of English at the University of Louisville.